THE BEST
HOME-BASED
FRANCHISES

THE BEST HOME-BASED FRANCHISES

Gregory Matusky
and The Philip Lief Group, Inc.

DOUBLEDAY
NEW YORK   LONDON   TORONTO   SYDNEY   AUCKLAND

Published by Doubleday, a division of Bantam Doubleday Dell Publishing Group, Inc., 666 Fifth Avenue, New York, New York 10103.

Doubleday and the portrayal of an anchor with a dolphin are trademarks of Doubleday, a division of Bantam Doubleday Dell Publishing Group, Inc.

Library of Congress Cataloging-in-Publication Data
Matusky, Gregory.
The best home-based franchises / by Gregory Matusky
and The Philip Lief Group, Inc.—1st ed.
p.   cm.
ISBN 0-385-42196-6
1. Franchises (Retail trade)—United States—Directories.   2. Home-based businesses—United States—Directories.   I. Philip Lief Group.   II. Title.
HF5429.235.U6M38   1992
381'.13'02573—dc20   92-13458 CIP

Designed by Rhea Braunstein

Produced by The Philip Lief Group, Inc.
6 West 20th Street
New York, New York 10011

CONTENTS

FOREWORD

This important new book by Greg Matusky provides an informed overview of two growing economic trends in our country today: (1) starting and growing a new business through the purchase of a franchise and (2) the tendency of many new small businesses to operate from the home.

Franchising in the U.S. economy continues to flourish. In a study recently compiled by the International Franchise Association, franchised sales of goods and services at well over 500,000 locations across the country have reached over $680 billion in 1990. Franchised businesses now account for well over 7 million jobs in nearly 100 different industries. From a global perspective, nearly 400 franchisors have sold franchises abroad, accounting for over 30,000 locations, in markets as diverse as Africa, Japan, Israel, France, and the Caribbean.

Home-based Franchises also offers insight into the growing trend toward operating a new small business from the home. A number of factors—many of which, no doubt, influence your own life—contribute to this trend: (1) technological advances in computer and telecommunications equipment; (2) the rising costs of establishing a business in a commercial office setting; (3) the flexibility of a home office to mothers and fathers of newborn and young children (especially during the baby "boomlet" that the country has experienced); (4) the high cost and hassle of commuting; (5) the trends in our nation toward a "service economy"; (6) the tax benefits of operating a business from your home; (7) the growing acceptance in the business world of operating a home-based office; and (8) the growing number of industries represented by home-based franchising.

This last point will be amply illustrated in this book. As you will see in the pages that follow, this book will provide you with critical profiles of the wide range of franchise opportunities that can be operated from your residence. These opportunities include mobile automotive and home services, interior decorating, residential and commercial cleaning, a variety of publishing ventures, educational tutoring, and home repair—just to give you a sense of the variety of enterprises available.

The continued growth of both franchising and home-based businesses should result in expansion for many years to come.

Is a Home-based Franchise Right for You?

What does all of this mean to you as prospective franchisees? Making the decision to buy a home-based franchise demands a fundamental understanding of the business and legal issues affecting the franchise relationship, as well as knowledge of your own ability—and willingness—to take on the rigors and responsibilities of owning and running your own business. There are a wide range of exciting business opportunities available for today's home-based entrepreneur. This book will help you make informed, thoughtful decisions on both counts.

Greg Matusky is uniquely qualified to offer you guidance and information on home-based franchises. As a veteran reporter, communicator, and franchising consultant, his experiences and insight are close to the heart of the trends that are at the cutting edge of franchising today. Greg not only walks you through the key issues in evaluating these opportunities but also has carefully selected the best and brightest new franchise offerings—all of which can be operated from the home, thereby offering flexibility and reduced overhead.

Evaluating Franchise Opportunities

Owning and managing a profitable small business is never an easy road; franchising may make it easier to travel, but it will never be a free ride. This is primarily because franchising certainly mitigates but does not eliminate the risk of business failure. However, anyone considering the purchase of a franchise should begin by looking for a franchisor with an established reputation, sufficient capitalization, quality products and services, and an existing network of satisfied franchisees. The franchisors that are among the final candidates for evaluation should be able to demonstrate to you that they have a strong foundation from which their franchising program was launched and is currently operating.

In the twelve years that I have served as both a franchisor and an attorney practicing primarily in the area of franchise law, I have determined that there are certain core components that should be found at the foundation of every franchise offering. These key components are set forth in the list that follows, and then are addressed in considerably more detail in the pages that follow. It is critical that the following elements are understood and used as evaluation tools in reviewing the franchisor's offering documents:

(1) A *proven prototype* location that serves as the basis for the franchising program and that is not too dependent on the presence or expertise of the founders of the system;

(2) A *strong management team* made up of internal officers and directors as well as qualified consultants who understand both the particular industry in which the company operates *and* franchising as a method of expansion;

(3) *Sufficient capitalization* to launch the franchising program and provide ongoing support and assistance to franchisees;

(4) A *recognized protected and distinctive trade identity* which includes federal and state registered trademarks as well as a uniform trade appearance and overall image;

(5) Proprietary and proven *methods of operation and management* which can be reduced in writing in a clearly written operations manual;

(6) A *comprehensive training program* for franchisees, initially at the company's headquarters and on-site at the franchisee's proposed location;

(7) *A field support staff* who are available to visit and periodically assist franchisees and monitor quality control standards;

(8) *A set of comprehensive legal documents* that reflect the company's business history, strategies, and policies. Offering documents must be in accordance with applicable federal and state disclosure laws and franchise agreements should strike a delicate balance between the rights and obligations of franchisor and franchisee;

(9) *A demonstrated market demand* for the products and services developed by the franchisor that will be distributed through the franchisees; and

(10) *A set of carefully developed site selection criteria* that are based on market studies and demographic reports that require sites which can be secured in today's competitive real estate market.

Legal Aspects of the Franchise Relationship

From a legal perspective, franchising is a contractual method of marketing and distributing goods and services. The parties to this commercial relationship are the franchisor, which has developed an established business format for delivering the goods and services, and the franchisee, who wishes to obtain a license to operate a site in conformity with the franchisor's prescribed system.

As will be explained in more detail by Greg Matusky later in this book, the offer and sale of a franchise is regulated at both the federal and state level. At the federal level, the Federal Trade Commission's trade regulation Rule 436 specifies the minimum amount of disclosure that must be made to a prospective franchisee in any of the fifty states. In addition to the federal rules, fifteen states have adopted their own rules and regulations for offering and selling franchises within their borders. Known as the "registration states," they include most of the nation's largest commercial marketplaces, such as California, New York, Illinois, Maryland, Virginia, and Wisconsin. These states generally follow a more detailed disclosure format, known as the "Uniform Franchise Offering Circular" or "UFOC."

Ongoing Relations With the Franchisor

Franchising is designed to be a long-term and mutually beneficial relationship. Franchisors need franchisees as a source of revenue and as the principal contact with the marketplace to preserve and enhance the goodwill of the business format and trade identity. Franchisees need franchisors for ongoing support and assistance, research and development of new products and services, cooperative advertising, negotiations for volume discounts from key suppliers, and the continuing license for the proprietary systems and trademarks. Even the courts have begun to recognize the need for achieving and maintaining a delicate balance of power between the franchisor and franchisee by reading "implied covenants of good faith and fair dealing" into certain franchise agreements which must also be interpreted in accordance with "traditional notions of fair play and substantial justice."

The relationship between franchisor and franchisee is often compared to that between parent and child. At birth, the franchisee looks to the franchisor for all of its guidance, wisdom, and support. Failure by the franchisor to nurture the relationship at its early stages will usually lead to the franchisee's financial distress or business failure. As the franchisee grows older, suddenly everything the franchisor says is wrong and rebellion sets in. Conflicts arise and a sense of independence sets in similar to the relationship between a teenager and a parent. Finally, as the franchisee grows to be an adult, they realize that the franchisor really is not so bad and that a peaceful and harmonious co-existence is possible. A genuine understanding of both your rights and responsibilities before and after the purchase of a franchise is essential to success.

This book will help you in each step of the process.

ANDREW J. SHERMAN, ESQ.

Andrew J. Sherman, Esq., is Of Counsel with the law firm of Silver, Freedman & Taff in Washington, D.C., where he regularly works with emerging growth companies in the areas of franchising, securities, and corporate law. He is the author of *One Step Ahead: The Legal Aspects of Business Growth* (AMACOM-1989) and *Franchising & Licensing: Two Ways to Build Your Business* (AMACOM-1991).

PART ONE

CHOOSING THE HOME-BASED FRANCHISE THAT'S RIGHT FOR YOU

1

HOME-BASED FRANCHISING: AN OPPORTUNITY FOR INDEPENDENCE WITH A LIFELINE

It happens every Saturday night in America. A group of friends gets together to play cards or watch a videotape and they start discussing their work. No one in the group is particularly happy with their jobs. One friend doesn't like his boss. Another doesn't agree with the direction of the company. Still another in the group is worried about being laid off, and most of them aren't happy with their level of income.

Suddenly the conversation turns to starting a business. "Why not?" they ask each other. "The guy down the street started a business five years ago, and he's now driving around in a Mercedes-Benz. We're just as smart as he is," they encourage themselves. "We could do it. We have the talent right here in this room. After all, Bob has an accounting degree. He could do the books. Sue is a great salesperson. She could head up our marketing. Sherri knows advertising and Tom could be the administrative assistant."

They then start throwing out ideas. "A restaurant? Maybe. Or how about a retail store?" It all sounds inviting.

The ideas continue to fly for a few hours. They're excited about the prospects.

But as the night wears on, these armchair entrepreneurs forget about their ideas as the conversation turns to other topics. Their plans to start a business lay scrawled on cocktail napkins which are thrown out once the evening ends.

It's just as well.

Business ownership, and especially small business ownership, is an extremely risky undertaking in this country. According to the U.S. Small Business Administration (SBA), 65 percent of all start-up businesses fail before their five-year anniversary. Of those that remain in operation, many limp along for years before they attain any real success in terms of sales or profitability. These failures take huge tolls on the entrepreneurs who try to build their businesses. Many lose everything—even their homes and their life savings—while trying to contend with the pressure of creating a successful business.

But all is not bleak for those who desire to open a business—and make it a success. There are ways to open a business with minimal risk and transform it into a viable livelihood. Home-based franchising offers an array of advantages that could stack the cards in your favor—if you're committed to owning and operating a business.

What makes home-based franchising particularly attractive is that it overcomes the two leading reasons for business failure in this country. According to the SBA, most businesses fail because (1) they are undercapitalized and (2) they lack the management know-how needed to build a successful enterprise. A home-based business can keep the lid on cost. At the same time, a franchise can provide the requisite business knowledge you need to succeed in a business of your own.

The Money Crunch

Starting a business, any business, requires a lot of money. A new owner can expect to invest in everything from office supplies to advertising, computers to fax machines—and that's before the business is even open!

Most new business owners vastly underestimate the costs associated with opening a business, and they vastly overestimate how quickly their business will start generating revenue. Consequently, most new businesses run out of money before they meet success.

In the parlance of marathon running, they hit the wall at about the twenty-second mile. It's a shame, because if many new businesses just had enough cash reserves to see them through another year, they would finish the race in fine fashion. Unfortunately, they run out of gas a little too early—right before they have unraveled the mysteries of how to market their business and profitably serve its customer base.

Home-based businesses are not without their share of expenses, but they are a much more cost effective way to open and operate a business. Home-based business owners save on rent, utilities, commuting, and even on professional clothing (you don't need a $300 suit to work from your home). If you are a parent raising a family, you may still need child care during working hours, but the expense is likely to be considerably lower, and there is less stress since you are at home—and can be flexible with your time as needed.

The cost savings often allow home-based business owners to stretch operating budgets and side-step the scourge of many new businesses: lack of investment capital. In effect, a home-based business could give you the added advantage you need to save money and make it through the first few difficult years of business ownership.

Buying Experience

Money is only half the battle to finding success in a business of your own. Management know-how, or rather a lack of management know-how, is the second leading cause of business failure in America, according to the SBA.

A home-based business won't help you here. If anything, working from your home, isolated from other professionals, might retard your ability to learn from others about how to effectively manage a business.

But here's where franchising comes into play. Franchising is a transfer process whereby experienced and skilled business people (that is, franchisors) communicate their knowledge to business neophytes (such as you, the franchisee) who have desire and enthusiasm to build a business.

Within a well-managed franchise organization, new franchise owners receive the training, guidance, and expertise they need to operate an effective business. Through training, technical support, ongoing seminars, and newsletters, franchisees learn via their franchisors how to build profitable, long-term businesses.

The results, in terms of success, are dramatic. While the SBA reports gloomy outlooks for your chances of succeeding in an independent business, another government agency, the U.S. Department of Commerce, reports that only 3 percent of franchises are discontinued every year. Sound too good to be true? Perhaps. That statistic has been challenged on a number of occasions primarily because it was compiled by polling franchisors, and they have a vested interest in keeping their reported failures to a minimum. But even if the number is not precisely correct, the success rate would still be impressive compared to non-franchised businesses.

The Home-based Option

While home-based franchising provides an attractive alternative for some fledgling entrepreneurs, it's not for everyone. As you will see throughout the course of this book, working from the home can be a lonely and difficult way to live your professional life. Franchising requires long-term commitments and investment. It's not for the faint of heart or for the armchair entrepreneurs.

As an option for self-employment, however, home-based franchising is a strategy that more Americans are waking up to. For the right people, it delivers the appropriate mix of structure and independence that fits a range of lifestyles, interests, pocketbooks, and personalities.

2

WHAT IS FRANCHISING AND HOW DOES IT WORK?

If you are contemplating buying a home-based franchise, it is vital that you have a clear understanding about what franchising is and what it is not. First, franchising is not an industry. There is no such thing as the franchise industry, even though many people often refer to one. And it's not a passive investment, like a stock, since it requires your active participation in order to succeed. Franchising is also not a scheme like a multilevel marketing opportunity where you make a little bit of money off each person you recruit into the business.

Franchising is a system that businesses choose to expand their operations. It's a method used to rapidly penetrate a market and distribute products to the consumer. The process starts when a successful business seeks to expand. But rather than draw on its own capital to finance that expansion, franchisors rely on franchisees who invest their own money to open and operate the business. In return for this investment, franchisees gain the right to use the franchisor's trademark and method of doing business. The arrangement also reduces franchisees' chances of failure due to the initial and ongoing training and support services they receive from the franchisor. For the consumer, franchises offer a wide range of products and services at consistent quality and affordable prices.

Franchises are most likely to succeed when they are based on successful businesses that have long track records of meeting the needs, wants, and desires of consumers. Franchises are less likely to succeed when they are based on fledgling businesses looking to franchising as a way to make quick money off franchise sales.

Consequently, the goal of reputable franchisors is to recruit, train, and support business people who work independently to create viable long-term enterprises. At the same time, franchisees are their own business people. Their mission is to build sales and profitability. They actively work in their businesses to pay bills, service clients, and claim market share.

What Constitutes a Franchise?

Three elements define a franchise company: (1) use of a trademark or trade name, (2) payment of fees or royalties, and (3) significant control or assistance provided by the franchisor.

Use of a Trademark or Trade Name

To be a franchise, a group of businesses needs to operate jointly under one distinctive name. Typically, the name is trademarked with the U.S. Patent and Trademark Office and, therefore, provides franchisees a measure of protection against other companies using the same name.

Decorating Den, Professional Carpets, and Molly Maids are all examples of home-based franchises where the trade name is an invaluable asset because of its consumer clout and recognition.

Trademarks serve as a company's name tag or ID bracelet. They allow the consumer to quickly identify the company's products and services.

Payment of fees or royalties

The second element that defines a franchise is the payment of a fee for the right to sell the product or service. The payment must be at least $500 at the time the contract is signed or within six months after the business opens. The charge can be an initial franchise fee, ongoing royalty fee, or advertising payment.

As an example, Video Data Services, a 286-unit videotaping franchise, charges franchisees a flat fee of $250 every six months as an ongoing royalty. Foliage Design Systems, a home-based plant maintenance franchise based in Ocala, Florida, requires franchisees to pay 4 percent of their gross sales back to the home office as royalty. The Sports Section, a home-based franchise opportunity in the photographic industry, doesn't charge a royalty per se. Rather, the company tacks on a service charge for the photo finishing services it supplies to franchise owners. All these fee arrangements qualify the companies as franchises.

Franchisor Control or Assistance

The third element of a franchise is defined differently by the Federal Trade Commission (FTC) and various states that regulate franchising.

According to FTC rules, a business is a franchise if it exerts control or provides significant assistance or services to franchisees. For instance, Triple Check Income Tax Services, a home-based tax preparation franchise, provides franchise owners ongoing support through a team of tax researchers and investigators who respond to franchisee questions and inquiry via telephone. Money Mailer, a direct-mail franchise, supports its franchise owners through a national accounts program that secures large direct-mail advertising orders from national advertisers and then portions out the work among many different franchise owners. Wheelchair Getaways, a home-based franchise that rents wheelchair-accessible vans to disabled consumers, supports its franchise owners through an aggressive advertising and public relations program that promotes the company and its franchise owners in leading publications for the disabled.

In most states that regulate franchising, the establishment of a prescribed business format which the franchisee must follow is the third element of a franchise. For instance, Fortune Practice Management, a home-based business consulting firm that specializes in medical and dental consulting, requires franchise owners to use a complete format for operating their businesses. The format includes the trade names, marketing procedures, and operational techniques franchisees must follow while building their businesses. In the states that regulate franchising, Fortune Practice Management easily meets the criteria of a franchise. It also qualifies as a franchise according to federal rules because of the control it exerts over franchisees.

Putting the Power of Franchising into Practice

In practice, franchising is a rich blend of mutual interests between franchisees and a franchisor. The best franchise opportunities build a strategic partnership between experienced business people, the franchisors, and enthusiastic franchisees whose main objective is to follow prescribed, proven systems for operating within their own markets.

In the best franchise companies, this unique structure creates a win-win situation between franchisor and franchisee.

Andrew Sherman of Silver, Freedman & Taff, a franchise attorney based in Washington, D.C., explains:

"When franchising works well, it gains its power from the interrelationship of franchisors and franchisees. Each needs the other to succeed and each supports and helps the other to grow and expand.

"Franchisors, for instance, need successful franchisees to sell more products and services to consumers and to generate royalties, which is the economic life blood of the company. Franchisees need successful franchisors to develop new products, test new concepts, stay current with market trends, and provide sophisticated business services that most independent business people can't afford to buy on their own."

How Franchising Works

Although there are two types of franchising—product franchising and business-format franchising—business-format franchising is the more common form of franchising and the kind you will be considering as a potential home-based franchisee.

As a point of information, product franchises are set up by manufacturers who sell the right to use a product's name and/or formula in the production or marketing of the product. Coca-Cola bottling operations are examples of product franchising.

Under business-format franchises, franchisees purchase a replica of the franchisor's business and agree to follow pre-set specifications in its operation.

Most franchise companies are comprised of the franchisor and franchisees.

Franchisors sell franchisees the right to use their trademarks and trade names as well as their methods for operating the business. Franchisors teach franchisees their method of operating a successful business and share their special expertise.

In return, the franchisee pays the franchisor initial and ongoing payments for these rights. The initial payment is a flat fee to the franchisor for the right to open and operate the business.

This initial license fee, which can range from a low of $1,000 to a high of $50,000 or more, grants the franchisee the right to open and operate the business and learn the franchisor's trade secrets and operating procedures.

Once the business is established, franchisees typically pay monthly ongoing fees or "royalties" to the franchisor. These ongoing fees are generally based on a percentage of gross revenues of the business— anywhere from 1 percent to 15 percent of gross sales.

Gross is the operative word. Royalties are not based on net earnings. As a result, the fees can sometimes be substantial.

For instance, if you own a franchise which generates $200,000 a year in gross revenue and are required to pay a five or six percent royalty, you will pay to your franchisor annual fees of $10,000 to $12,000.

Sound unfair? Reputable franchisors point out that they provide an extensive array of support services designed to increase your revenues and potential profitability. Consequently, you should be able to make up royalty fees either through increased revenue or the ability to create and maintain a long-term business venture that appreciates in value. Likewise, if you had to buy these services on the open market, you would spend much more than the cost of your royalty payments.

What are some of these valuable support services? Well, it depends on the franchise. But well-managed franchise companies can provide new product research and development; national, retail, and whole-sale account marketing; lead generation; public relations; advertising programs; management training and consultation; profitability reviews and financial evaluations; new sales and marketing initiatives; industry updates; competitive reviews; and other services.

Providing services is the prime responsibility of a franchisor. But what are the obligations of franchisees?

Those obligations can be stringent. For instance, they can govern the name of the business, the style of your business cards, how you answer your telephone, and the accounting system you use to track and report revenue—just to name a few.

The point is that most franchisors want you to operate your business in a systematic and consistent fashion—according to their rules. They believe that if you deviate or modify, your chances of success are lessened and it damages other franchisees in the system.

As Edward Van Artsdalen, founder and president of Wheelchair Getaways, tells it, "The best way to ensure your success as a franchisee is to follow the systems established by the franchisor. If you're a tinkerer and you like to make changes, you don't have the right profile for franchising."

A Brief History of Franchising

Franchising is not new. The Chinese were franchising rickshaw routes thousands of years B.C. During the Middle Ages, the Catholic Church established a franchise system for the collection of taxes.

The Singer Sewing Machine Company started the first modern franchise company during the Civil War to distribute its products in the United States.

But franchising didn't win widespread recognition until the 1950s, when Ray Kroc, a milkshake machine salesman, heard about a California drive-in restaurant that served thousands of customers each week. Kroc drove out to San Bernardino and there, outside of town, discovered the McDonald brothers' restaurant. The food, especially the french fries, was the best Kroc had ever tasted. The parking lot was crowded with customers who traveled from throughout Southern California to patronize the business.

Kroc bought the rights to franchise the McDonald brothers' restaurant. McDonald's quickly became the darling of Wall Street. When the company went public in April 1965, its stock price more than doubled in one month, skyrocketing from $22.50 a share to more than $50 a share.

The irony to the story is that Ray Kroc wasn't the originator of McDonald's. Rather, he simply packaged the business as a franchise and sold its trademarks and methods of doing business.

Kroc's success attracted other companies, some legitimate and others less reputable. During the 1960s and 1970s, franchising suffered from a number of disreputable franchisors who promised the sky and delivered very little to franchisees who invested their money in the opportunities. Perhaps the most notorious example was Minnie Pearl's Fried Chicken, which failed so miserably that it added the expression "Minnie-Pearling it" to the American vernacular.

The problems led to increased cries for government regulation.

California was the first to heed the call by passing a law in 1970. It required a franchise company to register prior to the offer or sale of franchises in California or to its residents, and imposed a cooling-off period before a sale could be finalized. It also compelled franchisors to provide prospective franchisees with a copy of the franchise agreement, a company financial statement, and a detailed disclosure document.

The Federal Trade Commission began to regulate franchising in 1979, when the Federal Trade Commission (FTC) promulgated a comprehensive, nationwide franchising rule. Like the California regulations, the FTC required franchisors to provide potential franchisees with pertinent information prior to the purchase of the franchise. The FTC rule made it unlawful to offer or sell a franchise anywhere in the United States without first providing a disclosure document at either the earlier of (1) the first personal meeting to discuss the sale of the franchise; (2) at least ten business days before the signing of any franchise or related agreement; or (3) at least ten business days before any payment to the franchisor. (See Chapter 7 for a full description of a disclosure document.)

Today, fifteen states have laws specifically relating to franchise disclosure. Although the FTC rule applies throughout the country, state laws that impose more rigorous standards than the federal law take precedence over FTC rules. You can determine whether your state regulates franchising, and whether a specific franchise company has complied with your state's regulation, by calling your state's Attorney General's Office. The telephone number is in the blue pages of most telephone books.

These rules and regulations helped rid franchising of many disreputable franchisors and add significantly to its esteem. Today, franchising is a respectable means of doing business—one that accounts for the lion's share of retail sales in this country and one that is projected to become more and more important in the years to come.

The Advent of Home-based Franchising

Home-based franchises are a relatively new phenomenon. While franchising's modern era traces its roots to the early 1950s, home-based franchises didn't become popular until the 1980s and the advent of personal computers, fax machines, personal copiers, and other technologies that allowed virtually anyone to communicate from virtually anywhere.

Franchising found a welcome place in the home for three main reasons. First, home-based franchises tend to be less expensive than those that require outside offices or storefronts. Consequently, franchisors discovered they could sell more franchises if they converted or developed home-based franchise opportunities.

Second, by keeping a lid on overhead, home-based franchises helped franchisees to become profitable more quickly than other types of franchises. Their success attracted other entrepreneurs to home-based franchising.

Third, the home became an increasingly popular workplace during the 1980s. As the stigma of working from the home waned, and as technology made communications easier, legions of Americans left the workplace to set up shop in an extra bedroom, a finished basement, a walk-in attic—even in expensive custom-built home additions that were specifically designed to function as office space.

These factors pushed home-based franchising into the forefront of entrepreneurship during the 1980s and they promise to contribute to the growth of many home-based franchise opportunities well into the year 2000.

What a Franchise Is Not

Now that you have a better understanding of franchising—what it is and how it works—it will be helpful to define what a franchise is not.

Franchising is not a get-rich-quick scheme.

Many people confuse franchising with those get-rich-quick opportunities that are advertised in the back of newsprint magazines. In reality, franchising is a legitimate strategy for building a business. A quality franchisor provides franchisees with a complete package for opening and growing a business. But that takes time and conviction. Franchising is a long-term commitment that in many cases becomes a lifetime of effort. If you're looking to get rich quick, do not become a franchisee.

A franchise is not a multilevel distribution system.

In other words, as a franchisee, you are not rewarded on the basis of sales achieved by those below you. Neither is franchising a multilevel marketing organization, where commissions are based upon the number of other people recruited into the organization. In contrast, a franchisee's income comes from his or her success in the sales of products or services. As a franchisee you will concentrate on expanding *your* sales and profits, not selling franchises or attracting other entrepreneurs to the company.

A franchise is not an agency where you serve as a representative of a large, distant company.

As a franchisee, you work within a system, but represent yourself. You own the show, make the decisions, and take the losses or enjoy the gains. Each franchise is locally owned and operated.

A franchise is not a distributorship or dealership.

Distributors are typically middlemen. They usually buy products wholesale from manufacturers to resell to retail stores. Dealers work much the same way except they usually sell directly to the public. In both arrangements, the dealer and distributor have the right to buy and sell products from and to anyone. They are not bound to quality or variety restrictions nor do they follow a business system prescribed by a parent company. They pay only for the products they sell or think they can sell and spend nothing on ongoing royalties for the right to use a particular trade name.

A franchise is not a security or passive investment.

Franchisees are usually active players in the business. They balance the books, hire and fire employees, sell the product, and close the sales. They aren't passive stockholders who buy a piece of the company and hope the stock's value increases. This active role will be clear to you since you're considering investing in a franchise.

A franchise is not a partnership or joint venture.

As a franchisee, you are not in partnership with your franchisor. If you or your franchisor should make a mistake, you are not liable for each other's actions. Neither party owns interest in the other's company. You're both independent businesspeople. The franchise agreement (see Chapter 7) is the only tie between a franchisor and franchisees.

A franchise is not an employer relationship.

Franchisees are not employees. As a franchisee, you work for yourself, and your salary comes from the profit *your* business generates. In other words, you're the boss! You punch no time clock and answer to no supervisors. You hire who you want, when you want. You are the sole decision maker regarding the day-to-day operations of your business.

A franchise is not a business opportunity.

A business opportunity is a simple arrangement between a company and a licensee. When you buy a business opportunity, you typically buy little more than some initial training and a manual that explains how to operate the business. There is little ongoing support and no common advertising or shared trademark. Licensees also do not pay royalties. Business opportunities do not enjoy the same degree of success as do franchises who support and train their franchisees and stay with them as they grow their businesses.

Now that you have a firm grounding in the fundamentals of franchising, it's time to move on and discover the keys to determining whether franchising and working from home is right for you.

3

UNDERSTANDING
THE NATURE OF
HOME-BASED BUSINESSES

The more things change, the more they stay the same. Americans were working from the home generations before the first fax machine scribbled a message to distant offices.

In colonial days, just about everyone worked from their home. The farmer's office was just out the back door in the barn. The storekeeper lived with his family in the back room. The blacksmith and cobbler often did business in a shop attached to their homes.

So why did Americans leave their homes? With the advent of the industrial age, work became a process whereby your job could no longer be performed in isolation. You needed a person in back of you, nailing the widget to the handle and then passing it to you for further assembly. Once your task was through, you passed the widget along to someone who would finish the job. Production lines and assembly plants became our new workplaces.

When the information revolution started in the 1950s and 1960s, management, administration, and communications were also divided into discrete units that, again, could not be performed in isolation.

Then came the revolution. It started with the personal computer. All of a sudden, American workers could create, produce, and work from a terminal or computer practically anywhere and do the same quality work as you could at the company's office. The computer, coupled with a modem (a peripheral that allows you to send data via telephone lines), allowed the computer literate to leave the office and return to the comfort of home.

The fax machine added to the new independence by allowing for instantaneous communication.

With these technologies in hand, the entrepreneur soon broke out of the office. If employees could work away from the office in the comfort of their homes, why couldn't the self-employed? If entrepreneurs are the ones who don't like to be told what to do and hate to be tethered to other people, then working at home presented a great opportunity.

And best of all, the home saved entrepreneurs plenty—on rent, commuting, and on lunch. It improved productivity and increased their efficiency. Focused and working at home, the entrepreneur didn't waste time lingering around water coolers, saying good morning to an office full of colleagues or finding a parking spot. Each moment could be channeled on doing business, not preparing to do business. And if you needed to talk to someone and exchange information, update, promote, persuade, or sell, the fax and the computer stood waiting in unwavering readiness.

An Objective View of Working at Home

It all sounds so inviting. But a reality check is in order. Working from the home brings its own set of challenges.

It can be lonely and isolating. The sameness can be stifling. You can be distracted and interrupted—by your family, spouse and those neighbors who really don't believe you have a job (after all you work from your home!).

When things get tough working from the home, there's always the temptation to tune it all out—pull out your favorite hobby, read a magazine, or flick on "Phil" or "Oprah." And the silence can be deafening. No support system. No camaraderie. Very few people to call and kibitz with.

A franchise alleviates many of these difficulties. In a franchise, you are part of a network. Not only do you regularly talk and communicate with your franchisor, but you can also network with other franchise owners.

Franchisees love to communicate with one another. They know that a telephone call to another franchisee can uncover some new technique for building their businesses or some overlooked procedure they could use to become more successful. So they regularly stay in touch with one another.

In a franchise, you're in the loop and part of a larger organization. You don't have to be alone. You can turn to any number of the franchise's resources to break through the silence and isolation of working from home.

Franchising can add another valuable element to your business: structure. When you're working on your own, it's easy to put things off, ignore matters that need attention, or simply become so self-absorbed that you forget to prioritize or build action plans.

A well-managed franchise will provide you with a framework for operating your business—and not just with general guidelines. The best franchises come with detailed operations manuals that identify the critical tasks you must accomplish to build your business. The manual will provide a day-by-day blueprint for operating the business. It should tell you what time to begin work. How much time to invest in marketing. How to make sales calls. When to call prospective customers. When to check on production. Who to contact and when. Where to go. Who to see. What to do and when.

That kind of structure can help you arrange the business in a sensible and productive fashion.

Finally, franchising provides a no-turning-back point to your self-employment. In my personal experience of working from the home, there was always a sense that I wasn't *really* working—that I was more unemployed than self-employed. When things went wrong, I would let my mind wander in non-productive directions because I hadn't made a commitment to building a business. I was in a holding pattern.

Franchising can take you out of the holding pattern. Once you invest in a franchise, there is no turning back. Franchising is a long-term commitment. The franchise agreement can run five, ten, even fifteen years into the future. You will need to invest money in the endeavor. You will need to commit—personally, professionally, and financially into the business. In short, you will put yourself on the hook. You will have taken risks and assumed responsibility. That's a smart course of action for an entrepreneur. When people are at risk—when they have to recoup an investment, live up to a contract, or support themselves—they work hard to achieve their goals.

In fact, that's one of the leading reasons why franchisors franchise their business in the first place. Franchisees are more motivated and energized than employees who can simply quit and go find another job.

Consequently, a franchisee's commitment is much greater than that of an employee or even a well-paid executive. While interviewing franchisors for this book, I asked why they charged so much for their franchise fee, if their real intention was to tap into the ongoing royalties that successful franchisees generate. "We want them on the line," said one franchisor. "We want them to know that there is no turning back. If they invest $10,000 or $20,000 they can't turn tail and run away. That's the type of long-term commitment most business people must apply to ultimately win."

Home-based franchising takes time and hard work. You have to commit to your mission and work to make your dreams a reality. If you do your homework beforehand and then dedicate yourself to your business, your chances of success will increase dramatically.

Five Who Have Thrived: Home-based Franchising in Action

Turning a Disability Into An Asset

As a teenager, Andrew Goodyear had every reason to look forward to life. Bright and ambitious, he was set to attend college and enjoy his studies. Then a car accident took away the use of his legs. Goodyear was confined to a wheelchair. The experience taught him an important lesson: life is too precious to do things you don't like.

After graduating from college and working for the government for a few years, Goodyear decided to start his own business in Florida, where he had always dreamed of living. But Goodyear knew that most businesses either fail right off the bat or struggle for years before making it. He couldn't afford that risk.

One day, while leafing through a magazine for the disabled, Goodyear saw an ad for Wheelchair Getaways, the home-based franchise that rents wheelchair-accessible vans to the disabled. The concept made sense to Goodyear, who knew the challenges he faced in finding wheelchair-accessible transportation.

He bought a franchise, set up shop in the second bedroom of his

Fort Lauderdale apartment, and went to work. Today, Goodyear is Wheelchair Getaways' top franchise owner, operating nine vans throughout southern Florida. His business generates more income than he made working for the government. It's enough to keep his standard of living high.

More importantly, his business has made him a respected part of the business community, and he has been featured in the *Miami Herald* and other local media.

"The franchise gave me the systems I needed to make the business a success," says Goodyear. "By working from the home, I kept my overhead low and was able to better accommodate my disability."

Goodyear is quick to tell people that they can emulate his success, if they do their homework beforehand and understand what they are getting into.

"Home-based franchising isn't for everyone," says Goodyear. "You have to believe in the product or service, and you need a franchisor who will work to help build your business. But in the end, it's up to you. If you work hard, you can be successful."

Mother Turned Entrepreneur

Beverly Parkinson faced the same dilemma as many American women. At age 27, she needed a way to generate some additional money for her family, but she also wanted to be with her three young children as much as possible.

A former gymnastics and pre-school instructor, Parkinson searched for a way to capitalize on her experience and still not rob her children of time with their mother.

In March 1990, she read about Pee Wee Workout, a home-based franchise opportunity that teaches children about health through aerobics and lectures on nutrition and physiology. She investigated it and quickly decided it was for her.

"The franchise matched my interests perfectly," begins Parkinson. "But it also fit my lifestyle to a tee. The business is set up so you can tend to the organizational and administrative work from home and schedule the classes around your family."

Parkinson credits Pee Wee Workout's support and training for getting her business successfully operating in less than two months. "The franchise supplied me with all the materials I needed to get going," she says. "The training was relatively simple, and because the franchisor had developed many of the programs, I didn't have to waste time choreographing routines or creating lesson plans."

Pee Wee Workout supplied the tapes, music, and class outlines for classes that Parkinson leads at day-care centers and pre-schools. That head start helped Parkinson to quickly sell her program to twenty-five organizations in suburban Philadelphia while still having time to spend with her daughters. And good thing. Parkinson recently learned that she is again pregnant. But she not concerned. The business's flexibility allows her to make scheduling adjustments. "I have already hired more instructors for while I am on maternity leave," says Parkinson. "We're confident that we can switch things around and still keep the business growing."

In fact, Parkinson recently purchased franchise rights for the entire state of Pennsylvania, which she might consider selling to other franchisees as a way to make even more money from her business. "Right now, I have more than enough classes scheduled to keep me busy, and I'll decide where to focus our marketing after my next baby. But one thing I am sure of is that the demand for our classes will always be there. Parents love the service because it keeps their kids active and alert," Parkinson says. "In that respect, the franchise has delivered everything I had hoped in terms of financial return and quality of life."

Married with Franchise

Henry and Paula Feldman had spent a lifetime living apart and catching up on the weekends. As a sales representative in women's apparel, Henry spent weeks, even months, on the road away from his wife.

When the couple decided to investigate franchise opportunities, their primary objective was to find a business that could support them financially and keep them close to home.

They chose Money Mailer, Inc., a home-based direct-mail franchise, that allowed Henry's sales experience to shine and easily accommodated the couple's desire to stay at home. "Money Mailer is a sales-driven business, which appealed to us because we wanted to control our financial future," says Henry. "But more than that, we wanted to work together in the convenience of our home."

The Feldmans started their business with nothing more than a table and telephone. Five years later, the couple now owns fifteen franchise territories and they rank among Money Mailer's most successful franchise owners. They still work from home, but their in-home office, complete with state-of-the-art office equipment, is a far cry from their modest beginnings. "We thought we would give the business a try and move on if it didn't work out," says Henry. "That's why in the beginning we didn't want to invest in a lot of fancy furniture and equipment. But the business quickly grew and became a way of life."

And a highly successful one at that. The Feldmans grossed more than $600,000 in 1991, and they have won a cabinet full of Money Mailer awards, including Rookie Franchisee of the Year. They have also been admitted into the company's President's Club, which recognizes and rewards the network's top ten franchisees.

But success didn't come without a price. The Feldmans spent hours and hours during the early days making cold call sales and living with rejection.

But the couple relied heavily on Money Mailer's proven systems for building their business. The company's program, designed to teach franchisees how to boost advertising sales, focused on cold calling and telephone sales techniques.

"We just stuck with the program and made it work," says Henry. "That's the value of being in a franchise. The systems are already in place. You don't have to develop them yourself. You just have to be willing to work hard, listen, learn, and do what you're supposed to do. There's no greater magic than that."

When You Can't Beat Them Join Them

Tony Impoco had a cushy job in his family's poultry business, but he wanted more. He wanted a business of his own. So in the late 1980s, Impoco founded a video production company and started making the rounds to caterers, offering to videotape local weddings. The business, however, never really took off. Something was missing in his marketing, and he couldn't figure out what.

Then he read an ad in a national business magazine about Video Data Services, a videotaping franchise that provided many of the same services that Impoco's business did.

Impoco conducted some investigation and realized that Video Data Services had what he needed: a proven marketing program that he could use to broaden his marketing approach and get into higher margin video production work. Impoco quickly converted his business, which he had always operated from home, to a Video Data Service franchise.

"It was perfect for me because I could run the business from my home in my spare time, and grow at my own speed," he says. "The training gave me everything I needed to get started. I may have known how to use the camera, but I was lost when it came to sales or post-production work."

Although the first few months were filled with weddings and bar mitzvah contracts, Impoco soon broke into new markets, including corporate promotional and sales videos. He used the proceeds from his early bookings to invest in new equipment and expand his services to consumers.

"I was happy to get the experience in the wedding market," says Impoco. "It was my 'boot camp' of video production. But to make it in this business, you have to move on. That's where the franchise's marketing and sales programs really helped me build the business."

Impoco also appreciates the opportunity to work from his home, an arrangement that saved him plenty of money during his early years as a Video Data Service franchise owner.

Ironically, saving money allowed him to grow his business and eventually to open an outside office and production studio. "Many Video Data Service franchise owners work from their home very successfully," says Impoco. "Frankly, I thought I always would, too. But the business grew steadily. It reached a point where we needed more room. I will always credit home-based franchising with giving me that little extra breathing space needed, in terms of keeping costs low, to grow your business and make it a success."

Overcoming Tragedy Through Home-based Franchising

Glenn Epley of Kearney, Nebraska, had lost the farm—literally. Epley was one of the countless victims of the American farm crisis that caused many farmers to lose their land when interest rates on loans skyrocketed and commodity prices plummeted during the 1970s and 1980s.

For extra cash, Epley started working for Complete Music, a mobile DJ franchise operating in his Nebraska hometown. "As a farmer you work a flexible schedule and I wanted the same flexibility with a job," says Epley. "DJ-ing provided that chance."

Epley liked performing so much that two years after signing on as an employee, he bought a Complete Music franchise, and operated from his home. "Frankly, I was as surprised as anyone. I am not known for being outgoing, but the business brought out a new side to my personality."

Today, Epley owns twenty-five sound systems and he employs thirty DJs to service his central Nebraska and northern Kansas franchise territories. But he is still home-based, operating the business from a four-car garage.

"This is a perfect home-based business because we spend most of our time at the scene of an event. The DJs only stop by to pick up their equipment."

Epley isn't about to forsake that convenience. "I like being there for my family," says Epley. "We just bought a new home with a larger garage for the business. I couldn't even imagine returning to farming. I love this business too much."

Home-based franchising certainly isn't for everyone. There is a substantial investment required, uncertainties, and a degree of risk. But for those people searching for a way to open a business while keeping costs in check, home-based franchising offers a sensible alternative. For couples seeking to work together, home-based franchising offers a way to work in tandem building a future. For women with children, home-based franchising provides a rare opportunity to customize work schedules to meet the demands of both family and career. And for people from all walks of life, home-based franchising can open new horizons for personal and financial prosperity.

4

ARE YOU A CANDIDATE FOR A HOME-BASED BUSINESS?

■ ──────────────────────────────────── ■

If you're serious about being an entrepreneur and building a business, then a home-based franchise could be the right opportunity for finding success while staying at home. How can you be sure? This test can help you answer that question. It was designed after interviewing ten home-based franchisors and gaining their insights into the home-based franchise option. Here are the questions that will help you determine whether home-based franchising is right for you:

1. *Are you willing to assume long-term responsibilities?* More than any other factor, franchisors believe that a high level of commitment is the deciding determinant in finding success in a home-based franchise. Franchising is not a short-term endeavor. It will require years of hard work and effort before it pays off big.

2. *Are you a self-starter?* Working from the home presents a range of motivational challenges. Without the structure of a workplace, you must be able to set goals and objectives, and achieve them. If you're a procrastinator or if you have a low motivational level, home-based franchising is not for you.

3. *Do you have a compelling reason for wanting to work from the home?* Many franchisors believe that people who want to work from their homes, instead of those who choose the option simply to save money, make the best home-based franchisees. Women top the list as likely home-based franchisee candidates because they often need the flexible schedules to juggle family commitments. But other important reasons for wanting to stay at home include physical disabilities that preclude commuting and an unwillingness to commute far distances to an office. The desire to live a more independent lifestyle can also be a strong motivator to work at home.

4. *Are you self-sufficient and resourceful?* Working on your own in your home requires a great deal of self-sufficiency. You will be the one who will type your sales letters, post the mail, keep your date book, and make sales calls. Are you the type of person who can juggle many different balls at once and keep them in the air?

5. *Can your home house a home-based business?* Practically, does your home have the necessary space and facilities you need to operate the business. Chapter 9 explains in detail the space and facility requirements of a home-based business.

6. *Are you sales oriented?* Every business depends on sales to grow and expand. As a home-based franchise owner you will have to sell your product and services to your target markets. Don't expect to hire others to sell for you. Chances are, if you own the business, you will be responsible for the bulk of the sales.

7. *Do you like solitude?* Are you comfortable going to the movies or out to lunch yourself? People who need to be around others don't make good home-based franchisees. To be successful on your own, you need to believe in yourself and feel confident working on your own.

8. *Will your family support your decision to buy and open a home-based franchise?* Opening a business is a family decision. There will be long hours that will take you away from growing children. There will be investments that might deplete the family checking account. There will be risks that your spouse and children need to know about. In a home-based franchise, the business will affect your family even more. There will be ground rules that children and spouses will have to respect. You might need to use the garage as storage or the walk-in closet as a fax room. Will your family support

these sacrifices? Are they behind you and your decision to buy a home-based franchise?

9. *Do you know how to use a computer? A modem? A fax machine? Can you type?* Efficiency is the key to success in most businesses, particularly in a home-based business where you will perform most of the assignments. Computers are key. Do you have computer experience? Can you quickly type your own letters? Your own memos? Or create your own promotions? If you don't understand computers or if you can't type, you might need to develop these skills before taking on the responsibility of running a franchise from your home.

10. *Are you a positive thinker?* Business is one part aptitude and two parts attitude. An effective franchisor can provide the aptitude through training and support. You, however, have to supply the attitude. Do you believe in yourself? Do you allow or attack challenges? Do you impose ceilings on yourself? On your accomplishments? Believing in yourself is critical to succeeding in a home-based franchise.

11. *Do you have support systems in place?* You can't do everything yourself. You can't be the primary parent, head landscaper, maid, spouse, nanny, and business owner all at once. You have to establish support systems so that you can focus on growing your business. Before opening a home-based business, make sure you have day care for the children, cleaning help for the home, car pooling delegated to others, outside clerical and bookkeeping help on call, as well as other services in place.

12. *Do you hold a healthy disrespect for authority?* Most entrepreneurs don't like to be told what to do. They object to "bossism," unless they are the boss. And they are willing to put in long, hard hours and follow a system—provided they benefit from the results. That's a great attitude to have when you're building a business. It can provide the incentive you need to achieve.

13. *Do you like making money?* Naturally, everyone says yes. The real question you must answer is: Can you live with a relentless focus on the bottom line? When you have your own business, money is how you will keep track of your victories and your failures. It is the

ultimate measure of a business's success. If money doesn't turn you on, if the prospect of receiving a check for $200 or $2,000 isn't truly exciting, you might not have the motivation it takes to build a business.

14. *Are you detail oriented?* Sounds trite, but business is a matter of details. Send a sales letter with typos and the prospect will dismiss you and your business as careless. Running a business requires you to do a thousand different tasks—all with accuracy. To pull it off, you have to be detail oriented.

15. *Are you searching for a flexible lifestyle?* Some people need structure to thrive. Others love the idea of taking off a morning and then working through the night. If you love the idea of working when you want—not when your boss says so—then a home-based business is the way to live that lifestyle.

16. *Can you separate your job from your personal life*, even if your job is only four feet away in an adjoining bedroom? To work effectively from the home, you have to be able to turn off work and relax.

17. *Are you organized?* Again, that sounds like an old cliché of business. But if you're going to operate a business from your home without much support, you must be able to organize your business and your life, and run both effectively. Good business people and great franchisees keep receipts, get their taxes done on time, do their filing, and organize their records.

18. *Can you stretch?* Good business people extend themselves to accomplish new goals and achievements. They can break new ground and work through novel challenges. Can you stretch both professionally and personally to reach a goal? Do you have the ability to break through barriers and achieve?

19. *Are you prepared to transform your home into a place of business?* Working from home adds a great deal of wear and tear to your home. You might have people coming to meet with you. You might have to store inventory in an extra bedroom or even have a secretary work part time in the kitchen. Is your home so immaculate

or well maintained that you don't want to use it as a place of business? If so, you will run into trouble operating a home-based franchise that might make it difficult to maintain your home in perfect condition.

20. *Can you feel good about yourself working from your home?* Some professionals can't imagine working without a secretary and all the support that accompanies a job and an outside office. Will you be embarrassed by working out of your home? Will you find it difficult to explain to friends and former colleagues that your office is next to your kitchen or that your fax machine is in the attic?

If you can answer yes to at least fifteen of these questions, then chances are you could succeed in a home-based franchise. But before rushing out to buy that franchise, there is still a lot of work to do— in finding, investigating, and financing the franchise of your dreams.

5

FINDING AND FINANCING
THE HOME-BASED FRANCHISE
THAT'S RIGHT FOR YOU

■———————————————————————————————————————■

There are scores of ways to find the franchise that's right for you. But the best strategy is to start by examining yourself. What do you hope to accomplish through a home-based franchise? Are you looking for a second income? Or do you need to support your family from the business? How much can you afford to invest in a franchise without overextending yourself? What franchises best fit your personality? Your likes and dislikes? Your perceptions of yourself?

You can answer all of those questions by following this simple process to direct your search process:

Look at as many franchises as possible.

The world is your oyster as a prospective franchise owner. The number of franchise opportunities has mushroomed during the past two decades. Most franchisors are anxious to find franchisees and keep their companies growing. So don't limit yourself.

Start by leafing through the second half of this book, which is devoted to reviewing some of the best home-based franchises in the country. It profiles each business and gives an overview of the challenges and opportunities their franchise owners face. The profiles were developed by surveying franchisors and then interviewing people inside the companies. Some of the companies, such as ServiceMaster, are well-known and established franchisors. Others, such as Handyman Housecalls, are new franchise opportunities that are worth considering. We tried to make the directory as all-inclusive as possible. However, some franchises, such as Jani-King, the large home-based commercial cleaning franchise, never responded to our questionnaires. Other franchises were purposely eliminated because they failed to meet our criteria of quality, which took into consideration the size, reputation, and age of the franchise. It's must reading for anyone who is serious about taking the plunge and buying a home-based franchise.

If you'd like to expose yourself to an even wider range of opportunities, consult the *Franchise Opportunities Guide*. It lists hundreds of franchise companies, all of which are members of the International Franchise Association (but, of course, only some of them will be home-based franchises). IFA members are typically more established than other franchise companies. The *Guide* is no guarantee to quality. The IFA doesn't police its membership. But it does require members to agree to their Code of Ethics and operate in a fair and honest fashion. You can receive the *Guide* by sending a $15 check to the IFA at 1350 New York Avenue, N.W., Suite 900, Washington, D.C. 20005.

Another comprehensive guide to franchising is *The Franchise Handbook,* which lists thousands of franchise companies in scores of industries. Published quarterly by Enterprise Publications, it's available in many bookstores and on newsstands. The *Handbook* gives brief overviews of various franchise companies and includes such relevant information as the number of franchises the company supports, capital requirements, and franchise fees. The *Handbook* provides a listing—and not a selective one. It doesn't review or reject companies that want to be listed. Consequently, it's just a resource for a broad overview, and again, only some of those franchises will be home-based.

Trade shows are another excellent place to find franchise opportunities. The IFA typically sponsors the biggest and best trade shows in the country. At an IFA show, every exhibitor is a franchise—not a business opportunity or a networking marketing company. So you don't have to be confused whether you're talking to the real thing or an imposter at an IFA trade show.

Other companies sponsor franchise and business opportunity shows in cities throughout the country. You can learn about them through the business opportunity classified advertising in major metropolitan newspapers.

In addition to trade shows, business magazines often report on franchises and home-based franchise opportunities. *Entrepreneur, Success,* and *Inc.* magazines are your best bets for learning about franchise opportunities. *Entrepreneur* sponsors a ranking of 500 of the best franchise opportunities each January.

Inc.'s reporting of franchising has become more aggressive during the past few years. The magazine publishes a special franchise section just about every quarter. It also reports on select franchise companies in the body of the magazine.

Success magazine reports on franchising in every issue. Its features about franchise companies offer candid, compelling glimpses into how franchise companies grow and function. It also publishes regular franchise how-to articles about breaking into franchising and not getting burned.

Once you have taken a survey of what franchise companies are available, start narrowing the field.

Your most important criteria—a home-based business—will eliminate many franchise companies you have gleaned from resources outside this book. You can skip many automotive and food franchises. They typically require store fronts. But there's always that odd exception. For instance, franchisees of Car Checkers of America, a franchise that provides used-car diagnostic evaluations to potential used-car buyers, run their businesses from their homes and work from vans to provide their service direct to the consumer. (Car Checkers is more fully described in Part Two of this book.)

Typically, franchise sales brochures and solicitation letters will tell you up front whether the business can be worked from home.

You will find two types of home-based franchise opportunities: those that can be started from home and those that are structured to stay in the home. Starting a business from home with the intention of someday moving out is an excellent way to keep overhead to a minimum during those difficult early years. It might be a strategy worth considering for getting your business off the ground. But the majority of this book is dedicated to those entrepreneurs who want to stay put in their own business in their own homes.

Keep pruning the choices.

Once you have identified the leading home-based franchises start zeroing in on the ones that most interest you. Don't be overly critical.

Instead, start a top ten list. What industries, products, or services would you be proud to promote? Sell? Or market? For instance, if you have a flair for the artistic, maybe Decorating Den might be worth considering. If sales is your bag, then you should strongly consider direct-mail marketing or financial services. Here's one trick. Sit down and fantasize about the business of your dreams. Would it be selling? Helping? Creating? Or producing? Then read through the directories with the intention of finding that franchise.

After you have identified your top ten choices, call them and re-quest their sales materials.

Identify the top three choices.

Once you know how much money you have to invest and you have narrowed the field to ten candidates, create a top three list of your dream franchises. To do it, pore over the franchisors' sales literature. Eliminate the franchises that are out of your price range or don't appeal to your interests and your personality. Once you have narrowed the field to three companies, it's time to start investigating the franchisor, which is the topic of the next chapter.

Financing Your Home-based Franchise

Finances will play a major role in determining which franchise is right for you. Consider how much money you have to invest in a franchise. Which franchises are in your price range? The cost of opening a home-based franchise ranges from a low of $999 for a Trade Labor franchise to a high of $138,000 for an Armor Shield franchise. How much money can you afford to invest without wiping out your life savings? How much money do you have on hand to invest in a home-based franchise? If you don't know, here's a quick way to find out:

First, add up the money in your savings, checking, money market funds, CDs, and other liquid asset accounts. How much of that money would you feel comfortable investing in a business? Thirty percent? Fifty percent? All of it?

Next, look to the equity in your home as a source of start-up capital. Home equity loans are a leading source of franchise financing. Banks typically allow individuals with good credit ratings to borrow up to

75 percent of the equity in their homes. To calculate that amount, take the value of your home, subtract your outstanding mortgage and any other liens against the property, and multiply it by .75. The advantage of using your home's equity to finance your business is that the interest is tax deductible. And the interest rate on home equity loans is usually more competitive than credit cards or signature loans—typically 1.5 to 2 points over prime.

Here's one tip if you're thinking of using the equity in your home to buy a franchise—don't quit your job before you apply for the loan. Lenders want to know you are gainfully employed.

Also, make sure that your debt ratio is less than 45 percent. That is the benchmark that most banks use to qualify applicants for a home equity loan. Simply defined, debt ratio is the amount of debt you have to pay out of your net income every month.

Also, determine the cash value of insurance policies. If you have an insurance-based savings or retirement fund, these policies often allow you to borrow against your own money at rates at prime or better.

Finally, consider borrowing from friends or family. It's said that the best way to lose friends is to ask them to loan you money. But if you're serious about getting into a business of your own, and you don't have the money, friends and family might be your only shot. If you borrow from a family member or friend, approach the deal as if you were going to a bank. Present the person with a business plan complete with projections for sales and profitability. Work out a payment plan that incorporates the same rate a bank would charge. And then stick to your payments. If you're smart and you're committed to paying the loan back, both you and your friend will benefit in the long run. You'll get the money you need to open your business. Your friend or relative will receive a return on his or her investment that surpasses the return he or she could make in a savings account or a CD.

But even if you can get part of the money from your personal savings and family or friends, chances are you'll eventually have to turn to a commercial lender to finance part of the start-up costs.

The good news is that many commercial lenders, money suppliers, and the U.S. government actually prefer to finance franchised businesses over independent businesses. They understand that their money is safer in a franchise than an independent business. Consequently, they are more willing to listen to potential franchisees—home-based or otherwise.

Here's where your understanding of franchising can really help to get your business off the ground.

Many franchisors have existing relationships with money suppliers such as banks, money brokers, and commercial lenders. These financial institutions work with franchisors because they know that the risk is reduced when a quality franchisor and a quality franchisee work together to build their business.

Who are some of the big lenders in franchising?

AT&T Commercial Finance, The Money Store, National Westminster Bank USA, First Bank of Minneapolis, ITT, and others are big financial boosters of franchising.

Some of these lenders, such as The Money Store, are Preferred Lenders of the Small Business Administration. This means that they can process a loan and submit it to the SBA for a government guarantee that backs up 90 percent of the loan.

The SBA guarantees more than $3.5 billion in small business loans every year. Interest rates are typically 2¾ percent over prime and vary for the life of the term. The big advantage in getting an SBA loan is that the pay-back period is stretched out up to ten years for working capital and up to twenty-five years for real estate and hard assets.

Consequently, your monthly payments are lower, which leaves you with more money to build your business. There are more than 100 SBA offices throughout the United States. (You can find the one nearest you by looking in the blue pages of the telephone book, or dial 800-827-5722).

Even if your franchisor has a relationship with a bank or money lender, you will still have to do your homework to get a loan. Lenders look at a number of factors when considering who to lend money to. First they will look at your historical experience. They'll run a credit report, check your debt ratio, and investigate the collateral you'll have for the loan.

Second, they'll consider your potential for repaying the loan. In other words, they'll want to know how much money you can realistically expect to make from your business. They will want to see a comprehensive business plan complete with cash flow and sales projections and a competitive analysis of similar businesses operating in the area.

Your franchisor can answer many of these questions. But lenders will also want your input. They will want to see that you understand the business and that you've tailored your business plan to your specific location and situation.

The rules to finding a lender to finance your franchise are simple:

First, look for experience in franchising. A lender who has worked with franchises before will be more open to your proposals and more willing to underwrite the cost of your business.

Second, find a lender who is interested in you and your mission. The best lenders take a personal interest in your dream. They will take time to visit with your franchisor, check out your marking materials, and talk to your vendors and suppliers. A lender who understands your business can serve as an important ally and confidant in building your company.

Finally, shop around for rates. Interest rates, years of the loan, and closing costs are all negotiable. Try to get the best rates possible and let lenders know when other banks or money suppliers offer better terms. They just might make adjustments, if they want your business.

Finding the franchise that's right for you requires you to investigate the franchises that are available and then match which ones best fit your interests, abilities, and bank account. The IFA estimates that there are more than 2,500 franchise opportunities now available to potential franchisees. Many of them can be successfully operated from the home. Your task is to narrow the field to the best likely candidates and then undertake a careful examination to determine which is best for you.

6
INVESTIGATING
THE FRANCHISE

With careful research, you can investigate just about any franchise opportunity and determine beforehand whether it delivers—personally, professionally, and financially—all that it promises and all that you need.

The people who end up regretting their decisions to buy a particular franchise are usually those who fall in love with a franchise at first sight and buy the franchise on emotion. They didn't do their homework.

Most franchisors will try to play to your emotions and woo you with an assortment of glossy brochures, smooth presentations, slick video presentations, fast-talking sales people, and a solid operation.

Take it all with a grain of salt. It's not just what the franchisor says that should make you buy a franchise. It's your own independent research that should be your final determinant.

Your research should fall into three broad categories: First, you need to evaluate the people behind the franchise. All great companies are built on quality people.

Second, you need to investigate the concept. Is it in a growing industry? Is it new or innovative? How real is consumer demand for the product or service? Can the business be duplicated in another environment? Has the business been operating long enough to determine its viability?

Finally, you need to investigate the potential of the franchise itself. Are current franchisees making money? Is there a track record of success among franchise owners? Does the franchisor have sufficient personnel to support franchises? Is the franchise marketing program sensible and designed to rapidly penetrate markets?

Investigating the People Behind the Franchisors and Their Operations

It's amazing how many potential franchisees fall in love with a franchise concept and ignore the people or the business behind it.

But a quality franchisor—someone who is dedicated to franchisees and has built an organization on that premise—can be the linchpin in your chain of success. Before buying a franchise, it's imperative to investigate the franchisor—both the people and the business.

You can start with the Uniform Franchise Offering Circular (UFOC), which lists the previous experience of the management team as well as any bankruptcies and litigation they are either currently experiencing or faced in the past.

You need to know the previous experience of the franchisor in the current business. How long have they been involved in the industry? What were they doing before starting the franchise? And how much experience do they have operating businesses like the one you are about to buy?

Many franchisors concentrate on just selling franchises—and that's the extent of their experience. You need a franchisor who understands how to make the business succeed for you and has devoted the appropriate resources to supporting and servicing franchise owners, not just selling franchises.

Next, investigate the franchisor's core business. How big is its staff? What is the management's qualifications? And how well capitalized is the company?

Franchise companies often appear much larger than they are in reality. Most franchise companies are very small businesses with home office revenue less than $10 million. For instance, a franchise with 100 units that average gross sales of $300,000 would generate only $1.5 million in home office revenue, if the royalty is 5 percent. Consequently, some franchise companies are undercapitalized and can't afford to provide the support their franchisees need and deserve.

Make sure to have your attorney, accountant, or advisor obtain a credit report from a company such as Dun & Bradstreet or TRW about the franchise company. Carefully review the franchisor's audited financial statements and determine the source of the majority of the franchise's income.

If the company is publicly owned, you can easily obtain its 10K statement—a public disclosure document similar to its franchise offering circular. All 10Ks are available through stockbrokers or from the company itself.

If the company is privately owned, as is often the case with smaller franchise companies, your research becomes more difficult. Financial reporting services can help you generate information about the company's profit and loss picture, but you should also work directly with the franchise company to obtain local bank and credit references.

When these references are obtained, each one should be contacted and asked relevant questions, such as how long they have conducted business with the franchisor, the terms of credit, and the franchisor's payment history. Solid franchisors should present credit references that reflect stability and a strong payment history.

As we discussed before, you also need to determine how the franchisor makes its money. If most of its revenue comes from the sale of franchises and initial fees rather than ongoing royalty streams, beware. A few slow sales months can knock an undercapitalized franchisor into oblivion—leaving you and other franchisees high and dry.

How can you tell how the franchisor makes its money? Ask them! Franchisors who have nothing to hide will tell you how much of their income comes from initial franchise sales and how much comes from royalties. Also, consult your accountant. With a little insight and a few calculations, your accountant should be able to determine the financial composition of the franchisor.

The Concept Behind the Franchise

Your next step is to evaluate the business and the industry in which it operates. You need to know if the business is in a growing market. Whether it is in a competitive industry. Who the industry leaders are. And whether the concept is new or whether it has a track record of success.

You can start your research at your local library. Ask your reference librarian to help you find trade associations and trade journals for the industry you are investigating. For example, if you're considering buying a home-based franchise that provides business training, *Training Magazine, Training and Development Magazine, Human Resource Executive,* and other trade journals can be a good place to begin your research.

Call the editors at these publications. Tell them you are considering buying a franchise in their industry. Most trade journal editors love to talk about the businesses and industries they track.

You will want to ask them such questions as:

- Is the industry growing? If so, by how much a year? Where is the information published?

- How common is franchising in the industry?

- Do franchises do better than independent businesses in this industry?

- What are the keys to success in this business?

- How competitive is the industry?

- What are typical retail prices for the product or service offered? What are typical profit margins?

- What major market forces affect the health of the industry?

- Where would I go for additional information about the industry? What research firms, analysts, and trade associations track the industry?

Profitability and Growth

Finally, you want to investigate the potential and profitability of the franchise. After all, making money is the reason for buying a franchise. You want to make sure the franchise can generate an adequate return on your investment.

Start by talking to the company's franchise owners—the people who will be your colleagues if you join the franchise.

Current franchise owners are listed in the franchise-offering circular. They are the best people to talk to. They will tell you about their problems and successes, often in direct language.

Beware, however. Some franchisors will try to steer you to those special franchisees who have either been coached to say only good things about the business or who are compensated on a commission basis to help sell franchises.

Call as many names as possible, choosing them randomly from the list contained in the offering circular. But don't rely solely on the list. Some unscrupulous franchisors conveniently delete the names of unhappy franchise owners from the document. When you talk with current franchisees, ask them for the names and telephone numbers of three other franchise owners. Then check to make sure they are also listed in the offering circular. If names are missing, something is wrong.

When talking with current franchise owners, you want to ask direct and penetrating questions that get to the heart of the matter.

Key questions to ask franchise owners are:

- Has the franchisor ever made promises he couldn't or didn't keep?

- Are you making the kind of money you thought you would?

- How responsive is the home office?

- How stable is the management?

- What was your previous career?

- Are you making as much money as you did in your previous career?

- When was the last time you took a week's vacation?

- How many family members work in the business? Are they compensated?

- How long did it take for your business to break even?

- Would you recommend that a friend or relative buy into this franchise?

- What was the biggest surprise in buying and opening your franchise?

- Does the franchisor work to help you build sales and profitability?

- How much will your business gross this year? How much did it gross last year?

What Franchisors Don't Want You to Know

Many franchisors ramble on and on about the positive aspects of their franchise. But they grow remarkably silent when it comes to telling you about the negatives of their business.

Every business has a downside. Here are some vital issues that franchisors may not bring to your attention:

- How long the franchisor's core business has been in operation. Too many companies franchise too early in their growth cycle. The best franchises have outgrown their entrepreneurial roots and have blossomed into professionally managed organizations. Franchises that are still operated by the founding entrepreneur typically do not have the stability and market savvy to be great franchisors.

- The number of units that close each year. No organization is perfect. Even conscientious franchisors can make mistakes. Ask your franchisor how many units have been closed or bought back. Ask for the names and telephone numbers of franchisees who have closed shop or sold their units back to the company. Call them to get their side of the story. You'll learn a lot.

- The profitability of franchise units. Many franchisors do not disclose information regarding earnings claims or forecasted sales, profits, or earnings. But many drop hints as to the profitability of their stores. Federal and state laws require earnings claims to be in a very specific and detailed format if they are made at all. Don't listen to innuendo. Do your own independent research to determine profitability. And remember, franchisors may be violating federal and state franchise laws if they give you information which is inconsistent with what is in the franchise offering circular.

- Lawsuits against the franchise company. Franchise companies always downplay their legal battles with franchisees. Get the names and telephone numbers of franchisee litigants and ask them the nature of the dispute. Some lawsuits are acceptable and just a part of doing business in today's society. However, if more than 10 percent of a franchisor's franchisees are involved in lawsuits against it, then that is a trend to be wary of.

- Arbitration against the franchise company. Many franchisors require disputes to first go to arbitration. But arbitration often doesn't have to be disclosed in the offering circular. Consequently, crafty franchise companies can easily hide serious disputes from prospective franchise owners. Contact the American Arbitration Association's local office and ask them if the franchise you are investigating is in arbitration with its franchise owners.

- The time and money spent selling franchises. If a franchisor spends more than 50 percent of its time and resources selling franchises, it's not adequately committed to its current franchise owners.

- The real scope of its research and development programs. Franchisors are famous for telling prospective franchisees about new products and services coming up in the future. Find out how many new products or services the franchisor has successfully launched during the past year.

- The break-even point. Building a business takes time. Many franchisors understate the time and money it takes to become successful. Find out from current franchise owners how long it took to achieve profitability.

- The franchisor's understanding of the end-user. Many franchisors are great at selling franchises. But you have to discover whether the franchise you are interested in is skilled at selling products and services to consumers. Ask franchisors for their marketing plan so you can determine how well they understand the ultimate consumer.

- The experience of the people who will train you. The quality of training can spell success or failure for a franchisee. Who performs the training for the franchisor? Is it an operations person who might not be able to communicate the nuances of operating the business? Or is it a professional communicator who understands the operation as well as how to convey information effectively?

- The exclusivity of your territory. Franchisors define exclusivity in different ways. Make sure you understand the terms of your territory. Is your territory a geographical area? Is it based on population? Some franchisors don't offer exclusive territories.

- The protection of the trademark. Check the offering circular to make sure whether the franchisor's trademark or service mark is protected through the U.S. Patent Office. If the trademark is not protected, it could be challenged down the road. You want to be sure that the trademark will always remain the same.

- The success of the franchisor's company-owned operations. Make sure to find out whether the franchisor operates company-owned outlets and how they perform. If the franchisor doesn't have any company-owned outlets, it's much more difficult for the franchise to test new products—and it could be a sign that the franchisor is not interested in the end-user or consumer needs. If the company has too many company-owned units, the franchisor could be more interested in operating their own businesses rather than supporting yours.

- The source of the products or services you will market. Typically, franchisors don't sell products to their franchisees. Instead, franchise companies approve select vendors who you can buy from. Find out who these vendors are. Do they have a financial relationship with the franchise company? It's cleaner and less suspicious if there's no financial quid pro quo between a franchisor and its vendors. You also want to know the financial stability of your suppliers. Are they large and respected? Will they be there when you need them?

• The franchisee input in the direction and management of the franchise. Great franchise companies listen to their franchisees, take into account their recommendation and act upon their ideas. Does your franchisor have a Franchise Advisory Council that channels communications between franchisees and franchisor? Does the franchisor listen and respond to its franchisees?

• The real structure of the franchise. Great franchise companies are fully developed management organizations. They have gone through the entrepreneurial first stages of growth and have blossomed into companies with job descriptions and professional management. Ask your prospective franchisor for the organizational chart of the franchise company. No one should wear more than one hat. Key personnel should have well-defined roles that will help you as you build your business.

• The real size of their franchise. Bigger is better. At least, that's what most franchisors think you want to hear. When you ask them how many franchises they have, they might tell you how many franchises they have sold or expect to sell—not how many they have opened. The difference can be dramatic and provide insight into the real size of the franchise—and the honesty of the franchisor.

You have a lot riding on your decision to buy a franchise. That's why it behooves you to do the research necessary to determine the viability of the franchise you want to buy.

7

CONTRACTS AND LEGAL ASPECTS OF FRANCHISING

If you remember back to the first chapter of this book, we briefly touched upon the Uniform Franchise Offering Circular (UFOC). Although the UFOC is a lengthy and complex document, it contains important information about the franchisor and the franchise program. Don't overlook just how valuable this document can be to your investigation of a franchise.

Above all else, UFOCs provide prospective franchise owners with a microscope they can use to peer into the operation of a franchise company. It's a single, convenient source on which to center your investigation. And it's unique to franchising. If you buy an independent business, you won't receive the type of thorough disclosures that a UFOC provides.

Coupled with the franchise agreement and a good franchise attorney, the UFOC represents your best bet for understanding what is entailed in the operation of a franchise. You need to read and reread the UFOC. Have your attorney, accountant, and/or business consultant examine it. The UFOC is open to anyone's inspection. It includes twenty-three points that examine every issue involved in the purchase and operation of the franchise. It can be lengthy, involved, tedious, and, at times, confusing. But it's well worth studying.

An Overview of the Uniform Franchise Offering Circular

The UFOC is comprised of five major sections: the narrative, financial statements, franchise contracts, other exhibits, and, in some cases, earnings claims.

The narrative is where you will find the bulk of the qualitative information regarding the franchise. Subjects covered in the UFOC include: background information about the franchisor, fees and financing of the business, and the products and services you will need to operate your business. The sections of the UFOC are explained later in this chapter.

It's imperative that you have an experienced franchise attorney or business consultant review the UFOC and interpret it. You should also read the UFOC before signing a franchise agreement.

Some franchisors include earnings claims in the narrative section of their UFOCs. Earnings claims are intended to portray the sales or profitability of the franchise business. But be forewarned. By manipulating numbers, franchisors can create inferences that might prove misleading when carefully scrutinized.

The UFOC will be accompanied by audited financial statements of the franchise company. Again, your accountant or attorney should evaluate these statements to determine the financial stability of the franchisor. But you should also know that many new franchisors establish separate corporations to operate the franchise company. Consequently, very good franchise opportunities might suffer from weak financial statements.

Finally, it's important to realize that franchisors are bound by law to provide you with a UFOC or disclosure document ten days before any money can change hands or contracts can be signed. If the franchise you are considering buying can't produce a UFOC, there's a serious problem and you should stop talking to the company immediately. If the franchisor tries to collect money or tries to make you sign a contract before the ten-day "cooling off" period is complete, that's a violation of FTC regulations and should cause you to disqualify the franchise as a possible business for you.

Understanding the Uniform Franchise Offering Circular

Here is a point-by-point examination of the UFOC:

Item One: The Franchisor and Any Predecessors

This item is a straightforward explanation of the historical background of the franchisor and the businesses that preceded the current franchise company. The item includes the franchisor's corporate name and trade name, where the business is headquartered, the state and date of incorporation, the franchisor's prior and current business activities, and the franchisor's qualifications for conducting this kind of business. Item One also includes a general description of the business that the franchisee will operate as well as a discussion of the competition a franchisee might face. In general, Item One introduces the franchise company and the industry it operates in. It's typically easily read and digested.

Item Two: Identity and Business Experience of Persons Affiliated With the Franchisor

Item Two identifies top managers and executives within the franchise company and provides a description of their backgrounds. It also identifies brokers and agents who are approved to sell the franchise, which can sometimes be surprising. For instance, some franchisors approve franchisees to sell the franchise. But franchisees don't have to identify themselves as sales agents anywhere except in Item Two of the UFOC. So if you've met a particularly positive franchisee who is anxious to see you join the network, refer to Item Two to determine whether the enthusiasm might be due to a commission earned the day you sign the franchise agreement.

Items Three and Four: Litigation and Bankruptcy

Everyone's closet houses a few skeletons. Item Four is where you can find those skeletons about a franchisor and determine whether they should affect your decision to buy.

Most franchise companies that have been in business for more than two or three years have or will have litigation against them. But how much is too much and when should a red flag be raised? Franchise attorney Andrew Sherman offers his insights: "Litigation isn't necessarily a bad thing. In fact, many of the cases listed in the document may have nothing to do with how well the franchisor serves franchisees. Litigation might even suggest a proactive franchisor who works diligently to protect the company from non-productive franchisees."

When investigating litigation, Sherman recommends that you look for patterns that could be tip-offs to serious problems within the franchise. Patterns might include franchisee-initiated litigation clustered around certain years. This might suggest a radical change in the franchise that franchisees rebelled against. Another red flag is a class action suit brought by a number of franchisees. This could suggest angry or disenchanted franchisees. Finally, Sherman recommends being alert to litigation brought by the government. The states and FTC usually don't get involved in frivolous claims.

Bankruptcy is another area that most franchisors would rather forget about but that the UFOC requires them to disclose. The true test of management's ability is their past track record. Recent or excessive bankruptcies should be a point of concern that needs to be investigated to determine whether they reflect poorly on the franchisor's management skills.

Items Five and Six: Initial and Other Fees

Items Five and Six describe the fees, payments, manner of payment, and refundability of the monies you will pay the franchisor. The items also describe how the fees must be paid. For instance, your UFOC might state that the total initial fee is $10,000 payable as follows:

1. $5,000 upon signing the franchise agreement.
2. $5,000 a week before training commences.

If the fees and payments identified in Items Five and Six are different than what you have been told by sales people or in sales literature, you should raise these issues with the franchisor.

Item Seven: Initial Investment

Item Seven gives you the bottom line for getting into your franchise. It will list all the costs associated with opening your home-based franchise, including computer equipment, supplies, inventory, stationery, insurance, and more. This item is often the source of much franchisee/franchisor litigation brought by franchisees who invest significantly more to open their franchises than estimated in the UFOC.

Items Eight and Nine: Product Purchase Requirements

These items are where you will find the franchisor's blueprint for quality control. If the franchisor requires you to buy products directly from the franchisor, that stipulation will be spelled out in these items of the UFOC. If the franchisor requires you to buy products from designated suppliers, those terms will also be disclosed. In addition, these items will tell you whether there are any financial ties between your franchisor and approved suppliers. The best franchise companies try to reduce or eliminate financial arrangements with suppliers to avoid conflict of interests.

Item Ten: Financing of the Franchise

If the franchisor offers financing, the terms and arrangements will be disclosed under Item Ten. If you were promised or were relying on internal financing to open your franchise, you had better carefully review this section of the UFOC.

Item Eleven: Obligations of the Franchisor

This item is one of the most important in the UFOC because it outlines the services the franchisor will provide to you. For instance, this item will tell you whether the franchisor intends to help promote your grand opening or assist in the training of your employees. Will the franchisor provide regional or national advertising programs? It's all laid out in Item Eleven. You need to carefully review this section to determine whether it in any way differs from the promises made by sales people or in sales literature.

Item Twelve: Exclusive Areas or Territories

Again, this is a vital section of the UFOC because it discloses how the franchisor determines the exclusivity of a territory—by population, geography, or any other parameter. The franchisor probably won't include a specific description of your territory in the UFOC, preferring to leave that for the franchise agreement. Nonetheless, it's vital that you understand the nature of the territory you are buying.

Items Thirteen and Fourteen: Disclosure or Trademarks, Patents, or Copyrights

Does the franchise have any trademarks, patents, or copyrights that are integral to the operation of the business? Trademarks, as we have discussed in Chapter 2, are an important part of any franchise. These items will tell you whether the franchise's marks have been federally registered. Patents and copyrights aren't as important as trademarks are to a franchise, but they can provide a competitive advantage by differentiating your business from others.

Items Fifteen and Sixteen: Owner/Operator and Restrictions on Goods and Services

Most home-based franchises will require you to participate in the actual operation of the business. This item will explain that provision. Franchise companies also typically restrict the goods and services that you can sell. That's so the owner of a home-based franchise in the pet care industry doesn't start diluting the image and reputation of the company by also offering car detailing services.

Item Seventeen: Renewal, Termination, Repurchase, and Assignment

This item is typically the most overlooked portion of the UFOC— but it's one of the most important. No one wants to think about how the franchise will be sold, terminated, or assigned if the business doesn't work out or if the franchisor disenfranchises a franchisee. But all these issues are vital to your investigation of the franchise. And they should play an important role in your decision to buy. A qualified franchise attorney can give you the best perspective on these issues.

Item Eighteen: Arrangements With Public Figures

This item requires the franchisor to tell you whether they have financial relationships with celebrities or personalities who promote the franchise. This item rarely has an effect on the franchisee/franchisor relationship.

Item Nineteen: Income Projections

By law, a franchisor cannot tell you how much money you will make operating the franchise anywhere else except in Item Nineteen of the UFOC, which must be presented in a prescribed regulatory format. Most franchisors choose not to make earnings claims under Item Nineteen. But if your franchisor has made claims outside of the UFOC, that should be a red light as to its credibility and legitimacy.

Item Twenty: The Number of Franchises, Addresses, and Telephone Numbers

Item Twenty is the mother lode for investigating a franchise. It's here where you will find the names and telephone numbers of currently operating franchisees. Make sure and call as many of them as possible when investigating the franchise.

Items Twenty-one, Twenty-two, and Twenty-three: Financial Statements, Other Contracts, and Receipts

To fully investigate the franchisor, your accountant or business advisor should review financial statements to determine the solvency of the franchisor. Item Twenty-two will provide you with all related contracts—including the franchise contract. Item Twenty-three is a receipt that you must sign to prove that you received the UFOC at least ten business days before any money changed hands or contracts were signed.

If you're serious about franchising, then you have to do your homework. Don't be intimidated by the scope and size of the UFOC.

It's the first of many documents you will have to become familiar with in order to find, evaluate, and open a successful franchise. At first, it might seem overwhelming. But it is essential that you learn to understand and interpret the UFOC. That knowledge will help you compare and contrast different franchise offerings and make the right business choice for you.

Understanding the Franchise Agreement

The UFOC tells you the cold, hard facts. It sets forth the who, what, when, where, and how of the franchise—the basic facts about the business.

The franchise agreement, on the other hand, is simply a contract. It binds you to the facts. The agreement commits you to operate the business according to the terms spelled out in the UFOC and in the company's operations manual. It also requires the company to perform as it promises.

Before signing any franchise agreements, it's imperative that you have your attorney review and explain its many nuances to you. You need to know exactly what you are getting into before you invest hard-earned money in a business.

The average franchise agreement contains anywhere from fifteen to thirty clauses, all of which will play a role in operating your business. When reviewing the franchise agreement with your attorney, find out where it is excessively strict on terms such as renewal of the franchise agreement. In other words, when your franchise agreement expires, what conditions and terms will you have to meet to renew it and how much will the renewal cost you? Terms of disenfranchisement are another important issue. If your franchise tries to "evict" you from the franchise network, will you be prevented from competing in the same industry by a covenant not to compete? And how about minimal performance requirements? Some franchises require franchisees to meet a minimum sales quota to retain their franchise. Are there any such restrictions placed upon you by your franchise agreement?

Here are key issues that you should consider when reviewing a franchise agreement:

The Fee Structure of the Franchise

What franchise fees, royalties, advertising, and other fees are included in the franchise? How are these fees paid? As a percentage of gross? As a flat fee? How often? To whom and when? When you're in business, making money should be your prime consideration. If the franchisor takes too much of the cut, you'll be left with significantly lower profits. Ask your attorney or business consultant whether the fees appear to be in line with the services offered by the franchisor.

Your Rights Concerning Trademarks, Trade Names

The most valuable asset of many franchise companies are the trade names that identify the business. After all, one of the reasons you are buying the franchise is to benefit from a known name that customers trust. Has the franchisor federally registered the logo and name of the business? If not, the trade name could be challenged at a later date. You could have to change your company's name on everything from stationery to uniforms. What are the restrictions that go along with the use of the trade name? Can you use it on all parts of your business? Are there any special reservations connected with the trade name?

Operational Requirements

What constraints does the franchise apply to the operation of your business? Does the franchisor control the types of products you can offer and sell? Must you maintain set hours of operation or are you free to open and close as you see fit? Does the franchisor mandate inventory requirements? Telephone answering procedures? Stationery design and logo presentation? All these issues are vital in the operation and growth of a business.

Financial Reporting Requirements

The franchisor has a vested interest in knowing how much money your business makes. After all, the more money you make, the more you will pay the franchisor in royalties. What financial reporting practices does the franchisor require of its franchisees? Must you maintain financial statements? Make them available to the franchisor? Some franchises retain the right to make franchisees produce audited financial statements, if a dispute over royalties arises. An audited financial statement can cost thousands of dollars and take months to complete.

The Size and Exclusivity of Your Territory

When you own a franchise, you don't want your franchisor to locate another franchise in the house next door to your home-based business. Your franchise territory will be identified in your franchise agreement. Some franchisors don't offer territories. Others make territories contingent on geography, population, or any number of criteria. Make sure you know exactly how big an area or territory you are purchasing before you sign your franchise agreement. Negotiate strongly to receive a territory that is large enough to support a profitable business.

Standards, Procedures, and Policies

How does the franchisor expect you to operate your business? What standards must you comply with to maintain a good standing within the franchise network? Franchisors are serious about controlling the quality of their products and services. The franchise agreement will list the obligations you must live up to as a franchise owner. In addition, the agreement will detail how you will be inspected and supervised by your franchisor. For instance, franchise representatives might make regular visits and give you forty-eight hours to make changes or come up to standards imposed by the franchisor. Make sure you understand how these standards will affect the operation of your business.

The Extent and Quality of Training, Support, and Guidance

A franchisor's main responsibility is teaching and directing. Your franchise agreement will outline the terms of initial and ongoing training as well as continuing education that will help your business to grow. In addition, it will explain the nature of the franchisor's ongoing assistance and how the franchisor intends to support you as your business grows and prospers.

Termination, Renewal, and Assignment

Too often, these topics get lost in the legalities of a franchise agreement. But as a potential franchisee, you need to know how a franchisor can terminate your contract and how you can renew your franchise agreement once your term is complete. What happens if you want to sell your franchise? Or give it to a son or daughter? Will you be restricted from working in the same industry through a covenant not to compete? Your franchise agreement will answer all these questions.

Marketing, Advertising, and Promotion

Exposure is everything in building a business. How does the franchisor support franchisees through advertising and marketing? What programs are in place and what can you expect to receive that will help promote your business to its target audiences? The franchise agreement will state how the advertising funds will be collected and used.

All these issues are critical to your understanding of how the business will operate. They should all be addressed in your franchise agreement. That's why it's imperative that you have an experienced franchise attorney review every point in the franchise agreement and explain how they could affect your business. Don't be afraid to ask your attorney to clarify specific issues so you can understand them. You will be living with your franchisor for many years. The franchise agreement will define the living arrangements. So make sure that every issue is clear to you before you sign on the dotted line. That way, you'll know what to expect.

Negotiating a Franchise Agreement

Can you negotiate the terms of the franchise agreement? It's always worth trying to negotiate. But will the franchisor make compromises?

That depends on many factors, including the size and strength of your franchisor.

Large, established franchise companies rarely make major changes in their franchise agreements. They will delete unimportant language, but they rarely concede matters that could affect the operation of other existing franchise owners. For instance, franchisors probably won't reduce royalty fees. That wouldn't be fair to other franchisees. They might, however, increase the geographical territory of a franchise agreement—if the change doesn't affect other franchisees.

As a prospective franchisee, you should always try to negotiate the best deal possible. But remember, once you're in the network, you don't want your franchisor to make concessions that might weaken the network or are unfair to you.

Tip-offs to Franchise Fraud

There are bad apples in every barrel. Franchising is no different. But in franchising, a bad apple can take your money, disrupt your life, and leave you with little to show for an honest investment and a lot of hard work.

But by doing your homework, reviewing the UFOC, staying alert, and knowing the tricks of the disreputable, you can protect yourself.

What are the tip-offs of a bad franchise deal? Here's a list of things to look out for and run away from:

1. *The franchisor cannot produce a UFOC.* By law, all franchise companies must have and present prospective franchisees with a UFOC at least ten business days before anything is signed or money changes hands.

2. *The franchisor makes promises or earnings claims that are not in the UFOC.* In franchising, there is no off the record. If the franchisor or its sales agent makes claims, ask for them in writing.

3. *The franchisor asks for money before the ten business days have lapsed.* The cooling-off period is law. No monies, no down payments, not even post-dated checks can change hands until ten business days have passed.

4. *The franchisor claims that other prospects are on the verge of signing for the same territory.* This is the oldest trick in the book, used to pressure prospective franchisees into buying. If someone is on the verge of buying your territory, why is the sales agent wasting time talking to you?

5. *The franchisor uses a negative sell and implies that you are not qualified to own the franchise.* This is a psychological game intended to make you buy immediately. If you aren't qualified, why are they talking to you?

6. *The franchisor implies that the business can be opened for less than the amount disclosed in the UFOC.* If it costs less, then why don't they change the UFOC?

7. *The franchisor can't or won't provide a list of its current franchise owners.*

8. *The franchisor uses a trademark that is similar to an established franchise.*

9. *The franchisor is new to the business but not franchising.* Some of franchising's most notorious scam artists skip from one franchise to another, duping the unsuspecting and then moving on.

10. *The franchisor promises that if you sign up now, a big customer is waiting to make a large purchase.* Again, this is a pressure tactic designed to make you buy.

11. *The franchisor tries to team sell you.* It's easier to pressure someone two-on-one. Only meet with one sales agent at a time.

12. *The franchisor downplays negative comments made by current franchisees.* Most franchisees say positive things about the business, unless there is something fundamentally wrong with the franchise.

13. *The franchisor tries to steer you to select franchisees.* Again, this is an old trick. The franchisor plants a ringer in the network and only lets prospects speak to this individual.

Finding a Franchise Attorney

Attorneys are everywhere. Millions now practice their craft throughout the United States.

Many of them would gladly review a franchise agreement and UFOC. But only a select few can provide the depth of analysis you need to protect yourself and negotiate the best possible deal for your franchise. The key is their experience in franchising.

The attorneys you choose to evaluate and help you buy a franchise should have substantial franchise experience. They should have worked with scores of other prospective franchisees—and franchisors—and know the intricacies of franchise documents and agreements.

Where can you find attorneys with special franchise talent? The International Franchise Association, in Washington, D.C., has a list of attorneys who serve on the association's Council of Franchise Suppliers. The American Bar Association also sponsors a franchise law division and can make member names available to you.

How can you determine whether an attorney has the right stuff for franchising? Here are the hallmarks of a competent franchise attorney:

1. *The attorney has current franchisee and franchisor clients.* By working both sides of the fence, an attorney has a better perspective of all the issues involved in franchising.

2. *The attorney is able to answer your questions clearly and concisely.* He should be able to do this without resorting to legal jargon or saying he will get back to you on it. If the attorney has to get back to you on basic issues, chances are he or she doesn't know much about franchising.

3. *The attorney can readily name specific franchise companies.* Most experienced franchise attorneys follow franchising closely. They keep current with the business of franchising and can demonstrate a working knowledge of the field.

4. *The attorney is willing to give you a flat fee for reviewing and analyzing franchise documents and franchise agreements.* An attorney who has gone through a previous purchase of a franchise should know the work involved and be able to quote you a price—nearly on the spot.

5. *The attorney demonstrates a capacity to negotiate realistically.* Experienced franchise attorneys understand that needless changes and overly aggressive posturing can kill a deal. If you're serious about buying a franchise, your attorney should be as interested in making the deal a reality as in protecting your interests.

6. *The attorney understands you, personally.* Franchising is more than a business deal. It requires you to change your life and assume risk. Your franchise attorney needs to know you—as a person—and what you're looking for. That way he or she can make sure the deal fits your personal needs.

The Legal Aspects of Franchising

Investigating a franchise takes time and effort. But the good news is that there are many tools to help you make sure you are investing your money wisely. The UFOC is a rare and vital document that potential franchise owners can use to examine the business they want to buy. Its twenty-three points can provide you with a realistic view of how the franchise works and what it offers franchise owners. Likewise, the franchise agreement, with its many clauses and provisions, spells out your obligations and responsibilities in advance of your signing on as a franchise owner. An experienced franchise attorney can steer you through your legal investigation of the franchise and point out any inconsistencies or concerns. Together, the UFOC, franchise agreement, and a franchise attorney can provide the protection and assurance you need to make a wise and informed decision about buying a home-based franchise.

8

PREPARING YOURSELF— AND YOUR FAMILY— TO WORK AT HOME

One thing you can be sure of working from home, you will be the envy of your friends, colleagues, and neighbors. It's amazing how many Americans harbor dreams of working from their home. When I spent a year working from my home, I heard time and time again how fortunate I was. I didn't have to commute. I wasted no time fighting traffic. There was no boss, no time clock, no one looking over my shoulder telling me what to do and when.

But to get the most out of the experience, you need to do some advance planning. You just can't one day choose to open your house for business. It's not fair to you or your family. And it might even be against local codes and ordinances. What do you need to know before starting to work from the home? What follows is a blueprint for setting up the home-based franchise of your dreams.

Codes and Ordinances

No city or county can stop you from working from your home. You have the right to toil at your kitchen table or to convert an extra bedroom into an office. But there are many codes and ordinances that could prevent you from using your home as a public place of business—particularly if you need parking or outside signage. Your local Chamber of Commerce and city planning departments can inform you of any zoning codes, laws, or regulations that could hinder the operation of your business. The Association of Cottage Industries, a trade group for home-based entrepreneurs, recommends that home-based entrepreneurs maintain a low profile while operating from their homes to avoid undue scrutiny by local officials. They also suggest that you use a post office box instead of your home address for business correspondence and keep traffic and noise to a minimum while operating your business.

Introducing the Idea

If you're single, the decision to work from your home will affect no one but yourself. But that doesn't mean you should make the decision lightly. Living and working from the same place can be monotonous and lonely. If you live by yourself, it can be even more isolating and difficult. So you will want to think long and hard about whether working from the home is the most productive and effective environment for you. Much of this chapter can help you answer these questions.

If you're married and have children, the decision to work from home can't be made in a vacuum. Your family must be a part of the decision-making process. If you fail to win their support beforehand, you're bound to cause a lot of stress between you, your spouse, and your children. With them supporting your decision, your chances of succeeding increase dramatically.

Your family needs to play a part in both the decision to buy a franchise and the decision to work from home.

Making Your Family A Part of the Franchise Decision

Buying a franchise is not like buying a new car or even a new home. A franchise isn't just an investment, it's a change of life. As a franchise owner, you will no longer be an employee, and most importantly, you will no longer have the security of a steady paycheck. Perhaps for the first time, you will be facing major financial risks.

You will be able to overcome these risks if your spouse supports your decision and understands what franchising is all about. Consequently, you will want to involve your spouse in the franchise decision as soon as possible. As you educate yourself to franchising, share what you learn with your family. Ask your spouse to meet with representatives of the company. Show family members the company's sales literature. Explain to them why you think franchising is the right option for you.

In short, you want to paint a picture for your family about what life will be like as a franchise owner. Write down what you think a franchise will allow you to accomplish personally, financially, and professionally. Document both the advantages and disadvantages of franchising for you and your family. Share your investigation with family members. For instance, your written evaluation might look like this:

THE PROS AND CONS OF OWNING A FRANCHISE

Advantages:

1. There's the possibility of making a lot of money which we can use to move, build a nest egg, or pay off bills.
2. I will be on my own, but I won't be all alone. The franchisor will be there to assist and help me, which should make the experience less stressful for the family.
3. The risks will be reduced because the business formula has been tested and proven. This should accelerate our success.
4. I will be able to share my ideas with other franchisees and learn from their experiences. This should accelerate our success.
5. I will be more confident in operating the business because the company has a track record of success that confirms my belief that the concept is sound and the business system works. This should improve my self-esteem at work and at home.
6. I will be free to create and act upon my own dreams. Again, this should improve my perception of myself and how I relate to the family.
7. I will not be confined by a boss or a company that is owned and managed by other people. This should allow me to grow as a person and contribute more to the family.
8. I will have the power of a known and recognized name behind me. This should help me build the business and reduce the early stresses of owning a business.
9. I will live a more flexible life—one where I decide when, where,

and how long I will work. This will improve the quality of life for the family as a whole.

10. I will be building equity in a business which can eventually be sold for a profit. This might fund our retirement or my children's college tuition.

Disadvantages:

1. There's a chance that this might not work. We could lose our investment and I might have to get a job.
2. The opportunity might not meet my expectations and the support of the home office may fall short.
3. We might not make as much money as we project. Reduced income could add new stress to the family.
4. The business might take much more hard work and time than I imagine. This might take me away from the family and impose upon our time together.
5. The business might require us to invest more money than projected. We might have to tap additional savings or take out loans that could add to the stress of managing the household.
6. Our expectations might be out of line with the reality of owning a franchise. Once the honeymoon is over, we might discover that the business is overly demanding and not as lucrative as we thought.

This kind of analysis will prepare you, your spouse, and your family for what to expect with a franchise. It will show your family that not only have you thought out the decision, but you have thought out how the decision will affect family life. When expectations are in line from the beginning, the chances of success are amplified.

And make your kids part of the process, also. Owning a business, any business, is bound to affect your relationship with your children. You might have to regularly work late. You might have to travel to far-off sales calls, meetings, and conventions. During that first year of operation, you might have to skip the summer vacation in order to save money or to get a big project completed for a client.

Let your kids know what to expect. Your life is going to change and so will the lives of your children. Make them a part of your mission. Share with them your dreams and hopes for the business.

Here's one strategy you might want to consider: When the time comes to sign your franchise agreement, have your family present. Your spouse might co-sign the agreement to reinforce the family's commitment to the decision. Make your children part of the ceremony. Buy a plaque and award it to them for their "unbridled support." Make them an honorary member of the board of directors or an honorary vice president. In short, get your family involved with the decision. Be sensitive to their concerns and fears and work to win their confidence.

Introducing the Work-at-Home Concept to Your Family

Once you have involved your family in the decision to buy a franchise, they now have to become part of your decision to work at home.

Working from the home places a new range of responsibilities on the family. You will want to involve your family in the decision to work from home just as you did in your decision to buy a franchise. But the work-from-home challenge requires you to go one step further. In addition to winning your family's support, you have to set some ground rules about how the family and business will share the home. You can't afford to go into a home-based business without first planning how the business and family will live and thrive together.

Set rules beforehand and then make sure everyone lives by them. What kind of rules will you need to establish? Here's a rundown:

1. *What will be off limits to your family?* We will talk later about the physical requirements of your home-based office. For now, however, it's imperative that you realize that some space—and hours of the day—will be off limits to your family while you are working from home.

2. *Who can and cannot answer your business telephone?* You will no doubt need separate business lines to operate your business professionally. But still, there will be the occasion when a family member has access to an incoming business call. Who can answer that call? What should they say? How will messages be taken? Nothing is less professional that a three-year-old answering a business telephone call and then screaming for mommy or daddy to pick up.

3. *Who can and cannot use your business equipment, such as fax machines and computers?* One perk of working from home is that some of the technology can be shared with your family. But when can junior use the computer for algebra? Who can use the fax machine and for what purposes? It's best to lay down the law beforehand.

4. *What space will be designated for the business?* In addition to your home office, you also might need an additional closet for office supplies or a corner of the garage to store inventory. Determine beforehand your space requirements, and then set those areas off limits for anyone not related to the business.

5. *When and how you can be interrupted.* There's always that temptation on the part of family members to tap on your office door and interrupt. Here's one strategy that works well. Tell your family to use the telephone if they need you. It tends to cut down on the interruptions and reinforces that fact that when you're at work, you're really working!

6. *The hours of operation of your business.* By setting hours for when the business is operating, you give notice to your family not to intrude on you when you are doing business.

7. *Who in the family will be responsible for what duties?* When you work from the home, it's easy for family members to expect you to contribute more to family life. "Can you run the kids to soccer camp? Can you tell the postman to stop cutting through the hedges? Can you take the car in for an oil change?" Some of this flexibility goes along with the work-from-home experience. But when these chores deprive you of valuable business time, they can eat away at your business. Set the ground rules beforehand and let it be known that just because you're at home, you are not the landscaper, house cleaner, launderer, and nanny. Chores have to be shared just as if you were working outside your home.

8. *Restrictions on noise.* You're on the telephone and suddenly your teenage son cranks up the stereo. Why not? It's his house, too. Sound travels easily in most homes. You'll need to set some rules on when stereos, televisions, radios, etc. can be played loudly or get some headphones with your profits.

9. *When you will and won't be working.* This is different from hours of operation. Sometimes, you will want to vary your schedule, working late one evening and taking a morning off. That's part of the beauty of working from the home. But to get the most out of this benefit, you will want to let your family know when you'll be working and when you won't. Keep a weekly datebook for your spouse and your children. Let them know what you will be doing so that you can synchronize schedules and maximize your time together.

10. *Don't become a workaholic.* The real temptation in working from home isn't that you won't work enough, it's that you will over-work. With your business and career only seconds away from your personal life, you'll be constantly reminded of projects that need to be completed and telephone calls that need to be returned. Don't become obsessive. When your business is closed, it's closed.

11. *Establish getaway periods.* If you spend all your time working and living from the same space, the world is likely to close in on you. You need time to get away from the house, see people, and spend time away from the pressures of work and family. If you like to work out, join a health club and attend regularly. If you have a close friend, set up a standing lunch date. Use sales calls and appointments as a respite from the monotony of working and living from the home. Establish regular getaway periods that can give you a fresh outlook on life.

The best way to introduce these rules to your family, again, is to involve them from the start in the decision to work from your home. Before buying a home-based franchise, call a family meeting. Lay out a game plan for how you think the business will affect family life. Let them know that changes are inevitable. But if these changes are implemented carefully, family life will improve. You will have more time to spend with the family and you will be happier because you will own a business of your own.

9

THE NUTS AND BOLTS OF ESTABLISHING YOUR HOME OFFICE

There are no hard and fast rules about the best way to establish a home-based business. Some entrepreneurs build elaborate, customized additions to their homes that they use specifically for a home office. Then again, I have seen home-based entrepreneurs operate their businesses from a desk in the corner of an extra bedroom—and earn six figures from their makeshift offices.

The best way to start setting up your home-based business is to consult with your franchisor. What does your franchisor say you need to operate an efficient home-based operation? Some franchises, for instance, require additional parking space for vans or equipment. Others require you to have enough room to inventory raw materials or supplies.

Your franchisor should be able to tell how much square footage you need to operate the business from your home. The franchisor should also provide you with an exact list of the equipment and office furniture you need to manage the business.

But also consult present franchise owners within the network. How did they set up and operate their home-based franchise? What equipment did they need? How much office furniture do they have? Do they have employees who work in their home office? What do they think you will need to operate your home-based franchise? Talk openly and frankly with them. And ask them whether the franchisor's view of the home-based office is realistic. For example, some franchisors allow their franchisees to initially work from the home, but expect them to move to commercial offices within a certain period of time. Find out the expectations of your franchisor right from the start. You will want to ask:

- Where do you operate your franchise from? An attic? Extra bedroom? Basement? Den?

- How much room do you designate for your franchise? What's the square footage? Does it take up more than one room?

- Are there any special requirements you need for delivery? Storage? Work areas?

- Do clients ever come to your home-based office? If so, how do you handle that situation?

- What furniture and equipment is necessary for operating the business out of the home? Is it more than what the franchisor thinks is necessary?

- What type of equipment—computers, fax machines, copiers, etc.—are needed to efficiently operate the business from the home?

- What are the biggest challenges of operating the business from the home?

- How many telephone lines do you have in your home office?

- Do you plan to keep your office in your home or eventually move into outside offices?

- How is your office separated from the family living space? Do you keep a door closed? Do you have to climb stairs?

- Do you find working from the home much of a stigma in getting accounts or new clients?

- In your estimation, what would the ideal home-based office look like for this business? What would it include?

- Do you have any tips for making a home-based office more efficient and productive?

Once you have the input of the franchisor and other franchisees, it's time to start converting portions of your home to a home-based business.

Step One: Finding a Designated Area

Your home-based office shouldn't be makeshift or temporary. You are going to own and operate the business for a long time—five, ten, fifteen years. You need a permanent, designated place to call your own. It should be separate and distinct from the family living area. It shouldn't be the corner of the kitchen table or a desk in the upstairs hallway. The office should have a door for security and privacy.

An extra bedroom, den, or extra room are your best bets. Short of that, you can consider an attic or basement. Wherever you choose, you have to make it comfortable and liveable. Basements and attics can work, but you might have to invest in insulation, upgraded electrical service, Sheetrock or plaster, quality lighting, and a bright coat of paint.

When I began working from my home, I chose an unfinished basement. But every month, I invested in upgrading the surroundings. One month, I insulated the walls and threw away my electric heater. The next month, I had a carpenter erect a wall between my office and the washer and dryer. I invested gradually over time. Within a year, I had a comfortable working environment that looked as if it were in a commercial office building—not the basement of my home.

The advantage of a basement, I found, was that it was very much separate from the family living area. The door at the top of the stairs kept my family from interrupting me or intruding at inopportune times. When I was downstairs, I was at work. The approach kept me focused and productive.

Step Two: Upgrading Your Home

Needless to say, you will need to make some physical changes to the area you choose for your home-based business.

First, consider lighting.

Most commercial office buildings are lighted specifically to encourage worker productivity. At home, however, lighting is more informal and diffused. One trick I discovered while working from home was to replace conventional incandescent lighting with fluorescent lights that emulate natural sunlight. The lights give a room an airy, open feel, even if it's in a basement or an attic.

Second, have an electrician look at your power supply in the room or area where you want to set up your office.

Most of today's technology requires a lot of electricity. A fax, telephone, computer, printer, copier, and desk lamp can easily overload a room's circuit. Most electricians will add outlets to your home-based office for between $50 and $200 a piece, depending on how far they must string lines and whether the office is on the first or second floor. Even if you have enough outlets, you will want to make sure that they are properly grounded. Improperly grounded outlets can do severe damage to computers and similar equipment.

If you're going to the bother and expense of having an electrician add outlets, you might want to consider putting your computer and other high-tech equipment on a power line of their own. This will reduce the chances of a power surge doing damage to sophisticated equipment. The cost will again vary according to where your office is in relation to the electrical box and whether your electrical box has an open circuit.

Third, consider telephone service.

The telephone company can run telephone lines to just about any room in a house. But you need to have some idea of where you plan to place the telephone within the room so the jack is close to the telephone. You also need to determine how many lines you will need to operate your business. If you need more than three, the telephone company might run into problems—especially in older neighborhoods where street wiring allows only one or two lines per home. Your franchisor should be able to tell you how many lines you will need. You will probably need at least two lines. A separate line for your fax machine could make the minimum three lines.

Fourth, do some soundproofing.

Soundproofing doesn't have to be extensive or expensive. But noise is often a problem in a home-based business, especially if you have young children around.

Fabrics are an inexpensive and attractive way to noiseproof a home-based office. Wall-to-wall carpeting, along with a good quality mat, will cut down on a lot of noise penetration. Draperies will also reduce extraneous noise. If you still have a problem, wall tapestries work as great noise barriers. You also might want to buy furniture that incorporates fabric. This tends to eliminate noise that bounces off hard surfaces, including chairs and desks.

Make sure that you keep your receipts for the work you do to upgrade your office. Also make sure the invoices clearly state that the work was done to a home-based office. All these expenses are business deductions which you will need to track.

Step Three: Furniture for Your Home-based Office

Here again, your franchisor should be able to give you insight into what you need. The franchise might even be able to secure discounts for you through their vendors.

If not, don't worry. Office furniture is easy to come by—and surprisingly inexpensive.

A number of office supply discounters sell brand-name office furniture at discounted prices. Many of these companies are buyer's clubs which require you to become a member to shop there. But becoming a member is often as easy as filling out a card. There's usually no expense. Buying clubs can save you a lot of money over the life of your business. I once surveyed office suppliers in the Philadelphia area and discovered that buyer's club prices are legitimately 15 percent to 30 percent lower than typical office supply stores. They can save you money on everything from fax paper to telephone answering machines.

Another alternative is to buy used office furniture. I have bought scores of used desks, chairs, and filing cabinets over the years, usually with good results. Used furniture is easy to find. Just look in the classified advertising sections of major metropolitan newspapers under the heading "Office Furniture." It usually has a heading of its own.

Because most office furniture is made to last, you can usually refurbish good-quality office furniture by spending an hour cleaning it and oiling its moving parts. The only drawback to used furniture is that you have to take what's available and the likelihood of finding matching pieces is slim.

Because of those drawbacks, I stopped buying used office furniture a few years ago and started investing in furniture that's made of pressboard (congealed sawdust) with formica tops. An oversize desk can cost as little as $300. You can often buy an entire office's worth of furniture (a desk, credenza, typing table, and two-drawer lateral filing cabinet) for less than $800. The only shortcoming is that this type of furniture is extremely heavy and difficult to move once it's assembled and set up in your office.

One other trick you might want to consider is buying floor models. Every office furniture store has scores of pieces on display. If you ask the sales person to knock 30 percent off the price of a floor model you're likely to walk away with an already assembled piece of furniture that looks and functions like new.

Unless you have the money to spend, it's wise to stay away from expensive, all-wood office furniture. When you're just starting your business, you don't know what your needs will be two years down the road. If you start inexpensively, you won't waste money when you make changes later.

Also, office furniture takes more of a beating than most other kinds of furniture. Along with all your other concerns in starting your business, you don't want to worry about scratching an expensive piece of furniture. And because you're home-based, the chances of clients coming to your office are slim. There's no need to worry about impressing someone. So save your money and invest it in other parts of your business. A desk or credenza won't make you money. But money spent on an advertisement or a sales letter just might.

One area you don't want to skimp on is a good desk chair. A cheap chair can damage your lower back and put you out of commission for days—even weeks—and that's a big blow to a home-based businessperson. A good office chair should support your lower back and come with enough adjustments so you can customize the position to your comfort. You'll also want a chair on wheels, so you can scoot around to the copier or the filing cabinet. And make sure it swivels. That way you can answer a telephone call by just turning around.

Step Four: Equipment for Your Home-based Business

The input of your franchisor will be imperative to investing wisely in equipment. A list of the equipment you need to open your business, along with prices, will be included in the company's Uniform Franchise Offering Circular. Some franchisors require you to purchase your equipment from designated sources. If that's the case, find out if your franchisor has a financial relationship with the vendor. You want to get the best deal possible on your equipment—regardless of whether your franchisor gets a cut or commission on the purchase price.

Other franchise companies provide specifications for equipment in Item Nine of the UFOC and allow you to purchase it anywhere. Either way, your franchisor should provide a detailed description of the equipment you will need to operate the business.

That equipment will vary from franchise to franchise and should be generally disclosed to you in Item Seven of the UFOC. But in this day and age, there are a number of basic tools you will need to operate your business. The shopping list might include computer equipment and software, printers, faxes, a telephone system and answering machine, and more. What follows are items to consider when investing in office equipment.

A Computer for Your Home-based Franchise

While some franchisors don't require you to use a computer in the operation of the franchise, it's difficult to imagine any business that couldn't benefit from computer technology. If you don't know how to use a computer, it might be wise to take a class in computers before investing in a home-based franchise. That way, you will have some idea of their power and potential and know whether they could help you in your business.

Computers can help you on many fronts in your home-based business. With a computer by your side, you can efficiently manage all your correspondence, including:

- balancing your business bank accounts;

- preparing your quarterly tax returns;

- communicating with other franchisees and maybe the franchisor;

- writing your own sales letters;

- managing your own mailing lists;

- tapping into electronic "bulletin boards" that might be specific to your industry;

- maintaining your Rolodex;

- keeping track of your schedule book;

- playing computer games (all work and no play makes a home-based franchisee a bore);

- ordering airline tickets, shopping for client gifts, finding stock prices, and accomplishing just about anything you can imagine.

But the key to maximizing the efficiency of a computer is understanding something about them. Computers are a world of their own, complete with a language straight out of "Star Trek." There are bytes and mips, hard drives and mother boards. Don't panic. You don't have to know anything about a carburetor to drive a car. You don't need to know much about electronics to know how to use a computer. You do, however, need to know some of the words that describe computers. Most bookstores sell basic handbooks on computers. But frankly, even the most fundamental book about computers can be confusing if you're starting from ground zero.

Here's one strategy I used while working from my home that helped me become competent in computers. I searched for and found a computer consultant who also worked from his home. Because we were both home-based, he had an intrinsic understanding of the type of computer, printer, and software I needed to operate my business. And because we both worked out of our homes, we could get together at off hours, at night, or early in the morning, when both our schedules were clear.

Consequently, he was able to teach me the basics of computing quickly with minor frustrations. And because I paid him a small retainer each month ($250), he was available for telephone questions.

This strategy is going to cost you money. But computers are marvels of productivity. They can help you do the work of three people. Never underestimate how much they can assist in organizing, managing, selling, and creating. The money I spent on a computer consultant came back to me in droves in terms of productivity and efficiency.

Buying a Computer That's Right for You

Now comes the great debate. Which computer should you buy for your home-based franchise? Obviously, your franchisor will have something to say regarding this decision. If your franchise uses computers, then they will be able to steer you in the right direction. If not, you will have to make up your own mind.

My suggestion is that unless your business is highly creative and requires graphic arts, stick with an IBM or a clone that uses DOS (Disk Operating System) as an operating language. Macintoshes have a clear advantage in the world of publishing, graphic arts, and printing. But in the business world, IBM has set the standards and DOS is the accepted operating system.

On average, a similarly powerful DOS machine is less expensive than its Macintosh counterpart. And while many people think DOS-based computers are more difficult to learn and use than Macintosh machines, DOS has made tremendous strides in ease of use with a program called Windows, which actually imitates Macintosh's uses of pictures instead of words to manage a computer.

Right now, the DOS standards in computing are 386 machines that operate at anywhere from 16 megahertz to 40 megahertz. The number 386 refers to the sophistication and speed of the computer's main processor. But again, don't get bogged down in words. Just use them the way you do to describe cars. Few people know what a turbo is. Few people know what a 386 is. Both make things go faster. And there is value in having a computer that can decipher information quickly.

In addition to the processor's speed, you will want to consider the size of the hard drive. A hard drive is the internal mechanism that stores information—both software and data—inside your computer. Think of it as your private library. The size of the hard drive determines how much information you can store. The standard size hard drive is 40 or 60 megabytes. That's more than enough to store most of your software and records. And if you need more space, you can always save old files or records on floppy disks.

The monitor is another important consideration. If you plan to use your computer extensively, you will spend a lot of time staring into its unwavering screen. A mono-color screen can save you money. But a color video display is easier on the eyes and more attractive with most programs. Color VGA (Video Graphic Adaptor) monitors can deliver nearly lifelike images with resolutions much higher than a conventional television set.

What are some good quality DOS-based computers? Virtually all manufacturers who offer warranties manufacture quality machines. Name-brand manufacturers might try to scare you with compatibility issues. But today, all major brands use the same processor and devices and have no trouble communicating.

How much can you expect to pay for a computer? Just wait three months and you will probably pay less. Technology is advancing so quickly that price decreases are a regular part of the game. The dollar you spend today on computers buys ten to fifteen times the computing power of only five years ago.

As an example, the computer I am writing this book on cost me about $1,800 (it's a 386 with a 60 megabyte hard drive and a color VGA monitor). Two years ago, if the technology were even available, I would have paid between $8,000 and $9,000 for a comparable machine. You should budget between $1,200 and $2,000 to buy a computer that meets your home office business needs. Anything more is probably overkill at this point. Anything less is probably limited in how it can be upgraded and used.

SOFTWARE FOR YOUR COMPUTER

It's not the computer that baffles most users, it's the software that's really frustrating. Training is the key to learning software quickly.

Local community colleges and high schools regularly offer night classes in specific computer software packages.

Your franchise might have a proprietary software package to help you manage the business, track sales, and build profits. If so, that will be a big advantage in developing your business. Many franchises, however, haven't advanced that far. Regardless, you'll probably have to augment what software the franchisor offers with off-the-shelf programs to manage your business.

Need some ideas? Following is a sampling of some of the best software for your home-based business.

WORDPROCESSING SOFTWARE

The wordprocessing software business is so competitive that just about every program on the shelf is a good package or else it won't have survived.

Right now, the leading wordprocessing programs are Wordperfect and MicroSoft Word. Both provide a huge array of choices and options for making your letters and proposals look terrific. MicroSoft Word relies heavily on mouse-activated icons for scrawling through pages and making stylistic changes. Wordperfect is driven by keyboard commands which many first-time users find tedious. Still, I am a big Wordperfect fan and recommend it because it's widely used, so exchanging files is rarely a problem.

CHECKBOOKS AND ACCOUNTING

As a businessperson, one of your prime responsibilities is tracking and recording the finances of your company. But that's a double-edged sword. On the one hand, you want to know what's going on financially in your business. On the other, balancing a checkbook doesn't make money for you or your business. The solution? Computerize your checkbook with any number of easy to use electronic checkbook programs now on the market. These software packages (Quickens3 and One Write Plus are examples) will help you account for all your income and expenses and even print out checks on a laser or dot matrix printer. Even if you don't use the check-writing function and prefer to carry your own checkbook, a computerized checkbook can still save you a tremendous amount of time when the time comes to balance your bank accounts.

In addition to balancing your checkbook, some small business accounting programs can help you budget and forecast, account for payroll taxes, and perform on-screen calculations. One of the biggest benefits to using these programs is that at the end of the year, you can spit out all your income and expenses by category. That one function can save you $500 to $1,000 a year on accountants who would otherwise have to rifle through receipts and bank statements to prepare your income tax return.

SALES AND PROSPECTING SOFTWARE

If you're growing a business, you have to be selling. Sales is often a game of numbers and contacts. The more people you contact, the more products and services you will sell. Don't keep those valuable contacts on index cards or scribbled on scraps of paper. Automate them with contact management software. Contact management software, such as ACT! and Telemagic, are simple-to-use programs that allow you to computerize your Rolodex and then quickly and conveniently call up the names and addresses of sales prospects, suppliers, vendors, colleagues, and associates by hitting buttons on your keyboard.

The programs can be customized so you can categorize your contacts on many different variables. For instance, if you operate a home-based interior design business, you could customize your contact management program to track your clients by town, by the cost of their home, or by whether they are a commercial or residential client.

If, for example, you want to do a mailing to just your commercial clients, you can quickly scan your client list and create a new mailing list. Or if you want to do an upscale mailing to people who live in homes worth $250,000 and more, you can find all of these clients quickly and easily if you have filed them away on your computer.

These contact management programs also prints labels, letters, and Rolodex cards. They can even be set up to dial the telephone for you through a modem.

DESKTOP PUBLISHING

Promotion is an important key to growing your business. Many off-the-shelf desktop publishing programs give you the power to create beautifully designed promotional pieces, everything from advertisements to flyers and even stationery.

PageMaker, Ventura, Ready Set Go, and Quark are just some of the desktop publishing programs that can make just about any document look as if it was professionally typeset.

Most of these programs are mouse-based and driven by on-screen icons, rather than keyboard commands. Consequently, moving or enlarging type, creating borders, and drawing lines can all be done quickly by even first-time users.

Top-quality desktop publishing programs are expensive—anywhere from $200 to $700. But if you like the creative side of business and plan to do your own promotions, these programs can save you money on graphic artists, typesetters, and designers.

Choosing a Printer

You can invest in the best computer made, but if your printer is poor quality, your sales letters, memos, proposals, and other correspondence will suffer. Dot matrix printers (those machines that use continuous form paper and compose images by putting down dots on a page) have been the accepted standard in home office computing for years. However, as prices of laser printers fall, the dot matrix is being replaced with the crisper and more exact lettering of lasers. Laser printers work by electrically charging a piece of paper to accept toner, which is then heated and adheres to the page. The end result is a true black image that looks even better than typewriter quality.

At today's prices, home-based franchise owners can purchase a quality laser printer for as little as $600 or $700. Hewlett-Packard, Panasonic, and Packard Bell all make reliable machines. One thing to consider, however, is the accessibility of supplies and toner for the machines. Obtaining supplies for off-brand laser printers can be a tough challenge and a frustrating one.

Fax Machines

Like the computer, fax machines are quickly becoming an indispensable part of home-based businesses. They are even more important to home-based franchisees because franchise owners have a compelling and ongoing need to communicate with far-off franchisors. The fax machine can make this communication easy and quick.

Sanyo, Murata, Panasonic, and other name-brand manufacturers all make quality machines. The prices vary dramatically according to the features you need. For instance, a cutting blade (the blade that cuts an incoming fax into pages) can add $200 to $500 to the price of a fax machine. If you want a fax that can be programmed to send faxes late at night when telephone rates are cheaper, this too will add to the cost.

Many home-based franchise owners start their businesses with basic fax machines, which range in price from $300 to $500. They then upgrade, if their volume of faxes warrants it.

Telephone Answering Machines

Time was, an answering machine was looked down upon as a poor man's alternative to a receptionist. Not anymore. Call a vice president at a Fortune 500 company and chances are you won't talk to a secretary. You will get a voice mail service. While voice mail is much more sophisticated than a traditional answering machine, it's nearly impossible for a caller to tell them apart. Consequently, the answering machine is no longer frowned upon in the business world.

Again, the major brands—Panasonic, AnswerPhone, General Electric—all make high-quality, reliable answering machines that can cover one, two, and even three telephone lines. If you plan to buy an answering machine, make sure it can be accessed remotely so when you're on the road you can pick up important messages.

The more remote options on a machine, the better. For instance, if you're calling long distance to listen to your answering machine, you might want to have the ability to fast forward over routine messages and only listen to important messages. You'll save money with the option. Also, an option that allows you to change your message remotely often comes in handy when you want to tell callers when you'll be returning to the office or if an emergency is keeping you away.

Answering services are an alternative to answering machines. But they have fallen out of favor in recent years and they offer few advantages over quality answering machines. Most callers can tell that an answering service isn't your own reception.

Another option is the answer call services now offered by local telephone companies. Answer call is an out-of-office voice mail service that picks up your messages while you're away or if your lines are busy. I have been using answer call for the past two years with tremendous success. It's easy to access remotely and the voice quality is as good as a telephone answering machine. By answering my telephone while my lines are busy, I never miss a telephone call. It's relatively inexpensive—$5 a month after a nominal installation fee. It does, however, run up your local telephone bill with repeated calls during the day to collect your messages. The service lets you know you have messages by stuttering the dial tone when you pick up the receiver. You can even add mail boxes to answer phones for other people on your staff. In that respect, it has the features of an expensive in-office voice mail system.

Your local telephone company can tell you whether answer call is available in your area.

The Nuts and Bolts

Outfitting your home-based franchise will take time and planning to do it right. Start with your franchisor and then turn to other franchise owners to help direct your buying. And don't overlook steals and deals—such as buying used furniture or joining buyer's clubs where prices are typically lower for supplies and furniture.

Finally, don't disregard how computer, fax, and laser technology can help you improve the productivity and efficiency of your business. As a home-based franchise owner, you're likely to do most of the work yourself. If you can handle more work in a shorter time, you will increase sales and profits for you and your business. Computers are your best bet for making that a reality.

10

MANAGING TAXES, RECORD KEEPING, BANKING, AND INSURANCE FOR YOUR HOME-BASED FRANCHISE

There are many misconceptions out there regarding the tax benefits of owning a business. It's assumed by the general public that if you own a business, you can write off just about any expense as a cost of doing business. Most people even believe you can write off a large portion of your home mortgage payment if you maintain a home office.

Truth is, however, tax breaks for home-based entrepreneurs aren't nearly as abundant as most people think. You're entitled only to legitimate tax deductions, and the mortgage write-off isn't as lucrative as you might imagine.

What are you entitled to write off as legitimate business expenses? You need to work with an accountant to answer that question. But certainly, any expense that is incurred during the process of building, marketing, or advancing your business can be written off as a business expense. Office furniture, equipment, stationery, and supplies are all business expenses. Advertising, employee wages, telephone bills, and other costs associated with the business are likewise deductible from your business's gross income.

But what about the gray areas? Can you write off repairs done to the roof of your house? After all, you can't do business if it's raining in your office. And how about the cost of the cleaning service that tidies up your home once a week? They also clean your office. Is that cost deductible? And how about your mortgage payment? A portion of it covers your home-based office? Can you deduct that?

The answer is that parts of all these expenses can be deducted when you maintain a home-based office. But just how much is a question that's best answered by your accountant. The way most accountants calculate these deductions is to determine how much of your home is used for business purposes. For instance, if you have a six-room home, and two of the rooms are used strictly for business, your accountant might argue that one-third of all maintenance, improvements, utilities, and rent payments are legitimate business deductions. One-third is an aggressive position for most home-based entrepreneurs. But if you can prove you use that much space to operate your business, then you're entitled to the deductions. Most home-based businesspeople write off between 10 and 30 percent of the expenses associated with their homes.

To qualify as an expense, those costs don't have to deal directly with the space in which you operate your business. For instance, if you report that 20 percent of your home is used for business, then you can write off 20 percent of your landscape bills, 20 percent of the cost of a new driveway, 20 percent of your condo fees, and 20 percent of the new vinyl siding you just had installed.

That might seem like a windfall for a home-based business owner. But all businesses are allowed to write off the costs associated with maintaining their offices or other facilities. The home-based business owner is given the same option with no greater or lesser advantage.

Writing off your mortgage payment is a little more problematic. Many home-based franchise owners wrongly assume that if 20 percent of their home is used for business, they are entitled to write off 20 percent of their mortgage costs. That's not the case. Most mortgage payments are comprised of interest and principle payments. The government already allows you to deduct mortgage interest payments from your income. So your only tax break as a home-based entrepreneur comes from deducting a portion of the principle you pay against your mortgage. If you use 20 percent of your home for business, that's a deduction of 20 percent of the principle. Because most people pay more in interest than principle against their home loans, this deduction for home-based business owners isn't as generous as it first appears.

Apartment renters are in better luck. They can deduct a straight percentage from their monthly rent payments as expense for maintaining a home-based business.

Writing Off an Automobile

Cars are another area where new franchise owners wrongfully believe that they can enjoy a tax windfall. As a business owner, you will have the option to maintain a company car and write off all expenses associated with that automobile. But you can't misuse this option. The car should be used for business purposes only. If the use is mixed between business and personal use, you must keep a detailed log and record mileage for both personal and business use.

Car expense is one area that the IRS will closely examine if you should be audited. If you have logs to prove your use, you're likely to stay out of trouble. If you have to re-create your use from memory, the IRS is much more likely to disallow expenses.

The cost of a car can be deducted in two different ways. One method relies on depreciation to write off the expense of buying a car. The other method involves deducting the actual cost of mileage and all related costs of operating the automobile. Again, your accountant can give you advice on the best way to account for these costs.

Tracking the Expenses of a Home-based Business

One of your primary responsibilities in operating your home-based franchise is to maintain clear and accurate records that will help you chart the progress of your business. Keeping track of your expenses is vitally important because expenses are deducted from your income at the end of the year. Those deductions lower the amount of money you have to pay in taxes and so put more money in your pocket once everything is accounted for.

There are two rules of thumb when it comes to tracking expenses: (1) keep every receipt; and (2) devise a system for recording those receipts.

As a home-based franchisee, you will pay expenses in three main ways: cash, credit cards, and checks. Here's what you need to know about maintaining accurate records in all three methods of transactions:

Tracking Cash

The life of a home-based franchise owner is a hectic one. You have to run to see clients, meet with vendors, talk to employees, and make sure everything is operating smoothly. You haven't time to collect receipts and account for every little penny. But you must. The name of the game in business is making money. First and foremost, you need to know where the money comes from and where it goes.

The accounting and check-writing software mentioned in Chapter 9 can help you track inflows of cash to your company. The great advantage of these programs is that in a keystroke they can help you discover who has been paying you and who hasn't. Computerizing your bookkeeping can also help track your cash outflows by showing you what checks have been written over any period and how these payments affect the net income of your company.

But for smaller transactions—typically petty cash purchases for supplies, tolls, or postage—you will have to collect receipts and account for the money on a weekly or monthly basis.

One simple trick is to buy petty cash envelopes at your local stationery store and start every month with $200 or $300 in the envelope. As you spend money, replace the cash with receipts. Note on the front of the envelope the date and the reason for the expense. At the end of the month, simply add up your expenditures. If there's cash remaining, carry it over to the next month. If you're short, reimburse yourself any monies you might have used to supplement the expenditures. Start every month with a new envelope and keep the old envelopes, complete with receipts, for your records.

Credit Cards

With plastic becoming the primary means of transaction in this country, it's probable that many of your business purchases will be done with credit cards. After all, they are convenient and the monthly statements offer an excellent means of keeping records. You should maintain separate personal and business credit cards and try never to mix their uses. Also, when choosing credit cards, look for the lowest interest rates possible. Typically, businesspeople maintain higher daily credit card averages than consumers. Over the course of a year, these higher averages can result in substantial interest payments.

Here's one budgeting strategy for using credit cards. When you make a substantial purchase on your credit card, write the check to pay the bill immediately after returning to your office. It's easy to overuse your credit card and then discover at the end of the month that your credit card balance is much higher than you imagined.

If you pay as you go, you will always have a bead on the cash flow of the company and you will be better able to manage your bills.

Keeping Track of Your Checkbook

With the computers and technology of today, you can easily operate a home-based franchise without ever paying a bookkeeper to balance your checkbook or send out invoices. In my own case, my company bills more than $250,000 a year, and we don't have a bookkeeper. All records are kept on the computer and the checkbook is balanced once a month. The entire process takes about 30 minutes. The advantage of doing your own bookkeeping is that it keeps your finger on the financial pulse of the company and lets you know how much money you are making.

Regardless of whether you use a bookkeeper, you will still need to use an accountant to help with year-end taxes, payroll taxes, and estimated tax payments throughout the year. But even here, computerization will save you hundreds of dollars by providing your accountants with exactly what they need in the way of profit and loss statements and financial reports.

When running your own business, it's vital to set up separate checking, savings, and/or money market accounts for your business. Most banks will force you to open a commercial checking account to operate your business. These accounts are typically more expensive than consumer accounts. But you can often avoid service charges by maintaining a minimum monthly balance in your commercial account.

Because commercial checking accounts don't bear interest, you want to keep your balance at a level that doesn't trigger service fees but also doesn't tie up too much of your money in a non-interest bearing account. The solution is to maintain two business accounts—a checking account and a savings and/or money market account. Keep your checking account low and when you need money transfer it from your savings account. Over the course of a year, this simple strategy can earn you hundreds of dollars in interest.

When dealing with banks, it's vital that you build a personal relationship with the staff and personnel. You will want to personally meet the branch manager to introduce yourself and your business.

Most businesspeople only meet with their bankers when there's a problem or if they need a loan. But it's more difficult to get a loan when you don't know anyone who works at your bank.

A personal relationship with your banker can help you learn a lot about operating the financial side of your business. For instance, my banker once suggested that I beef up my credit rating so that if I ever needed a commercial loan the process would be less difficult. He recommended that I establish a track record of borrowing money and paying it back on time. I started with small personal signature loans of only $1,000 or so. I used the same strategy with my credit cards. It cost me money in interest payments but today I have an open line of credit for $35,000 through my bank and three credit cards with $10,000 limits. That's ready cash that I could tap tomorrow if my business needed it.

As a businessperson, you need to plan and think in advance about financing future growth and sales. Just about every business, from time to time, needs to borrow to pay bills or buy new equipment. Your banker can teach you how to lay the groundwork for accessing the money you will need to grow a business.

Insuring Your Home-based Business

Most homeowners insurance have a low cap on the amount of coverage they will extend to office equipment and computers in the home. That's why it's vital that you purchase an additional insurance policy to cover your home office equipment, supplies, and inventory if a fire, flood, or burglary occurs. These policies are extremely reasonable—as low as $100 to $200 for $35,000 worth of coverage. You can get a policy from the same broker who wrote your home-owners' or apartment insurance.

In addition to office insurance, you might need car, liability, or other types of insurance as specified by your franchisor. The franchise agreement should provide the details.

Maintaining Other Records

You will want to make sure that your records are safe and accessible. If you plan to work on computer, record keeping is simplified because you can save copies of just about anything in a computer's hard drive. You should back up your computer hard drive at least once a week and store your back-up diskettes off-site—at a friend's office or in a safe deposit box. Computers fail much more often than most people assume. If your computer goes down, you can lose vital billing, accounting, bookkeeping, and client information. If you leave your back-up diskettes in your office, a fire or burglary could deny you of everything. By storing your back-up diskettes off-site, you will make sure to avoid losing valuable information in case of fire or burglary.

In addition to all your business records and files, you will want to keep special track of information integral to your relationship with your franchisor. Your franchise agreement and disclosure document should be kept separate and secure. Any lease contracts or long-term notes or obligations should be protected and kept out of the way of day-to-day business. Insurance policies, warranties, and guarantees should be afforded special consideration and kept in a safe location that you can access easily.

Finally, you will want to keep record of your dealings with your franchisor. Records should be kept pertaining to royalty payments, sales performance, and any material correspondence over the course of your relationship. Chances are, you will never become embroiled in litigation with your franchisor, but the risk always exists.

Franchise owners are notoriously poor record keepers. When a lawsuit arises, franchisees often are unable to present an accurate accounting of the actions that precipitated the suit. Many franchise owners can't even find a copy of their disclosure document and have to subpoena their franchisor's records for it.

Don't let yourself fall into this trap. Keep detailed records of your communications with your franchisor. If you call your franchisor, write down the nature of the call. How was it managed, directed, and acted upon?

If you're visited by a franchise representative, take notes of the meeting and file them. Ask for a copy of any reviews or evaluations that the franchisor makes of you or your business. If your franchisor doesn't respond to an issue or concern, make a note of it. If you call your franchisors and don't receive an answer or call-back, make sure you record the incident and file it somewhere safe.

In addition, keep all your telephone bills that show your communications with the home office. If four years from now your franchisor accuses you of not communicating with the home office, a telephone bill could be a valuable piece of evidence.

Record keeping for taxes, banking, accounting, and franchise relationships is an important part of the franchise success equation. In your zest to build a profitable business, you might be tempted to overlook the less glamorous aspects of tracking your business. But as a home-based franchise owner, it's imperative that you know how well your business is doing. Records will keep you informed, keep you clean with the IRS, keep you up-to-date with expenses and income, and maybe even keep you out of court with your franchisor. Don't overlook the need to track your business closely and keep tabs on its progress.

11

STAYING WITH THE PROGRAM AS A HOME-BASED FRANCHISE OWNER

Working from the home can be difficult because you have to rely on yourself to move forward. There's no boss to goad and threaten. There may not be colleagues to kick around ideas and share the excitement.

It's all up to you. You have to look to yourself for motivation and direction. You have to pull from within to move yourself and your business forward.

What are the keys to self-motivation in a home-based business? Some of the points we touched upon in Chapters 4 and 8. In general, you have to discipline yourself to make every day a great day in the development of your business. It's a matter of attitude and outlook. But it also depends on how you run your life and how seriously you approach your business. When your motivation starts to wane, these rules can help empower yourself to achieve your goals:

1. *Start every day at the same time*. It's amazing how this simple trick can help add to your motivation level and productivity. If you live with a floating starting time, there's the tendency to get going later and later in the day. Don't let it happen. Start every day at eight or nine o'clock, whenever you choose. Make it a personal rule, and never deviate. That will help you set the tone for the day and impose structure on your home-based business.

2. *Start your day before any of your employees*. Most home-based franchises start with few employees. But as you grow your business, you're bound to need help. After you hire people, make sure you start your day before they come to work. That way, you can prepare their assignments and organize the day.

3. *Overcome any tendency to procrastinate*. In business, putting things off until tomorrow means losing sales and profits. From the first day you operate your business, make it company policy to respond to all telephone calls, letters, and inquiries on the day they are received. And always tackle the most difficult challenges first. If you put those off until last, you're bound never to get to them. So attack those telephone calls you don't want to make. Get the paperwork you dread done early in the morning. Then reward yourself by saving the easier, more likeable tasks for once you have completed those jobs you like least.

4. *Reward yourself often for jobs well done*. As the boss, you have to be a motivator, just like any great leader. When you land a big contract, take the afternoon off. If you break your sales goals, go out and buy you or your spouse a gift. If you don't reward yourself for jobs well done, there will be little motivation for replicating your performance in the future.

5. *Network yourself with successful people*. A franchise gives you entree to other franchisees—some successful and some not so successful. If you spend your time talking with negative franchisees, you will become negative. If you spend your time talking with the franchise's top performers, you will learn their tips and tricks. Their positiveness and enthusiasm is likely to rub off—on you. Block negative thinkers out of your life. They will sap your energy and drag you down.

6. *Break down large assignments into small units*. One of the quickest ways to demoralize yourself is to try to tackle large projects all at once. You need to break them into small, manageable tasks that can be more easily completed. After you finish

these smaller tasks, reward yourself—even if it's just a cold soda from the refrigerator.

7. *Visualize success.* Working on your own, it's often easy to lose sight of your goals and objectives. Don't let it happen. Spend time every day concentrating on what success will look and feel like. Build a dream in your head and hold on to it through difficult times.

8. *Formalize your goals.* Success is an ethereal thing. It can't be quantified. To motivate yourself you need tangible goals that you can relate to. Maybe it's a new home, a new car, or more quality time with your family. Whatever your goal is for buying a home-based business, write it down on paper and refer to it often.

9. *Motivational books and tapes can inspire and provoke action.* Keep your books and tapes handy. If you begin to lose motivation, start reading or listening. They will help recharge your batteries and gear you up for success.

10. *Learn to take the blows.* Anytime you set out to build a business, you're bound to become a target for competitors and other people who are jealous of you. Expect it. Don't get emotional. If you're thrown a left hook, bob and weave. Don't play other people's petty games. Successful franchise owners take their lumps and move on. They don't labor over mistakes. They don't become negative or bitter.

11. *Take full advantage of the lifestyle working from home offers.* If you're a woman with children, a home-based franchise offers an excellent way to combine career and family. But you need to set ground rules and you'll need some help. With the right people working alongside you—either in your business or in your home—you will be free to build the business of your dreams.

12. *Don't waste your time pointing your finger at your franchisor.* There's a tendency among franchise owners to rely too heavily on franchisors for support on every issue. In franchising, you're in business on your own. Quality franchisors build busi-

nesses. They don't do the work for you. If you point fingers, you'll only breed ill will between you and your franchisor. If you did your homework beforehand, you should know and trust your franchisor. Don't destroy that relationship over petty issues.

13. *Have faith in the operating system.* You bought a franchise because it provides a proven method of operating a business. Use your manuals and the skills you learned during training to manage your business. That doesn't mean you will find success every day. Most franchises take time to build and develop. When tough times come your way, just remember that the system has worked before, and it will work again.

14. *Follow the procedures and policies of the franchise company.* If your motivation starts to wane, open your franchise's operations manual and start reading. It details how the business was designed to work. If you follow those procedures, you can overcome a temporary lack of direction or enthusiasm and once again get back on the track to success.

15. *Get out of your office and home at least once a day.* One of the challenges of a home-based business is that you run the risk of becoming stagnant. By staying in the same place all day, you don't give yourself time to clear your mind and look at problems and issues in a new light. If you don't have any meetings scheduled during the day, go out to lunch with a friend.

16. *Build and stay in contact with a network of business associates.* Working alone from the home, it's easy to feel isolated and unimportant. Your business is one of the most important things in your life. It's going to broaden your horizons and hopefully bring you prosperity. A network of business associates will help lift your spirits when times are tough and can share your excitement when sales and profits skyrocket.

Motivating yourself could be one of the great challenges in finding success in a home-based franchise. If you follow the rules set down here, you will have taken a giant step forward in winning the battle to build a successful home-based franchise.

PART TWO

PROFILES OF
THE BEST
HOME-BASED FRANCHISES

PART TWO

INTRODUCTION

To select potential candidates for inclusion in this book, we reviewed franchise directories, the membership of the International Franchise Association (IFA), and industry rankings compiled by major business publications. We also consulted with industry insiders, IFA officials, attorneys, and franchise owners.

The franchises we chose to include in this section responded in a straightforward manner to our surveys and questionnaires, and in many cases provided supplemental information in the form of interviews with representatives of the franchises and franchisees.

These profiles represent a strong field of franchise candidates. In that respect, this list serves as one of the most comprehensive overviews ever developed on home-based franchising.

Keep in mind, however, that a company's appearance here does not serve as an endorsement of the company or its franchise opportunity. Consider these profiles as a starting point for your own research once you've decided to pursue your investigation seriously.

Some home-based franchises were disqualified from this book because they chose not to return their Uniform Franchise Offering Circular with the questionnaires. There were a few well-known home-based franchise companies that could not be included because they simply failed to respond to our telephone calls and requests for information in time for our publication deadline.

In some instances, we included home-based franchising opportunities that have not yet sold a significant number of franchises. Although you must take into account that these companies do not offer you a track record, we deemed them worthy of consideration because of other advantages, including a low-cost, ground-floor entry into home-based franchising.

Each profile begins with a brief overview of the company, its fees, location, and contact person. This information is followed by a brief history of the company and then an in-depth discussion of the opportunity.

Franchise fees are defined as one-time payments made by franchisees in return for the right to use the company's name and benefit from the company's initial training. Royalty fees are ongoing payments that franchisees pay to the franchise company for the right to remain part of the franchise network. Advertising royalties are the investments that franchisees make in a pool or group advertising programs. The total initial investment comprises all costs associated with opening the business and can include such items as initial advertising, working capital, the franchise fee, stationery, computer equipment, and other start-up investments.

All information reported in Part Two of this book is current as of September 30, 1991.

12

BATHROOM FIXTURE REFINISHING

---

1. BATHCREST, INC.

FRANCHISE FEE: *$3,500*

TOTAL INITIAL INVESTMENT: *$24,500*

FINANCING AVAILABLE: *Yes*

ROYALTY FEE: *None*

ADVERTISING FEE: *None*

ADDRESS: *2425 S. Progress Drive, Salt Lake City, UT 84119*

TELEPHONE: *1-801-972-1110*

CONTACT PERSON: *A. Lloyd Peterson*

INDUSTRY OVERVIEW
- *Resurfacing fixtures is far less expensive than replacing them.*
- *Refinishing allows homeowners to match new fixtures to styles and tastes.*

BENEFITS OF THIS COMPANY
- *Bathcrest has a long history of success in its industry.*
- *The franchisor demands quality work from franchisees and closely supervises franchisees to ensure that quality.*

COMPANY HISTORY:
- **IN BUSINESS SINCE:** *1979*
- **FRANCHISING SINCE:** *1985*
- **NUMBER OF FRANCHISE UNITS:** *165*

In the $100 billion home-remodeling industry, the bathroom reigns supreme as the most remodeled room in the house. When consumers decide to redo a bathroom, they usually consider two options: fixture replacement or fixture resurfacing.

Bathcrest has won international recognition for its patented chemical process, Glazecoat, which resurfaces bathroom fixtures at 20 percent of the cost of replacing them.

Fixture refinishing may not be the most exciting line of work, but it's in demand. Bathcrest's home office revenue totals more than $1 million. The company supports 165 franchises throughout the United States and Canada. Bathcrest hopes to expand its operation to include at least 225 franchises by 1995.

Although the company is known for its resurfacing techniques, it also provides customers with a variety of services, including whirlpool conversions, acrylic spa repairs, brass plumbing fixtures, and non-skid fixture treatments.

Even though the business sounds technical in scope, no previous plumbing experience is needed to become a Bathcrest franchisee.

An initial investment of $3,500 buys a one-year contract to an exclusive territory with a minimum population of 300,000 residents. The contract is renewable each year for $1,200. A franchisee can expect to need $24,500 to $33,500 to get the operation off the ground. The additional money includes the cost of training, equipment, supplies, and promotional materials.

Bathcrest doesn't require that franchisees buy equipment from headquarters, but it does make franchisees buy its unique resurfacing products, which it produces in its own 10,000-square-foot facility in Utah.

Bathcrest's five-day training program covers techniques for resurfacing fixtures as well as managing and marketing the business. Franchisees also receive an operations manual, a trouble-shooting manual, and how-to VHS tapes.

For veteran franchisees, Bathcrest conducts regular mini-seminars across the United States and Canada, and holds an annual conference to introduce new services and products to all franchisees. Six *WATS* lines are in place at headquarters to handle franchisees' problems, and training programs are held regularly to enhance technicians' skills.

FORECAST AND ANALYSIS

The home service industry shows no signs of slowing—not even during the recession of the early 1990s. Bathcrest products are safe, effective, and economical—three qualities that draw consumers. The one-year franchise agreement is very short. Make sure a qualified franchise attorney reviews this provision of the franchise agreement before investing.

2. PERMA-GLAZE, INC.

FRANCHISE FEE: *$24,500*
TOTAL INITIAL INVESTMENT: *$26,500*
FINANCING AVAILABLE: *Yes*
ROYALTY FEE: *None*
ADVERTISING FEE: *None*
ADDRESS: *1638 S. Research Loop Road, Suite 160, Tucson, AZ 85710*
TELEPHONE: *U.S., 1-800-332-7397; International, 1-602-722-9718*
CONTACT PERSON: *Dale R. Young*
INDUSTRY OVERVIEW
- *The American consumer is more cost-conscious than ever.*
- *With the change in economic times, Americans are looking for ways to improve the appearance and value of their homes without spending a fortune.*

BENEFITS OF THIS COMPANY
- *Perma-Glaze has a distinct reputation for quality products which don't pose environmental or safety hazards.*
- *Competitors' products contain toxic substances which tend to break down over time.*

COMPANY HISTORY
- **IN BUSINESS SINCE:** *1978*
- **FRANCHISING SINCE:** *1981*
- **NUMBER OF FRANCHISE UNITS:** *138*

Chipped, discolored, or stained household fixtures can detract from a house's value. With the high cost of fixture replacement, many homeowners choose to live with the embarrassing condition rather than replace them. Perma-Glaze, a Tucson, Arizona–based company consisting of 135 franchises nationwide, has developed a solution to the problem.

With its non-toxic, synthetic porcelain glaze, Perma-Glaze successfully refinishes porcelain, fiberglass, acrylic, and enameled metal fixtures at a fraction of the cost and time it would take to replace them. Fees vary from $5 per square foot for tile to $95 for a sink to $295 for a standard-size tub.

Franchisees perform most of the refinishing work themselves. The business requires only one technician, and all equipment and tools fit into the trunk of a car.

For an investment of $24,500 franchisees receive everything needed to operate the franchise. The company charges no royalty or advertising fees, and it encourages franchisees to run the franchise from home to lower operational costs.

Perma-Glaze requires franchisees to attend a five-day training course at the company's headquarters in Tucson. During the training session, franchisees learn the technical process of refinishing, as well as how to develop their marketing and sales skills. The company provides national promotion and advertising campaigns, and post-training support is also available for franchisees with concerns or problems.

FORECAST AND ANALYSIS

Perma-Glaze has a strong reputation for quality in the service industry. Few companies match its organization and its product quality. The investment is reasonable and the market potential continues to grow.

3. WORLDWIDE REFINISHING SYSTEMS

■──────────────────────────────────────■

FRANCHISE FEE: *$9,000 to $18,000 depending on size of territory*
TOTAL INITIAL INVESTMENT: *$17,450 to $26,450*
FINANCING AVAILABLE: *Yes, but limited*
ROYALTY FEE: *5 percent*
ADVERTISING FEE: *2 percent*
ADDRESS: *508 Lake Air Drive, Waco, TX 76710*
TELEPHONE: *1-800-369-9361 or 1-817-776-4701*
CONTACT PERSON: *Charles Wallis*
INDUSTRY OVERVIEW
- *Refinishing services are gaining popularity because they are less costly than replacing bathroom fixtures.*
- *A refurbished bathroom adds significant resale value to a home.*

- *Worldwide has gained international recognition for its methods and the size of its franchise network.*
- *This is not a ground-floor opportunity. The company is established and has been operating since 1971.*

COMPANY HISTORY
- **IN BUSINESS SINCE:** *1971*
- **FRANCHISING SINCE:** *1978*
- **NUMBER OF FRANCHISE UNITS:** *420*

The bathroom takes more punishment than any other room in the house. But despite the traffic, it's often the last room to be remodeled. Prices for replacing porcelain or fiberglass fixtures are high, so very few consumers are willing to shell out the money for a new tub and toilet bowl.

Worldwide Refinishing restores old, chipped, and faded fixtures with its own chemical refinishing and polishing process at a price much lower than fixture replacement.

Since 1971, the company has successfully promoted itself not only in the United States but also internationally, and today reports that networkwide revenue exceeds $6.78 million. There are 420 franchises worldwide.

A $9,000 to $18,000 franchise fee buys a 10-year contract to an exclusive territory based on population.

Worldwide says franchisees need $17,450 to $26,450 to operate the business, with the additional capital allocated to lease or buy a company van, equipment, inventory, and marketing materials. The figure includes approximate traveling expenses for the mandatory training program. Franchisees pay a 5 percent monthly royalty and a 2 percent advertising fee.

The company offers some financing but admits sources are limited. Franchisees should have as much up-front capital on hand as possible.

A major attraction for franchisees is the low overhead for a franchise like Worldwide. Sales calls and work are performed at a customer's home, so there's no walk-in traffic. Only one or two people can operate the franchise efficiently. The business can be operated in as little as 400 square feet—enough for a desk, telephone, file cabinet, and refinishing equipment. Approximately 80 percent of franchisees work at home. No plumbing or related experience is necessary.

Two weeks of training covers chemical processes which restore and refinish porcelain, fiberglass, formica, tile, and ceramic products. Then, Worldwide urges franchisees to use an 800 line for technical questions. Each year, there are several regional franchisee meetings and an annual convention.

FORECAST AND ANALYSIS

Worldwide's mark has been made in an industry that's quickly gaining competitors. At the same time, consumers are searching for economical ways to improve their homes without breaking their bank accounts. Worldwide is part of the Dwyer Group, a consortium of franchise companies based in Waco, Texas.

4. MIRACLE METHOD BATHROOM RESTORATION

FRANCHISE FEE: *$11,500*
TOTAL INITIAL INVESTMENT: *$16,500*
FINANCING AVAILABLE: *Yes*
ROYALTY FEE: *7.5 percent sliding down to 5 percent as business grows*
ADVERTISING FEE: *3 percent if and when local advertising group is formed*
ADDRESS: *3732 W. Century Boulevard, Suite 6, Inglewood, CA 90303*
TELEPHONE: *1-800-444-8827 or 1-213-671-4995*
CONTACT PERSON: *Brian Pearce*
INDUSTRY OVERVIEW
- *Bathroom refinishing is a cost-effective alternative to the expensive undertaking of fixture replacement. The industry provides safe and long-lasting products which appeal to customers.*

BENEFIT OF THIS COMPANY
- *Miracle Method has a fifteen-year history in bathroom refinishing. The company has experienced tremendous growth since it began franchising in 1979.*

COMPANY HISTORY
- **IN BUSINESS SINCE:** *1977*
- **FRANCHISING SINCE:** *1979*
- **NUMBER OF FRANCHISE UNITS:** *136*

Thirty-five million bathrooms in the United States are in need of refinishing. This statistic may not thrill the average consumer, but it certainly warms the heart of Miracle Method franchise owners.

An Inglewood, California–based company, Miracle Method has been refinishing dated, chipped, and rusted tubs and other bathroom fixtures for fifteen years. Using its own molecular-bonded coating, the company, which had network-wide revenues in excess of $5.4 million in 1991, has expanded its operation to include 136 franchises. Miracle Method expects to have 225 franchises in operation by the mid-1990s.

The concept of refinishing fixtures has attracted both consumers and franchisees alike. The exclusive process, which works on porcelain as well as fiberglass, costs as little as 20 percent of the cost to replace fixtures.

A franchise fee, which ranges from $7,500 to $12,500, purchases the rights to an exclusive territory for a five-year period. Territories are based on the number of homes in an area that are at least twenty years old. Franchisees can expect to need an additional $6,500 to $8,000 to cover the costs of equipment, marketing, and working capital. Although equipment is listed as the largest expense, Miracle Method does not require much in the way of specialized instruments. However, franchisees must lease or purchase a pick-up truck to carry the refinishing materials.

Since all work—including sales calls—are accomplished at the customer's home, Miracle Method franchisees have few overhead costs when it comes to running their businesses. Few employees are needed, and most franchisees hire labor on a job-to-job basis. The light inventory and portable equipment require little storage room— only 100 square feet according to the company's recommendations. For these reasons, more than 50 percent of franchisees opt initially to run their Miracle Method business from home. But more than 80 percent of franchisees eventually move to commercial space.

FORECAST AND ANALYSIS

Miracle Method is a veteran in the fixture refinishing industry. As American consumers become more cost conscious, they are searching for ways to save money on home repairs. The Miracle Method service fits well with this new austerity. There is competition. Many franchises are now providing similar services.

13

BUSINESS CONSULTING AND SERVICES

---

5. GENERAL BUSINESS SERVICES

FRANCHISE FEE: *$15,000 to $25,000*

TOTAL INITIAL INVESTMENT: *$30,000 to $40,000*

FINANCING AVAILABLE: *No*

ROYALTY FEE: *Technically a support fee which totals a minimum of 7 percent of gross receipts*

ADVERTISING FEE: *None*

ADDRESS: *7134 Columbia Gateway Drive, Columbia, MD 21046*

TELEPHONE: *1-800-638-7940 or 1-410-290-1040*

CONTACT PERSON: *Ed Arrington*

INDUSTRY OVERVIEW

- *Small business owners need to stay current with changes in tax or business law. GBS and similar consulting companies play to that need.*
- *Most business owners don't have the time to manage their financial concerns and turn to outside professionals for help. Business consulting can be a lucrative endeavor because businesses will pay for quality service and expertise that improves profitability.*

BENEFITS OF THIS COMPANY

- *GBS is the nation's leading organization of professional business counselors.*
- *The company brings thirty years of experience to its franchisees and customers. The franchise network is extensive, with 415 outlets located throughout the United States.*
- *Franchisees can operate as home-based businesses.*

COMPANY HISTORY
- **IN BUSINESS SINCE:** *1962*
- **FRANCHISING SINCE:** *1962*
- **NUMBER OF FRANCHISE UNITS:** *415*

The 20 million small business owners in the United States can't afford to make mistakes in their tax or financial planning. To cement their financial future, many entrepreneurs enlist the help of an outside bookkeeping or tax planning business such as General Business Services (GBS).

From its beginnings in 1962, GBS has worked with small business owners who neither had the time nor expertise to handle all the financial aspects of their firms. Thirty years later, the company still targets small businesses and has learned some tough lessons along the way.

Most notable was a period during the 1980s when the company lost more than 600 franchises—going from a 1,000-unit chain in 1980 to about 415 franchises in 1991.

The company blames poor support for its franchise network. Since that time, it has worked to improve its ability to serve franchisees. The company's size is no longer decreasing and a number of new financial services and products should increase franchisee sales and profitability. In fact, GBS recorded network-wide sales of $30 million in 1991 and plans to have 585 franchises open by 1995.

Franchisees offer their clients a full range of financial support services, including tax preparation, bookkeeping, and long-term financial planning strategies.

Depending on the experience of the franchisee, GBS offers two distinct packages. The first costs $25,000 and entitles a franchisee to two weeks of basic training and one week of advanced training at headquarters. This plan assures a franchisee 40 hours of field support training, an extensive inventory package including computer software, marketing, and promotional material, plus training for his or her spouse under an Associate Spouse Program.

The $15,000 package entitles a franchisee to two weeks of training at GBS headquarters and sixteen hours of field support training and assistance. Neither option provides franchisees with exclusive territories. Contracts run for ten years.

Franchise costs may vary, but basic training is the same for all franchisees. No matter which package franchisees select, they receive instruction in marketing, promotion, and management. Field representatives visit them at their location and offer on-site advice and consultation on building the consulting practice. Those who attend the advanced training seminar receive instruction in other aspects of consultation, such as financial analysis and tax planning.

GBS also provides franchisees with post-training support. The company conducts summer and fall tax seminars and bi-annual conventions. Telephone consultation is also available to franchisees, and the home office helps with collection problems as they arise.

There are no inventory costs in the operation of this business. Most franchisees elect to operate at home. GBS encourages this and estimates that only 15 percent of its franchisees have given up the convenience of a home office for more expensive outside space.

FORECAST AND ANALYSIS

GBS has undergone a major downsizing over the past decade due to internal management problems. Potential franchisees should be aware of this and carefully investigate the profitability of present franchisees before investing.

Small business consulting is extremely competitive. Accountants, bookkeepers, and insurance brokers all vie for the same market. Savvy marketers can still build successful businesses by consulting to other entrepreneurs.

6. COMPREHENSIVE BUSINESS SERVICES, INC.

■───■

FRANCHISE FEE: *$17,500*

TOTAL INITIAL INVESTMENT: *$40,000*

FINANCING AVAILABLE: *Yes*

ROYALTY FEE: *6 percent*

ADVERTISING FEE: *2 percent*

ADDRESS: *1925 Palomar Oaks Way, Suite 105, Carlsbad, CA 92008*

TELEPHONE: *1-800-323-9000 or 1-619-431-2150*

CONTACT PERSON: *Robert Anderson or Peter Nelson*

INDUSTRY OVERVIEW

  • *Small business financial services play an important role in an entre-*

*preneur's success. Record-keeping, business analysis, and sales fore-
casting can mean the difference between profit and loss.*

- *Part of a business owner's responsibility is to recognize his or her
  financial limitations and seek outside assistance. Avoiding this type
  of assistance can cause a business to fail.*

BENEFIT OF THIS COMPANY

- *Comprehensive has been helping the business owner for more than
  twenty-five years. The company has built a reputation on accurate
  and efficient record-keeping.*

COMPANY HISTORY

- **IN BUSINESS SINCE:** *1965*
- **FRANCHISING SINCE:** *1965*
- **NUMBER OF FRANCHISE UNITS:** *225*

Small business owners juggle customers, inventory, and employees, and they still must find time to maintain accurate records. For
more than twenty-five years, Comprehensive Business Services of
Carlsbad, California, has relieved businesses of the burden of financial record-keeping, income tax preparation, and long-term financial
planning.

Established in 1965, Comprehensive Business Services includes
225 franchises throughout the United States. The company projects
that it will have 1,000 franchises by 1995.

Comprehensive accepts as franchisees only accountants, preferably
CPAs, or experienced financial analysts, and all must have a minimum
net worth of $100,000.

The franchisee's main role is that of all-around financial consultant.
Franchisees travel to the client's office or store and work with the
owners to establish the best possible financial plan. Franchisees are
expected to understand all aspects of their client's business from
inventory control to personnel benefits.

An up-front fee of $17,500 assures a franchisee of an exclusive
territory, based on business population, for twenty years. The fee
also pays for the use of the company name as well as its logo,
trademarks, and marketing materials. Franchisees should expect to
invest an additional $5,000 to $20,000 for the set-up of a 500-square-
foot office equipped with a computer system, fax machine, telephone,
and modem.

Comprehensive allows franchisees to initially operate from home
because consultation is generally conducted at the client's site. But

Comprehensive encourages franchisees to view the home-based office as a temporary location and advises them to move to commercial space as their business prospers. Presently, 20 percent of all franchisees operate from home.

Comprehensive Business Services also charges franchisees a 6 percent royalty fee and a 2 percent advertising fee, and the company will finance qualified investors.

Franchisees attend a two-week training course at the company's California headquarters. Comprehensive teaches franchisees the various company programs offered to customers as well as strategies for marketing and managing the consultation business. Franchisees also learn computer maintenance and use. Comprehensive provides in-field training for all franchisees plus it sponsors regional and national seminars regularly which include round-table discussions and advanced training workshops. Comprehensive also conducts direct marketing programs to assist franchisees in the sale of their services to area businesses.

FORECAST AND ANALYSIS

Business consultation is a needed service. A business owner does not automatically become a business expert, and the stresses of running a business too often take precedence over the financial recording procedures.

7. PDP, INC. (PROFESSIONAL DYNAMETRIC PROGRAMS)

■——■

FRANCHISE FEE: *$29,500*
TOTAL INVESTMENT: *$29,500 plus personal operating expenses*
FINANCING AVAILABLE: *Yes*
ROYALTY FEE: *None*
ADVERTISING FEE: *None*
ADDRESS: *P.O. Box 5289, Woodland Park, CO 80866*
TELEPHONE: *1-719-687-6074*
CONTACT PERSON: *Bruce Hubby*
INDUSTRY OVERVIEW
  • *Management and employee consulting firms are gaining popularity*

in today's competitive marketplace. PDP analyzes a company's management structure and how each can better fit into that structure.

- *Management consulting firms can establish repeat business when clients see improvement in employee performance or morale.*

BENEFIT OF THIS COMPANY

- *PDP focuses its consultation on finding the best employee for a specific job. PDP uses scientific research data and psychological profiles to reveal the strengths and weaknesses of clients and employees. This process allows companies to better fit the job to the appropriate person and improve productivity.*

COMPANY HISTORY

- **IN BUSINESS SINCE:** *1978*
- **FRANCHISING SINCE:** *1980*
- **NUMBER OF FRANCHISE UNITS:** *32*

Employee performance can make or break a corporation. PDP (Professional Dynametric Programs) preaches this concept to its clients on a daily basis.

Established in 1978, the management consulting franchise uses scientifically proven survey data and psychological profiles to match a company's employees to jobs best suited to their skills. The psychological survey material determines employees' personality strengths and weaknesses as well as their tolerance to stress and their logic capabilities.

PDP franchisees personally administer the written and oral psychological surveys to a company's employees. The results of the profiles are then discussed with the company's management, who can decide which employee would perform best in certain job situations.

PDP franchisees also conduct training seminars for the client's management staff. The seminar teaches managers how to administer and interpret the psychological surveys without the assistance of PDP. The company also supplies its customers with computer programs and survey materials as part of their initial consultation fee.

The PDP franchisee is expected to maintain a professional image. Most clients are large corporations that need to improve their efficiency or productivity. Franchisees must be able to present and sell the PDP consulting program to executive management.

Franchisees invest $29,500 to purchase the rights to use the PDP name and techniques. The company finances half of the initial investment for one year at no interest. There are no exclusive territories, but PDP tries to avoid overlapping franchisees in an area. PDP also supplies to franchisees operating manuals, training videos, computer software, and demonstration disks which explain in detail the consulting role of PDP.

PDP recommends that franchisees purchase a personal computer, fax, copier, and a separate telephone line. The franchisor does not require franchisees to lease professional office space since all consulting is done at the client's site. Most PDP franchisees maintain their home-based office even after substantial business growth.

PDP receives 30 percent of the contracted fee negotiated between franchisees and their customers or $150 of the revenue earned from the sale of materials in the customer training class—whichever is greater.

All franchisees receive individualized training at their home-based site. A professional trainer assists franchisees in the sales and marketing of PDP. The in-field representative will also conduct the first on-site customer training program for each franchisee. PDP also holds seminars and conferences for franchisees, and the home office encourages telephone contact as often as needed.

FORECAST AND ANALYSIS

PDP differs from its competition in that it teaches customers how to implement PDP programs without the help of a PDP representative. Companies can repeat the program without paying additional fees to PDP. PDP will also provide to customers at their request updated research materials and programs.

PDP is a highly professional company. Because of this, PDP takes care in selecting franchisees, which has slowed franchise growth. The company foresees more rapid expansion, as more and more companies request their survey and training service.

8. RESPOND SYSTEMS

■——■

FRANCHISE FEE: *No initial fee*
TOTAL INITIAL INVESTMENT: *$35,000*

FINANCING AVAILABLE: *None*
ROYALTY FEE: *None*
ADVERTISING FEE: *None*
ADDRESS: *P.O. Box 39925, Denver, CO 80239*
TELEPHONE: *1-800-621-2900 or 1-303-371-6800*
CONTACT PERSON: *Steve Carson*
INDUSTRY OVERVIEW

- *Respond Systems and companies like it sell medical supplies and CPR classes to small companies that do not have staff-operated infirmaries, but need first-aid supplies and over-the-counter medications.*
- *The industry provides a practical, preventative service that can save business and company owners time and money by keeping workers on the job.*

BENEFIT OF THIS COMPANY

- *Respond is the second largest mobile, medical supplies franchise in the United States today. The company offers customers an array of products as well as emergency care training. The company is sales oriented, which requires a great deal of telephone and cold calling.*

COMPANY HISTORY

- **IN BUSINESS SINCE:** *1979*
- **FRANCHISING SINCE:** *1983*
- **NUMBER OF FRANCHISE UNITS:** *50*

In small companies, every worker counts. One ill or injured employee can inhibit or cripple production. Respond Systems reduces this threat with its sales route service that delivers to smaller companies a range of medicinal, injury prevention, and first-aid products.

Established in 1979, Respond targets and sells to companies with less than 250 employees an assortment of products ranging from aspirin to bandages to safety glasses. The company, whose goal is to keep workers on the job, expects to have more than 100 franchises in operation by 1995.

The role of the Respond franchisee is to establish and maintain a successful sales route business through person-to-person sales and telemarketing campaigns. Respond franchisees are also trained to teach customers CPR and other emergency medical procedures.

For a total investment of $35,000, Respond franchisees purchase the rights to an exclusive territory containing 7,000 small businesses for ten years. The investment also pays for the lease of a standard three-quarter-ton van painted with the Respond logo. Franchisees may need additional money for personal expenses, but the company does not estimate this amount. Respond charges no royalty fees, but franchisees purchase all products through the home office.

Initially, the van is the only office franchisees need. However, franchisees who expand their territories and lease additional vans may need to move to a commercial facility with parking. Sixty percent of Respond franchisees eventually lease commercial office space.

Respond trains a franchisee for a minimum of one week at the franchisee's site. Franchisees learn about the various remedies and the pharmaceutical companies that manufacture the products they sell. They are also trained and certified in CPR and other medical emergency treatment. The company holds a four-day conference annually which introduces franchisees to new products, and it conducts regional sales seminars on a regular basis.

In-field assistance is available whenever it is requested, and Respond maintains daily contact with many franchisees.

FORECAST AND ANALYSIS

Respond targets companies that would not know where to turn to get these services. The smaller companies rely heavily on their employees, and Respond's program is designed to make sure employees stay on the job effectively and safely.

Entrepreneurs who like to sell can build a profitable business with this franchise. It takes a sales-oriented person to develop and maintain a profitable route.

9. SANDLER SYSTEMS, INC.

■━━━━━━━━━━━━━━━━━━━━━━━━━━━━━━━■

FRANCHISE FEE: *$25,000*
TOTAL INITIAL INVESTMENT: *$25,000*
FINANCING AVAILABLE: *None*
ROYALTY FEE: *$908 per month*
ADVERTISING FEE: *None*
ADDRESS: *10411 Stevenson Road, Stevenson, MD 21153*
TELEPHONE: *1-800-638-5686 or 1-301-653-1993*
CONTACT PERSON: *David Mattson*
INDUSTRY OVERVIEW
 • *Sales training is a top priority for businesses in America. Many com-*

panies rely on sales productivity and efficiency as a way to grow and generate profits.

- *Companies know that a more confident sales force with high morale brings in more revenue for the company.*

BENEFITS OF THIS COMPANY

- *Sandler has been in existence for twenty-five years. It has had ample time to develop and test programs.*
- *Competition has used Sandler as a prototype to develop competitive programs.*
- *Sandler has learned to change with the times and examine their programs to meet the needs of the changing work force.*

COMPANY HISTORY

- **IN BUSINESS SINCE:** *1967*
- **FRANCHISING SINCE:** *1983*
- **NUMBER OF FRANCHISE UNITS:** *65*

It's a jungle out there, and every businessperson knows it. Sales people need more than a quality product to win customers in a crowded and fickle marketplace. Sandler Systems of Stevenson, Maryland, guides sales people to success with programs designed to set and achieve goals, build self-confidence, and master time management.

Through a series of seminars and one-day workshops, Sandler Systems offers clients the chance to evaluate and improve their sales ability. In these workshops, professionals from all backgrounds learn to identify their personal and career goals and implement strategies to achieve them.

Started in 1967, The Sandler Systems method of sales, personal, and career development has established a nationwide customer list. The demand for the seminars opened the doors for expansion, and since 1983 Sandler Systems has opened sixty-five franchises throughout the United States and in 1991 grossed more than $1.8 million in home-office revenue. The company expects growth to continue and predicts that 125 franchises will exist by 1995.

The business's success depends entirely on the ability of the franchisee to sell the service to individuals, corporations, or organizations. Anyone who is timid about selling a service or intangible product should look elsewhere for a franchise opportunity.

The company neither monitors nor takes a percentage of franchisee revenue. It does, however, charge a flat, ongoing fee of $908 per month. Although Sandler's territories, which are based on population, are not considered exclusive, Sandler will only approve one franchise for every 500,000 people.

With sales calls and smaller seminars conducted at the client's location and all larger programs held at hotels, a franchisee has little need for a commercial office. With this in mind, more than 90 percent of Sandler Systems franchisees opt to work from their homes.

Franchisees receive six days of extensive instruction on all programs. They also participate in quarterly training conventions, which teach seminar techniques and presentations. Visits to other franchise locations are encouraged so franchisees can learn from their peers.

Sandler also offers franchisees aid in making sales calls and in conducting programs and seminars. The company is available for daily telephone contact with all franchisees. It also publishes a monthly newsletter outlining developments and sales techniques to all franchisees.

FORECAST AND ANALYSIS

More companies are participating in workshops and seminars to build their salesforce's confidence and determination. All industries have learned that a salesforce's performance depends on how well it's trained. Corporations are investing big money in providing their salesforces with the knowledge, techniques, and motivation they need to succeed.

10. WORLDWIDE CANADIAN MANAGEMENT CONSULTANTS, INC.

FRANCHISE FEE: *$20,000*
TOTAL INITIAL INVESTMENT: *$60,000*
FINANCING AVAILABLE: *Yes*
ROYALTY FEE: *8 percent*
ADVERTISING FEE: *4 percent*
ADDRESS: *P.O. Box 639, Rickering, Ontario, Canada LIV 3T3*
TELEPHONE NUMBER: *1-416-686-0469*
CONTACT PERSON: *Kelly Rogers*

INDUSTRY OVERVIEW

- *New businesses are in vital need of business advice and guidance. Worldwide provides new businesses with an array of marketing and management consulting tools.*
- *Nearly 65 percent of independent businesses fail during their first five years of operation. Many of these would succeed if they had access to sensible consulting advice.*

BENEFITS OF THIS COMPANY

- *Worldwide works with a range of entrepreneurs from the small start-ups to full-scale investment partnerships.*
- *Worldwide has sixteen years of business experience behind them and operates internationally.*

COMPANY HISTORY

- **IN BUSINESS SINCE:** *1976*
- **FRANCHISING SINCE:** *1980*
- **NUMBER OF FRANCHISE UNITS:** *35*

The world is full of would-be entrepreneurs who fail because they do not understand market conditions. Worldwide Canadian Management Consultants helps entrepreneurs not only understand these market conditions but build a business plan around them.

Established in 1976, the international company includes thirty-five franchises throughout North America. A $20,000 franchise fee buys the rights to an exclusive territory for three years with a maximum population of 50,000 people. Worldwide estimates that franchisees will need a total of $60,000 to cover the costs of equipment, inventory, marketing and advertising materials, and working capital. The company also charges franchisees an ongoing royalty of 8 percent and an advertising fee of 4 percent.

The business requires only standard office equipment and runs smoothly with a computer, fax machine, and telephone. Worldwide estimates that franchisees need a maximum of 400 square feet to operate their business successfully. Outside office space is not a requirement since all sales calls and consulting is completed at the client's location. More than 80 percent of current franchisees run their consulting businesses from home.

Franchisees need no previous financial or consulting background. They must be willing to promote the service extensively on an individual and corporate level. Franchisees need to become versed in developing business plans and analyzing marketing trends for products and services.

Worldwide conducts an on-the-job training program which ranges from three to twelve months. The program teaches franchisees marketing and operational procedures. The company also sponsors regularly scheduled seminars and regional meetings, and is available for in-person and telephone consultation.

FORECAST AND ANALYSIS

New businesses are in dire need of expert business consulting. Ironically, however, they often can't afford to invest in these services because of limited cash flow. Franchisees who can serve this market, while keeping their fees in line, may find a ready market. The company has more than fifteen years consulting experience, and it works hard to convey this knowledge to franchise owners.

11. PROFORMA, INC.

■━━━━━━━━━━━━━━━━━━━━━━━━━━━━━━━━━━━━■

FRANCHISE FEE: *$39,500*
TOTAL INITIAL INVESTMENT: *$45,000*
FINANCING AVAILABLE: *Yes; up to 50 percent of franchise fee for a period of twelve to eighteen months*
ROYALTY FEE: *7 percent*
ADVERTISING FEE: *1 percent*
ADDRESS: *4705 Van Epps Road, Cleveland, OH 44131*
TELEPHONE: *1-800-825-1525 or 1-216-741-0400*
CONTACT PERSON: *John Campbell*
INDUSTRY OVERVIEW

- *The $136 billion business-forms and products industry continues to grow. Small and large businesses need office products and want to buy them conveniently.*
- *Computer supplies are a burgeoning part of the industry, and as more companies depend on computers, the demand for related products will swell.*

BENEFITS OF THIS COMPANY
- *ProForma not only sells paper product lines, but it analyzes a cus-*

tomer's needs as well and offers advice on how to best use these products.

- *ProForma has built a company around its franchisees and works with them intensively to make them successful. The company could have expanded more quickly, but chose a more careful and planned growth course to optimize its chances for success.*

COMPANY HISTORY

- **IN BUSINESS SINCE:** *1978*
- **FRANCHISING SINCE:** *1985*
- **NUMBER OF FRANCHISE UNITS:** *103*

The more automated a business becomes, the more paper, office, and computer supplies it needs. Computer technology hasn't eliminated the need for business forms and products, it's accelerated it. Today, the industry is a $136 billion market. ProForma, Inc., is a major franchised player.

Started in 1978, ProForma, Inc., has left an indelible mark on the business products industry by offering customers all types of products from customized invoice forms to computer system accessories.

ProForma supports 103 franchises nationwide and generated networkwide revenues in excess of $30 million in 1990. The company estimates that 180 franchises should exist by the year 1995.

A franchisee's main role is to sell ProForma products to companies of all sizes. Franchisees market the ProForma supplies through telemarketing, direct mail campaigns, and direct sales.

ProForma discourages franchisees from leasing a professional office since most sales calls are conducted at a customer's site. Most franchisees work from their homes.

As part of the franchise agreement, the company handles all billing for its franchisees and operates an answering service at its headquarters for them as well. Most franchises run efficiently with one or two persons, and husband-wife teams are prevalent throughout the organization.

ProForma franchisees are usually between thirty-five and forty-five years of age with liquid assets totaling $75,000 to $100,000.

Franchisees pay an initial investment of $39,500, which purchases the right to use the ProForma name and sell ProForma products for ten years. The company assigns no exclusive territories, but it will protect customer lists for its franchisees.

Franchisees should expect to invest an additional $5,000 for business telephone-line hook-ups in their homes, office equipment, and an optional software package and computer modem. Franchisees also pay a 7 percent royalty fee and a 1 percent advertising charge which pays for direct mail, telemarketing, and other promotional campaigns.

ProForma requires franchisees to attend a one-week training seminar at the company's Ohio headquarters. Franchisees also receive as part of their contract three months of free telemarketing service, and most begin operation with potential customers in hand. The company also has developed a large pool of manufacturers for office products from which ProForma franchisees can order business forms and products for their customers.

Along with regional meetings and an annual convention, ProForma also has established a franchise advisory council which interacts with ProForma corporate management. Franchisee controlled, the council offers comments and opinions on new and current policies. The company relies heavily on the council for franchisee input and concerns.

FORECAST AND ANALYSIS

ProForma is nationally recognized as a franchise leader in the business products industry. The company's reported networkwide sales of $30 million translates into average gross sales of just under $300,000 per franchisee. That's a strong return considering that the total initial investment is only $45,000.

ProForma works hard to keep the channels of communication open between franchisees and franchisor, an important trait for a franchise company.

12. PRIORITY MANAGEMENT SYSTEMS, INC.

FRANCHISE FEE: *$29,500*
TOTAL INITIAL INVESTMENT: *$44,500 to $49,500*
FINANCING AVAILABLE: *Yes*
ROYALTY FEE: *9 percent*

ADVERTISING FEE: *1 percent*
ADDRESS: *500 108th Avenue N.E., Suite 1740, Bellevue, WA 98004*
TELEPHONE: *1-800-221-9031 or 1-206-454-7686*
CONTACT PERSON: *Todd Schmick*

INDUSTRY OVERVIEW

- *More companies are looking for outside assistance when trying to improve sales and professional staff.*
- *Outside consulting services can provide specialized services at a fraction of what companies would spend to develop the expertise on their own.*

BENEFITS OF THIS COMPANY

- *The firm was put together by an education professional and a business expert. The pair formed a bond and has won support from hundreds of companies in corporate America.*

COMPANY HISTORY

- **IN BUSINESS SINCE:** *1984*
- **FRANCHISING SINCE:** *1985*
- **NUMBER OF FRANCHISE UNITS:** *257 in eleven countries*

Employee productivity determines a company's success or failure. Priority Management offers companies more than fifty employee programs to develop communication, self-motivation, task delegation, and time management.

Established in 1984, Priority was the dream of an ex–college science professor who realized that businesses could benefit from the training procedures long used in academics. What was a one-man operation is now a 275-franchise international network with revenue that exceeds $37.5 million.

Through an exclusive four-phase program over six to eight weeks, Priority conducts workshops, face-to-face interviews, and seminars to focus on strategic planning and product management. The program's cost varies, but corporations pay an average of $495 to $750 per person for ongoing counseling. Priority also offers clients bi-annual reviews, a newsletter, and access to future seminars at no added charge.

The $29,500 franchise fee pays for the right to use Priority's name and curriculum and covers a perpetual contract for an exclusive territory based on business populations. Priority emphasizes that another $15,000 to $20,000 may be needed for an office. That cost can be minimized by operating at home. Priority encourages this and

95 percent of the franchisees choose that avenue. As volume grows, more than 40 percent eventually opt for an outside office.

Franchisees attend a seven- to ten-day training class in Vancouver to learn Priority techniques and programs and receive instructions in sales, management, marketing, and administration. Later, each new franchisee works with a regional coach to build sales presentations skill and improve marketing tactics and conduct of programs and seminars.

The company holds two regional meetings per year and an annual international conference to inform franchisees of new programs and strategies.

FORECAST AND ANALYSIS

More companies want ways to improve management productivity. Priority is a product of the scientific and educational worlds and has been successful in integrating its system into the corporate world. Its revenue of $37.5 million reflects its own success, and its philosophy of professionalism and convenience has made it a reputable consulting firm.

13. SUCCESS MOTIVATION INSTITUTE, INC.

■──────────────────────────────■

FRANCHISE FEE: *$20,000*
TOTAL INITIAL INVESTMENT: *$20,000*
FINANCING AVAILABLE: *Yes*
ROYALTY FEE: *None*
ADVERTISING FEE: *None*
ADDRESS: *5000 Lakewood Drive, Waco, TX 76710*
TELEPHONE: *1-800-880-0745 or 1-817-776-1230*
CONTACT PERSON: *John Appel or Bill Garner*
INDUSTRY OVERVIEW
- *Never has self-improvement been so popular in this country. Americans want proven methods to improve their lives in terms of money, fitness, and relationships.*

BENEFITS OF THIS COMPANY
- *Success Motivation Institute, which is part of the Dwyer Group, has twenty years of experience in teaching Americans how to improve.*

- *Corporations are always looking for programs to inspire improved performance by employees. Business knows that in competitive markets, employees must be effective and positive if they are to win.*

COMPANY HISTORY
- **IN BUSINESS SINCE:** *1960*
- **FRANCHISING SINCE:** *1962*
- **NUMBER OF FRANCHISE UNITS:** *1,263*

Emotions, attitude, commitment and many other factors can stand between a person and their goals for success. For more than twenty years, Success Motivation Institute (SMI) has taught people how to maximize their performance to achieve their goals in all aspects of their lives.

Established in 1960, SMI uses audio tapes and manuals to teach clients the secrets of time management, personal goal-setting, creative sales techniques, and wealth-building strategies. Written by renowned motivational author Paul J. Meyer, all programs are designed to provide practical advice on how to gain control of the future.

The concept of charting one's own destiny has won many fans, as SMI's success proves. Total home office revenue exceeded $5.8 million in 1990. SMI, which offered its first franchise in 1962, now has 1,263 franchises nationwide, and SMI projects that total to increase to 1,400 by 1995.

SMI is a sales-oriented franchise. Franchisees who succeed need to effectively market their programs to corporations and individuals. The $20,000 initial investment includes all office set-up, inventory, training materials, use of the SMI name, headquarters training, and assistance.

SMI charges no royalty or advertising fees, and franchisees are under no obligation to report their income to headquarters.

A franchise contract runs three years, with the franchisee holding the right to renew. The company offers financing assistance at its discretion to qualified applicants. All sales calls are conducted at a client's home or place of business, making this well-suited for home-based franchisees. At present, 70 percent of all franchisees work from home.

SMI instructs franchisees in all aspects of their operations. Marketing directors are required to contact franchisees daily. SMI also sends its directors out with franchisees to make presentations at clients' homes or businesses. The home office sponsors monthly training conferences, and franchisees are encouraged to attend as often as they want.

FORECAST AND ANALYSIS

SMI is a twenty-year veteran franchisor that has succeeded despite sometimes skeptical reviews from those unattuned to its purpose. SMI seems able to find a market of professionals, as well as individuals willing to invest in its programs that stress motivation and improved personal performance.

14. BUCK-A-STALL, INC.

■──────────────────────────────■

FRANCHISE FEE: *$3,995*

TOTAL INITIAL INVESTMENT: *$3,995*

FINANCING AVAILABLE: *No (the company does offer discounts to operating companies that convert to the franchise)*

ROYALTY FEE: *None; franchisees buy paint supplies from franchisor*

ADVERTISING FEE: *None*

ADDRESS: *P.O. Box 1156, Madison, TN 37116*

TELEPHONE: *1-800-321-BUCK or 1-615-824-2825*

CONTACT PERSON: *Jim Shafer*

INDUSTRY OVERVIEW

- *Parking-lot striping is a service that is always in demand since most parking lots and airports restripe their facilities at least once every two years.*
- *This is a specialized industry. Few national companies perform this task.*

BENEFIT OF THIS COMPANY

- *With more than twenty years of experience in the industry, Buck-A-Stall has fully developed its procedures and methods. The company is based on a solid concept and owner Jim Shafer is knowledgeable and realistic as to future success.*

COMPANY HISTORY

- **IN BUSINESS SINCE:** *1971*
- **FRANCHISING SINCE:** *1989*
- **NUMBER OF FRANCHISE UNITS:** *8*

■──────────────────────────────■

Parking spaces are a necessity, but few of us stop to think that someone has to paint those lines—and get paid to do so. Buck-A-Stall, Inc., based in Madison, Tennessee, is a leading franchisor in the paint-striping industry.

Established in 1971, Buck-A-Stall paints boundary lines for parking spaces, special zoning areas, airport runways, and sports arenas. The company offered its first franchise less than two years ago, and currently supports eight franchises. The company projects that fifty franchises will be in operation by 1995.

Buck-A-Stall franchisees usually operate from their homes and use a lawn-mower–sized painting machine to perform contracted work. Franchisees work with real estate developers, mall owners, and airport managers to design and paint parking areas, roads, and other surfaces.

For a total investment of $3,995, franchisees purchase an exclusive territory, equipment, an initial inventory of paint, training, and the rights to use the Buck-A-Stall name. Buck-A-Stall charges no ongoing royalty or advertising fee, but it does require its franchisees to purchase their paint from the home office.

Franchisees who enjoy the outdoors and working alone are best suited for this business. Buck-A-Stall trains its franchisees for three to four days either at the Tennessee home office or at the franchisee's site. Franchisees learn the techniques of paint striping, parking-lot layout, and blue-print interpretation, and they also receive instruction in marketing and managing the business. The company also provides in-field support with sales and will assist on troublesome jobs if necessary.

FORECAST AND ANALYSIS

Buck-A-Stall is a relatively new franchise company, and as with any new franchise there's risk. But parking-lot striping is always in demand. There is, however, competition. Local companies provide the service and compete vehemently for customers. Some malls and airports maintain their own striping equipment. As in most franchises, success depends on sales ability and customer service.

15. FORTUNE PRACTICE MANAGEMENT

FRANCHISE FEE: *$60,000 for one territory; $50,000 for three territories*
TOTAL INITIAL INVESTMENT: *$76,000 to $98,000*
FINANCING AVAILABLE: *Yes*
ROYALTY FEE: *10 percent*
ADVERTISING FEE: *5 percent*
ADDRESS: *6490 S. McCarren, Suite D-43, Reno, NV 89509*
TELEPHONE: *1-800-628-1052 or 1-702-827-8000*
CONTACT PERSON: *Kathy McHenry*

INDUSTRY OVERVIEW

- *Health care is the third largest industry in the United States, grossing more than $640 billion. Although doctors and other health-care professionals receive technical training, few of them understand how to establish or manage a practice.*

BENEFITS OF THIS COMPANY

- *Fortune Practice Management is the result of a partnership that combined Quest Seminars, a twelve-year-old company that teaches business and practice management theory, and Robbins Research, a company founded by Tony Robbins, the best-selling author who developed neurolinguistic programming.*
- *Fortune Practice Management also has marketing agreements with companies like Conquest Technologies, which provides ancillary management consulting programs such as financial, computer, and real estate services.*

COMPANY HISTORY

- **IN BUSINESS SINCE:** *1990*
- **FRANCHISING SINCE:** *1991*
- **NUMBER OF FRANCHISE UNITS:** *20*

Doctors and dentists spend years in school learning the intricacies of the human body, but many of them never learn the secrets of operating a profitable practice. To help them manage their practices, many doctors and dentists turn to outside business consultants, such as Fortune Practice Management.

Established in 1990, Fortune Management is a full-service medical and dental management consulting company targeting physicians and dentists. Franchisees use seminars, coaching programs, and one-to-one consultations to aid physicians and dentists develop practices that are profitable and efficient. Fortune Practice is the result of a well-orchestrated partnership that combines the talents of Quest Seminars, a twelve-year-old leader in business and practice management consultation, with the management and personal development techniques of Tony Robbins, the best-selling author and personal motivation guru.

The company reported networkwide revenue in excess of $3.5 million for 1991. Demand and volume are projected to grow and lift the number of Fortune Practice franchisees from 20 to 300 by the year 1995.

Franchisees have to be sales-oriented professionals who can persuade and motivate dentists and doctors—a skeptical audience. When they're not conducting seminars, franchisees concentrate on selling the consulting service through one-on-one sales presentations and other proprietary techniques.

The initial investment for this franchise is $60,000. Fortune Practice will finance half of the fee and allows franchisees to operate from home, if a regional office exists somewhere within a franchisee's region. Home-based franchisees are free to use company offices for meetings, seminars, and presentations.

Fortune Practice charges franchisees a 10 percent royalty on gross revenue and a 5 percent advertising fee.

The company conducts an intensive four- to ten-day training seminar for all franchisees at its San Diego office. Along with learning Fortune Practice's products and services, franchisees learn the "polling process" marketing method. This provides franchisees with a novel strategy for marketing to doctors and dentists by first surveying them and using the results to tailor sales presentations and consulting packages.

Fortune Practice Management holds post-training seminars twice a year for established franchisees and regular telephone contact is also encouraged. Field representatives are available to handle franchisee concerns in person if needed.

FORECAST AND ANALYSIS

The health-care industry is growing daily and so is the complexity of running a medical or dental practice. Fortune Practice Management franchisees serve as consultants, motivators, and business advisors to highly paid doctors and dentists. This is a lucrative market and a competitive one. Accountants, lawyers, and financial planners provide similar consulting services.

Fortune Practice's marketing programs are among the most advanced in the industry. Its partnership with best-selling author Tony Robbins provides franchisees with visibility and credibility in an industry where name and reputation are everything.

16. LIBERTY EXPRESS CORP.

FRANCHISE FEE: *Ranges between $15,000 and $20,000 depending on experience of franchisee in industry*

TOTAL INITIAL INVESTMENT: *$76,000 to $98,000*

FINANCING AVAILABLE: *Yes*

ROYALTY FEE: *5 percent*

ADVERTISING FEE: *½ to 2 percent in advertising fund*

ADDRESS: *928 Alton Place, High Point, NC 27263*

TELEPHONE: *1-800-356-3139 or 1-919-434-5077*

CONTACT PERSON: *Andy Klein*

INDUSTRY OVERVIEW

- *It is difficult for furniture and cabinet manufacturers to get ancillary supplies such as hinges and drawer knobs from one vendor. Most have to use at least two or three distributors, and this can hold up production on furniture and other wood products.*

BENEFIT OF THIS COMPANY

- *Liberty Express is the child of Liberty Manufacturing, a forty-nine-year-old furniture accessory manufacturer.*

COMPANY HISTORY

- **IN BUSINESS SINCE:** *1991*
- **FRANCHISING SINCE:** *1991*
- **NUMBER OF FRANCHISE UNITS:** *2*

North Carolina is known as the furniture manufacturing capital of the world. It is no accident that Liberty Express Corporation chose this state as its home base for its new franchise network that distributes cabinet and wood furniture accessories directly to furniture manufacturers. Liberty Express is the offspring of Liberty Hardware

Manufacturing, a forty-nine-year-old-company that makes accessory furniture products such as hinges and doorknobs.

"Cabinet and wood manufacturers have always found it difficult to purchase hinges, knobs, and other products," says Lothar Mayer of Liberty Express. "Liberty Manufacturing has made furniture for forty-nine years, and we knew the problems associated with purchasing these types of products. Production can be seriously delayed if manufacturers do not have these products at their disposal."

Liberty Express offered its first franchise on July 1, 1991, and it sold two territories within six months. The company expects the growth to continue and hopes to be established in most markets throughout the United States by 1995.

The franchise company relies on Liberty Hardware Manufacturing's expertise to fill customer orders. Franchisees store all inventory in the company's twelve regional warehouses. Customers place their orders with franchisees who in turn call the warehouse and have the merchandise shipped usually within a twenty-four-hour period. Franchisees can network with other franchisees to trade or sell merchandise to each other since all inventory is stored in the same locations.

Liberty Express takes on responsibilities for billing as well as other administrative duties for its franchisees. This practice allows franchisees to set up operations from home without the expense of an outside office or warehouse space.

A $15,000 to $20,000 initial franchise fee purchases the rights to a protected territory for up to twenty-five years. The company estimates that franchisees will need an additional $50,000 for the purchase of the cabinetry accessory inventory, and $6,000 to $12,000 more for working capital. The company recognizes that the total investment may be steep for a home-based franchise operation, so Liberty Express offers limited financing to qualified franchisees.

As a condition of the contract, all franchisees attend a one-week training session at the High Point, North Carolina, headquarters. After this training period, regional sales managers visit with franchisees for a minimum of one week to assist them with sales calls and the everyday operation of the business.

Liberty Express conducts regional and national sales seminars which will take place on a more regular basis as the franchise network grows. The company also attends national trade shows and markets the franchise company nationally to the furniture manufacturing industry.

FORECAST AND ANALYSIS

This company has a forty-nine-year-old track record in the furniture hardware industry. The franchise network is geared to provide franchisees with ongoing support. Customer satisfaction is the theme for the franchise and the regional warehouse practice is an insurance policy against out-of-stock merchandise. The regional warehouse practice also promotes an interdependence among franchisees who swap or buy merchandise from each other as needed.

Liberty Express is for the sales professional. Knocking on doors is the key means of gaining customer loyalty. Although the franchise is new, it is well conceived. The company plans to promote the opportunity aggressively throughout the United States.

14

CHILDREN'S FITNESS
AND EDUCATION

■——■

17. KINDERDANCE

■——■

FRANCHISE FEE: *$6,000 to $9,000 depending on size of territory*
TOTAL INITIAL INVESTMENT: *$7,000 to $10,000*
FINANCING AVAILABLE: *Yes*
ROYALTY FEE: *10 percent to 15 percent*
ADVERTISING FEE: *3 percent*
ADDRESS: *P.O. Box 510881, Melbourne Beach, FL 32951*
TELEPHONE: *1-800-666-1595 or 1-407-723-1595*
CONTACT PERSON: *Bernard Friedman*
INDUSTRY OVERVIEW

- *Educators have always been aware of the advantages of combining play activities with learning. Unfortunately, few school systems can take the time to find the right combination or develop the most appropriate programs. Private companies are becoming a teacher's aide with their choreographed and enjoyable classes that combine a child's love of activities with everyday learning.*

BENEFIT OF THIS COMPANY

- *Kinderdance teaches pre-school and early elementary grade children the basics of ballet, tap, jazz, and aerobics and combines the movements with basic learning skills. The result is a happy and fit child who enjoys the prospect of learning.*

COMPANY HISTORY

- **IN BUSINESS SINCE:** *1979*

● **FRANCHISING SINCE:** *1985*
● **NUMBER OF FRANCHISE UNITS:** *28*

From their earliest days, children express themselves through movement. One company uses this love of jumping and hopping to teach children the joy of dance and the benefits of physical fitness.

Kinderdance was launched more than ten years ago when owners Carol Harsell and Bernard Friedman wanted to bring the benefits of dance to as many young people as possible.

Marketing its service to day-care centers and nursery schools, Kinderdance teaches children ages two through eight the basics of ballet, tap, jazz, and aerobics. The lessons, which incorporate colors, shapes, and other educational themes, are geared to nurture children's respect for their bodies through a program that's fun.

For the franchisee who has the commitment and desire to work with young children, this may be an excellent opportunity. Kinderdance franchisees typically work directly with the children, serving as part performer, educator, and dance teacher. Although love of dance is a prerequisite, training and education in dance isn't.

Franchisees pay a $6,000 to $9,000 fee, depending on the size of the exclusive territory. This fee covers most costs involved with establishment of the franchise, including training, supplies, equipment, program curricula, and training videotapes.

Although the franchise is affordable, the company offers to finance for up to 50 percent of the cost. Franchisees pay an ongoing royalty of 10 to 15 percent of gross revenue, depending on the size of their territories, plus an advertising fee of 3 percent. Franchisees should have an additional $1,000 to handle miscellaneous expenses, such as office equipment and a telephone line. All programs and classes take place at the day-care or school facility, making a leased office unnecessary. All eighteen franchisees, who account for twenty-eight franchised territories, maintain home offices, a policy Kinderdance encourages.

Training includes one week of study at headquarters in Florida, where franchisees learn the four dance programs. Franchisees also receive instruction in marketing, sales, and management.

Kinderdance offers franchisees post-training support and assistance on an as-needed basis. The company makes itself available to franchisees through telephone and in-field consultations.

FORECAST AND ANALYSIS

Kinderdance combines fun, physical fitness, and education—a potent mix for today's young people. Parents love the programs because they're part of a day-care or elementary school curriculum. There's no lugging the kids to a dance studio or outside location.

For franchisees, the investment is very affordable and financing is available. As day care becomes more a part of American life, programs like Kinderdance will continue to grow and prosper throughout the 1990s.

18. GYMBOREE CORP.

FRANCHISE FEE: *$19,000 for one location; additional locations receive discounts*

TOTAL INITIAL INVESTMENT: *$35,000 to $40,000*

FINANCING AVAILABLE: *None*

ROYALTY FEE: *6 percent*

ADVERTISING FEE: *1¾ percent*

ADDRESS: *577 Airport Boulevard, Suite 400, Burlingame, CA 94010*

TELEPHONE: *1-415-579-0600*

CONTACT PERSON: *Bob Campbell*

INDUSTRY OVERVIEW

- *More and more parents are taking an active interest in their children's motor development. Parents are looking for ways to teach children fitness and make it an important and enjoyable part of their lives.*
- *The concept of "Learning Can Be Fun" has won many supporters over the past ten years.*

BENEFITS OF THIS COMPANY

- *Gymboree was one of the first companies to promote organized children's play that does not focus on competition.*
- *The Gymboree program involves both parents and children in the games, which develop motor and sensory skills.*
- *The company has more than fifteen years experience in child development.*

COMPANY HISTORY
- **IN BUSINESS SINCE:** *1976*
- **FRANCHISING SINCE:** *1979*
- **NUMBER OF FRANCHISE UNITS:** *325*

From infancy to kindergarten, a child's development can depend on a myriad of factors. Gymboree of Burlingame, California, has developed programs which give children the opportunity to explore and challenge their own levels of motor and sensory abilities through song, dance, exercise, and fun.

Established in 1976, Gymboree conducts nine- to thirteen-week classes for infants and children up to age five. The programs require participation from both parent and child, and they are held at churches, schools, or other community centers.

Although the classes must take place at a leased or donated site, the administrative work involved in the operation of a Gymboree franchise may be done from home. This set-up has attracted many female entrepreneurs, who use Gymboree to launch new careers without having to leave family behind. Gymboree estimates that 94 percent of its 325 franchisees are women. The company expects this trend to continue as it strives to reach its expansion goal of 400 global franchises by 1995.

Franchisees are responsible for establishing the franchise in an area, finding a site, hiring teachers, and promoting the Gymboree name. They do not have to teach the classes. Most franchisees hire one or more instructors. No previous teaching experience is required, but most franchisees are college educated and have completed some post-graduate work.

A $19,000 franchise fee purchases the rights to one territory, but many franchisees opt to buy two or more territories immediately. The cost for each territory is discounted as an incentive for a potential investor. Gymboree also estimates that franchisees will need an additional $10,000 for equipment purchase and $1,000 to $5,000 for the purchase of office supplies and Gymboree accessory items such as tee shirts, audio tapes, and Gymboree clown dolls.

Franchisees are also required to pay a 6 percent royalty fee and a 1¾ percent advertising fee monthly to the company.

Gymboree requires franchisees to attend ten days of classroom instruction at the home office. Franchisees learn how to conduct all programs using the special tumbling and play equipment. The training also focuses on marketing, management, and administrative procedures.

For the first three months of operation, Gymboree regional franchise consultants will make frequent visits to a franchisee's site. For both new and established franchisees, there is telephone support and annual visits from Gymboree field managers. The company uses radio, television, newspapers, and direct mail to conduct a national advertising campaign, but local advertising is up to the individual franchisee.

FORECAST AND ANALYSIS

Gymboree is the most established and recognized child development program in the market today. Although there are regional competitors, few national companies effectively compete against Gymboree. The Gymboree program is geared toward fun. The classes are non-competitive and innovative, and individual accomplishments are emphasized.

Gymboree is also diversifying into retail stores. The company's retail products do not compete with those sold in class by franchisees.

19. COMPUTERTOTS

■──────────────────────────────────────■

FRANCHISE FEE: *$19,500*
TOTAL INITIAL INVESTMENT: *$24,900*
FINANCING AVAILABLE: *None*
ROYALTY FEE: *6 percent*
ADVERTISING FEE: *1 percent*
ADDRESS: *P.O. Box 340, Great Falls, VA 22066*
TELEPHONE: *1-703-759-2556*
CONTACT PERSON: *Erin O'Grady*
INDUSTRY OVERVIEW

- *Computer education is essential for today's schoolchildren. The sooner children are exposed to computers, the less likely they will be intimidated by them.*
- *Computer classes which teach children through fun are in demand.*

Day-care centers and nursery schools are looking for ways to intro-duce computers to students.

BENEFITS OF THIS COMPANY

- *The company's founders come from educational backgrounds, and all classroom instructors must be certified teachers.*
- *Computertots is based on a program developed at the Massachusetts Institute of Technology (MIT).*
- *The company believes in steady growth through skilled and well-trained franchisees.*

COMPANY HISTORY

- **IN BUSINESS SINCE:** *1983*
- **FRANCHISING SINCE:** *1988*
- **NUMBER OF FRANCHISE UNITS:** *46*

In order to succeed in tomorrow's world, children must learn computers today. By the year 2000, 95 percent of all jobs will require computer skills. Computertots, a Virginia-based franchise company, combines games with technology to teach children the computer skills they need.

Established in 1983, Computertots uses a prototype educational program developed by the Massachusetts Institute of Technology to teach these vital skills. The concept has attracted many followers, and Computertots estimates that 205 franchises will be in operation by 1995.

Computertots teachers conduct thirty-minute lessons at day-care centers, nursery schools, libraries, and other community centers. Classes meet four times per month. Students range in age from three to eight years old. Classes focus on shapes, colors, and activities that are designed to hold a child's attention. Computertots familiarizes children with both computer hardware and software. Each program costs $22 per student, and the class size ranges between four and twenty-two pupils.

Franchisees do not have to teach, and they do not have to be certified teachers. They can take on the managerial role only, promoting the program to the schools and day-care centers in their areas and hiring teachers to handle the classes. However, Computertots requires that all teachers be certified teaching professionals. Most franchisees are former managers and corporate executives who have left their positions in search of their own businesses.

An initial franchise fee of $19,500 purchases the rights to an exclusive territory for ten years as well as the right to use the Computertots' curriculum and its twenty-three software packages.

Computertots recommends that franchisees keep in reserve $4,000 to $6,000 for the purchase of two computers plus other start-up expenses. Computertots charges a 6 percent royalty and a 1 percent advertising fee.

Computertots franchisees need not lease professional office space. All sales calls are completed over the telephone or at the school's site. The company suggests that franchisees forgo the expense of a professional office and operate the franchise from their homes. More than 44 percent of franchisees run their businesses from home.

Franchisees attend a five-day training seminar at the home office in Virginia where they learn the curriculum for the computer program. After the initial training, the company maintains phone contact with all franchisees and remains available for personal assistance if necessary. There are also several two-day seminars throughout the year which focus on the educational techniques of the franchise.

FORECAST AND ANALYSIS

Computertots has been in existence since 1983 and has regulated itself to a slower but steady growth. The emphasis on quality over quantity has contributed to the company's success.

The Computertots program is centered on fun and is taught only by certified teachers, an advantage that other companies may not offer. Computers will become more important during the decades to come, and all parents want their children to compete and achieve. More and more, that achievement depends on a youngster's understanding of computers.

20. Pee-wee workout

■───■

FRANCHISE FEE: *$1,500*
TOTAL INITIAL INVESTMENT: *$2,300*
FINANCING AVAILABLE: *None*
ROYALTY FEE: *10 percent monthly gross*

ADVERTISING FEE: *None*
ADDRESS: *34976 Aspen Wood, Willoughby, OH 44094*
TELEPHONE: *1-800-356-6261 or 1-216-946-7888*
CONTACT PERSON: *Margaret J. Carr*
INDUSTRY OVERVIEW

- *Children's fitness is becoming a focal point for parents and educators.*
- *Schools often don't have the time or expertise to provide children with adequate aerobic workouts or the education of caring for their cardiovascular systems.*

BENEFITS OF THIS COMPANY

- *Pee-Wee Workout can be run administratively as a home-based business. The company literally takes its service on the road to various schools, day-care centers, and community centers.*
- *There is a great emphasis today on physical fitness and education. Pee-Wee Workout teaches children early the benefits of caring for their bodies.*

COMPANY HISTORY

- **IN BUSINESS SINCE:** *1986*
- **FRANCHISING SINCE:** *1987*
- **NUMBER OF FRANCHISE UNITS:** *25*

American children are woefully out of shape. Television and Nintendo have replaced outdoor exercise and play as the entertainment of choice for many children. Pee-Wee Workout is helping to reverse this trend.

Established in 1986, Pee-Wee Workout uses exercise, dance, and music to whip kids into shape and to have fun at the same time. The franchise differs from Gymboree or Kinderdance by focusing as much on fitness as on fun.

Franchisees are in essence wandering physical fitness instructors who travel between locations to involve children through lectures and fun workouts. Franchise owners target schools and day-care and community centers. The classes meet once a week for thirty minutes and go through all the basic components of an aerobic workout including warm-up, cardiovascular workout, cool-down, and stretching. Programs are available for children from pre-school age to grade eight.

Along with physical exercise, children also learn through games and lectures about the cardiovascular system and other parts of their bodies.

Costs for the class vary, but the program is affordable to most parents, and the average price per class is less than a meal at a fast-food restaurant.

There are twenty-five Pee-Wee Workout franchises throughout the country, and Pee-Wee expects that number to double by the mid-1990s. Franchise owners tend to be educated women who have left the job market to raise families and are now in search of more flexible work schedules.

The affordable $1,500 price tag is also attractive. The company, whose owner, Margaret Carr, has a long history in adult fitness as well as children's fitness, wants to build the network slowly to ensure the quality of the Pee-Wee programs.

Franchisees pay an ongoing 10 percent royalty to the company. There's no other continuing charge to the company. In addition to the franchise fee, franchisees should have on hand another $500 to $1,000 for working capital and $200 for a Pee-Wee Workout starter kit, which contains props, music, and choreographed routines.

Pee-Wee suggests that franchisees run their operations at home. It requires no minimum office space for operation nor any special office equipment.

Franchisees learn all dance programs and music through video-tapes and manuals. Most franchisees have a keen interest in aerobics and are familiar with the various stages of the exercise so the training comes easily to them. Pee-Wee uses its own music for the exercise programs, and the home office choreographs all routines. Although there's no formal classroom training initially, Pee-Wee Workout holds regular meetings with franchisees and observes some classes as well. Headquarters is available at all times for franchisee questions and problems, and regular telephone contact is recommended.

FORECAST AND ANALYSIS

Pee-Wee Workout is one of the few children service franchises that focuses on fitness instead of just play. Youth physical fitness is a major concern among health-care administrators in this country. Heart disease, diabetes, and cancer may all be linked to early childhood habits.

Pee-Wee franchisor Margaret Carr has served on the President's Fitness Council as well as in other high-level fitness positions. The franchisees we contacted were extremely positive about the business. They take pride in being part of an enterprise that makes a difference in the lives of young people.

15

CLEANING, COMMERCIAL

---

21. COVERALL NORTH AMERICA, INC.

FRANCHISE FEE: *$4,000 to $33,000*
TOTAL INITIAL INVESTMENT: *$5,000 to $38,000*
FINANCING AVAILABLE: *Yes*
ROYALTY FEE: *10 percent (plus 5 percent management fee)*
ADVERTISING FEE: *None*
ADDRESS: *3111 Camino Del Rio N., Suite 1200, San Diego, CA 92108*
TELEPHONE: *1-800-537-3371 or 1-800-752-6910 or 1-619-584-1911 (in CA)*
CONTACT PERSON: *Jack Caughey*
INDUSTRY OVERVIEW

- *Commercial cleaning services are always in demand—whether the economy is good or bad. It's estimated that the demand for commercial cleaning services will increase from the $20-billion level at present to $40 billion by the mid-1990s.*

BENEFITS OF THIS COMPANY

- *Franchisees can test the waters for a modest investment and expand at their own pace.*
- *Coverall offers an incentive for expansion but never pushes franchisees before they're ready to assume new responsibilities. Financial assistance is available and encouraged.*
- *Coverall has won international acclaim for its growth. Its $30 million networkwide revenue is an impressive accomplishment for a company not yet ten years old.*

COMPANY HISTORY
- **IN BUSINESS SINCE:** *1985*
- **FRANCHISING SINCE:** *1985*
- **NUMBER OF FRANCHISE UNITS:** *1,900*

On the surface, commercial building maintenance may lack the professional polish of other franchises. Look beneath the cleansers and rags and you'll find an industry bursting with potential. Started in 1985, Coverall is one of the scores of commercial cleaning franchises that is capitalizing on rising demand for office cleaning services. But with 1,900 franchises in North America alone, Coverall ranks as one of the largest players in the market. The company is now targeting international growth and plans to open offices in France and the United Kingdom while it pursues added growth in the United States and Canada. The company projects that it will have more than 4,500 franchisees by 1995.

What has spurred Coverall's growth? The company relies on a two-tier franchise program that uses master franchisees to market the opportunity and train smaller franchise owners, called subfranchisees. Master franchisees pay between $100,000 and $250,000 to open their territories. Subfranchisees pay a graduated franchise fee that depends on the value of the contracts they purchase from their master franchisees. The price of the subfranchise opportunity starts at $4,000 and climbs to $33,000.

Financing is available for all franchise programs. The contract spans ten years.

Depending on the franchise arrangement chosen, franchisees can expect to invest an additional $1,500 to $10,000 for inventory, equipment, marketing, and advertising materials, plus working capital. There's also a 10 percent royalty and a 5 percent management fee for account generation and maintenance.

Coverall's hands-on support system places much of the administrative burden on master franchisees. Subfranchisees do little marketing or management of their businesses. Regional offices throughout the United States make it unnecessary for franchisees to support an office outside their home. For this reason, 100 percent of subfranchisees run their Coverall franchises from home.

Before Coverall franchisees pick up their first dust rag, they receive two to six weeks of training in all aspects of commercial cleaning.

The training is customized to the franchise package purchased. Training can include classes in account management, personnel recruitment, scheduling, and marketing.

FORECAST AND ANALYSIS

Commercial cleaning services are very much in demand across the globe; still, the work is menial, low-paying, and usually performed at night. Coverall's two-tier franchise keeps most of the dollars in the pockets of master franchisees.

Subfranchisees can often work hard and end up with little to show after paying a high 10 percent royalty, 5 percent management fee, and financing charges, and covering the cost of supplies. Have an accountant carefully review this opportunity to determine whether it can achieve a reasonable return on investment.

22. COUSTIC-GLO INTERNATIONAL, INC.

FRANCHISE FEE: *$12,000 (may be higher depending on territory)*
TOTAL INITIAL INVESTMENT: *$13,500 (may be higher depending on territory)*
FRANCHISING AVAILABLE: *None*
ROYALTY FEE: *5 percent*
ADVERTISING FEE: *1 percent*
ADDRESS: *7111 Ohms Lane, Minneapolis, MN 55439*
TELEPHONE: *1-800-333-8523 or 1-612-835-1338*
CONTACT PERSON: *Scott Smith*
INDUSTRY OVERVIEW
- *More than 25 billion square feet of acoustical ceiling exists in the United States, and most of it needs regular cleaning and maintenance.*
- *Dirty acoustical ceilings can conceal a wealth of health problems that are now becoming widely recognized and addressed.*

BENEFITS OF THIS COMPANY
- *Coustic-Glo has more than thirteen years experience in the ceiling maintenance industry. Its franchising record is impressive and its steady growth also lends to the company's high standing.*
- *Coustic-Glo has its own research and development team which is responsible for bringing to market the patented cleaning materials*

the network uses. An on-site research lab develops new products and services ahead of its competitors.

COMPANY HISTORY
- **IN BUSINESS SINCE:** *1978*
- **FRANCHISING SINCE:** *1982*
- **NUMBER OF FRANCHISE UNITS:** *193*

Staring at the ceiling may be a restful pastime, but some of the solace is lost when the ceiling is saturated with dirt, grime, mold, and bacteria. It is a gruesome image, but for Coustic-Glo of Minnesota it is an image that spells success.

Started in 1978, Coustic-Glo is the oldest and largest ceiling maintenance company in the world. The company's network, which now includes 193 franchises throughout the United States and Canada, reports revenues in excess of $6 million, and Coustic-Glo estimates that 250 franchises will also be in full operation by 1995. Spurring growth has been the company's patented cleaning methods.

Marketed primarily to hospitals, laboratories, and clinics, Coustic-Glo services eliminate the infectious bacteria that may gather in acoustical ceilings and infect patients and employees alike. In the past few years, skyrocketing costs of remodeling have also attracted clients who could not afford the high price associated with installing new acoustic ceilings.

For an entrepreneur looking for a specialized opportunity, Coustic-Glo fits the bill. It is a niche within the niche of the cleaning industry, and the quality of its work is evidenced by the company's success.

For a minimum initial investment of $12,000, a franchisee purchases a ten-year exclusive and renewable territory based on population. Along with the right to use the Coustic-Glo name, a franchisee receives inventory, cleaning materials, equipment, marketing and advertising material, and training. Franchisees pay a 5 percent royalty and a 1 percent advertising fee each month.

All Coustic-Glo franchisees operate their business from their homes. There is limited inventory and little space is required to store equipment and materials.

To learn the Coustic-Glo cleaning processes, franchisees attend a one-week training program at company headquarters. Here, instruction is given in the patented cleaning processes, but more importantly, franchisees learn how to market and sell their service to both commercial and residential customers. The company also conducts on-site training and regular sales and management seminars. Coustic-Glo publishes a periodic newsletter and updated training materials to keep franchisees abreast of new research and development. Franchisees also have access to an 800 number they can call for assistance.

FORECAST AND ANALYSIS

Each year, 1.5 billion square feet of acoustical ceiling is installed in American homes and offices. Coustic-Glo provides a convenient and cost-effective way to clean and restore acoustical tile. The company's commitment to research and development offers a clear market advantage to franchise owners. The company has the potential to keep growing throughout the 1990s and beyond.

23. BUILDING SERVICE AND MAINTENANCE

FRANCHISE FEE: *$12,000*
TOTAL INITIAL INVESTMENT: *$19,000*
FINANCING AVAILABLE: *Yes*
ROYALTY FEE: *7 percent decreasing to 3 percent*
ADVERTISING FEE: *None*
ADDRESS: *575 Airport Boulevard, Gallatin, TX 37066*
TELEPHONE: *1-800-826-9586 or 1-615-451-0200*
CONTACT PERSON: *Richard Isaacson*
INDUSTRY OVERVIEW

- *Commercial cleaning is a sales-oriented business. For franchisees to succeed, they must convince customers they provide better service than competitors.*
- *There's also a great deal of competition in commercial cleaning. With so many companies out there, a nationally recognized name may attract customers looking for honest and quality work.*

BENEFIT OF THIS COMPANY

- *Building Service and Maintenance has its own franchise network to depend upon as well as ServPro Industries, its founding company. Franchisees from both networks work together and refer business to each other and occasionally assist each other.*

COMPANY HISTORY
- **IN BUSINESS SINCE:** *1987*
- **FRANCHISING SINCE:** *1987*
- **NUMBER OF FRANCHISE UNITS:** *24*

A sister franchise to ServPro Industries, Building Service and Maintenance applies many of the techniques and strategies proven by ServPro.

Established in 1987, Building Service and Maintenance (BSM) was developed to fill the commercial janitorial void when ServPro franchisees were unable to do so. Burdened with residential cleaning and restoration contracts, many ServPro franchisees found little time to handle the growing commercial cleaning portion of their businesses.

BSM franchisees serve commercial cleaning accounts in ServPro franchise territories where the ServPro franchisees choose not to pursue commercial cleaning accounts.

ServPro and BSM franchisees interact with one another and refer business to each other, but no competition for business contracts exists. BSM currently supports twenty-three franchises, and the company projects it will grow 25 percent annually.

BSM franchisee owners differ from ServPro franchisees in that they perform most of the cleaning work themselves. The business is for smaller investors who typically work at night. BSM franchise owners also do their own marketing and account solicitation. Referrals from ServPro franchise owners and ServPro headquarters account for the majority of a BSM franchisee's sales leads.

As is the case with franchisees in its sister company, BSM franchisees may find that an increase in business volume requires roomier quarters to accommodate increasing staff.

Although ServPro views BSM as a separate entity, it extends BSM franchise owners the same financing courtesies as it does ServPro franchise owners.

To qualify for the franchise, franchisees need only $10,000 down, and ServPro Industries will finance the balance for up to five years. Royalty fees, which range from 7 percent to 3 percent, decrease as business volume increases. There's also the potential that a 3-percent advertising fee written into the franchise contract four years ago will be activated.

The initial $12,000 fee purchases the rights to a non-exclusive but protected territory for five years, and the contract is automatically renewable. Franchise owners should have another $7,000 in reserve to buy cleaning equipment and products, pay for a business telephone exchange, as well as pay for Yellow Pages advertising.

BSM franchisees undergo the same intensive training as ServPro franchisees, where they learn cleaning, marketing, and management techniques through an "on-the-job" training program. BSM franchise owners also receive personal help in the set-up of their business from a general trainer franchisee. The company also holds an annual convention, and the general trainers and state directors also conduct four seminars per year in their area franchises.

ServPro publishes newsletters for BSM franchisees, and the company also maintains a technical and sales support staff to handle any franchisee concerns.

FORECAST AND ANALYSIS

Building Service and Maintenance was an offshoot of ServPro's highly successful residential cleaning and fire restoration experience. ServPro is adamant that the BSM franchisees coexist peacefully with ServPro franchise owners, but because BSM relies on ServPro franchisees for referral, there's some question of what would happen if a BSM franchisee and ServPro franchisee didn't get along.

Financing makes this opportunity attractive. ServPro's experience in residential cleaning is no doubt an advantage for franchisees in commercial cleaning.

24. TOWER CLEANING

■——————————————————————————————————■

FRANCHISE FEE: *$3,250 to $33,000 depending on number of guaranteed business contracts*

TOTAL INITIAL INVESTMENT: *$3,400 to $33,400*

FINANCING AVAILABLE: *Yes*

ROYALTY FEE: *15 percent of all billings*

ADVERTISING FEE: *None*

ADDRESS: *565 E. Swedesford Road, Wayne, PA 19087*

TELEPHONE: *1-800-67-TOWER or 1-215-293-2000*
CONTACT PERSON: *Adam Beck*
INDUSTRY OVERVIEW

- *Competition in commercial cleaning is stiff. The work is relatively easy, and the barriers to entry are low. Mom-and-poppers, who often undercut contract prices, are everywhere.*

BENEFITS OF THIS COMPANY

- *Tower solicits and contracts all business for its franchisees. Tower takes on all billings and accounts receivable for franchisees.*
- *One hundred percent of all franchisees (with the exception of master franchisees) run the business at home at the encouragement and request of Tower Cleaning Services.*

COMPANY HISTORY

- **IN BUSINESS SINCE:** *1988*
- **FRANCHISING SINCE:** *1990*
- **NUMBER OF FRANCHISE UNITS:** *230*

Another entry into the commercial cleaning industry, Tower Cleaning was established only four years ago and has grown dramatically to support more than 230 franchises.

Franchisees perform light to moderate office cleaning, usually after hours or at night. Franchisees perform the work themselves and hire a minimal number of employees to help. The company offers similar financing and franchisee services as Coverall, Jani-King, and other commercial cleaning franchises.

Franchisees do no marketing, administration, or bill collecting. Headquarters provides these services for hefty royalty fees of 15 percent and financing fees that cover the initial investment as well as any late payments by customers.

The company, which reached networkwide sales of $10 million in 1991, estimates that between 1,500 and 2,000 franchises will exist by 1995.

Like Coverall and Jani-King, Tower employs a two-tier franchise structure, with master franchisees selling and servicing smaller subfranchisees. The master franchise opportunity isn't for home-based franchisees. Tower subfranchisees work from their homes exclusively.

The franchise fee ranges from $3,250 to $33,000 and buys a guaranteed number of contracts that range in annual sales value from $6,000 to $120,000. Franchisees need only an additional $150 to $400 investment capital to cover the costs of insurance.

Training for a Tower franchise includes one week of classroom instruction at headquarters in Pennsylvania. During this period, franchisees are taught Tower's cleaning and safety procedures as well as customer relations. Tower encourages frequent telephone contact with its franchisees, and field representatives are available to handle concerns in person. The company also conducts seminars for its franchisees which are in part sponsored by local cleaning equipment and product suppliers. The seminars bring franchisees up-to-date on new products and developments in the commercial cleaning industry.

FORECAST AND ANALYSIS

Tower is another of the "pyramidal" commercial cleaning franchises that are now popular with franchisees who have limited investment capital. The opportunity allows subfranchisees to begin part-time and "tailor" their businesses according to how many cleaning contracts they choose to buy from the franchisor. Master franchisees pay much more to buy their franchises and typically receive a higher return on their investment than subfranchisees.

The hours are usually long and late at night. This franchise requires careful investigation. Prospective franchisees should call currently operating subfranchisees to determine whether the return is worth the investment. If everything checks out, Tower Cleaning could be a viable ground-floor opportunity for those without much money and willing to start at the very bottom and work their way up.

16

CLEANING, MISCELLANEOUS

---

25. SPARKLE WASH MOBILE POWER CLEANING

FRANCHISE FEE: *$17,500*

TOTAL INITIAL INVESTMENT: *$65,000*

FINANCING AVAILABLE: *Yes (from Sparkle Wash and from Ford Motor credit, which makes Sparkle Wash vehicles)*

ROYALTY FEE: *5 percent*

ADVERTISING FEE: *None*

ADDRESS: *26851 Richmond Road, Cleveland, OH 44146*

TELEPHONE: *1-800-321-0770*

CONTACT PERSON: *Franchise Sales*

INDUSTRY OVERVIEW

- *There isn't much competition in this industry. Mobile power wash, which cleans the exterior of buildings and the interior of warehouse space and industrial sites, has been dominated by companies that pioneered the industry, of which Sparkle Wash is one.*
- *This is a service which many companies and real estate owners use to enhance the appearance of their properties.*

BENEFIT OF THIS COMPANY

- *Sparkle Wash pioneered the mobile power wash industry. The company has established itself throughout the world, and it holds international patents on its equipment and products.*

COMPANY HISTORY

- **IN BUSINESS SINCE:** *1965*

- **FRANCHISING SINCE:** *1967*
- **NUMBER OF FRANCHISE UNITS:** *180*

The original entrant into the exterior cleaning industry, Sparkle Wash continues to be the largest franchise network that provides customers a power wash process to clean building exteriors, truck fleets, railroad cars, plus the interior of warehouses and factories.

Established in 1967, Sparkle Wash has seen competition enter and exit the market. The company sponsors more than 180 franchise units throughout the United States. Franchisees use a patented diesel-powered pressure pump that delivers 3,000 pounds of hot water per square inch to clean the exterior walls of buildings and large vehicles.

Sparkle Wash has also developed a patented natural wood restoration process that allows franchisees to offer customers a cleaning and restoration service for wood siding shingles.

Franchisees need no cleaning experience or background in the power wash industry, but they must enjoy outdoor work. Most franchisees run their power cleaning service as a one- or two-man operation and perform the power cleaning services themselves.

Franchisees need $10,000 of the $25,000 franchise fee to secure an exclusive territory, which contains an average population of 250,000. Sparkle Wash will finance the balance at terms agreeable to the franchisor and franchisee. Franchisees should also have in reserve $7,200 for a down payment on a one-ton Ford truck, which is specially designed to hold Sparkle Wash equipment. They can also purchase a computer system with software specifically tailored to the Sparkle Wash operation, although it's not required to operate the business. Franchisees pay the company a 5 percent royalty and buy cleaning equipment and supplies from the company, too.

Sparkle Wash provides franchisees with five days of training at the corporate office. At that time, franchisees learn to use the equipment and become knowledgeable in EPA- and OSHA-approved standards for the application of cleaning chemicals to buildings and walls. Sparkle Wash also instructs franchisees in its own management and marketing methods.

The company periodically sends representatives to franchisee sites and maintains a hotline for franchisees who need assistance. Sparkle Wash conducts seminars throughout the year at various locations and holds an international convention annually at headquarters.

FORECAST AND ANALYSIS

Sparkle Wash has continued to improve its operations since it founded the power wash industry more than twenty-five years ago. It has demonstrated strength in research and development and protects its patents vehemently. This protection allows the company to eliminate competition in the marketplace.

26. SHADE SHOWER, INC.

FRANCHISE FEE: *$8,500*
TOTAL INITIAL INVESTMENT: *$8,500*
FINANCING AVAILABLE: *None*
ROYALTY FEE: *None*
ADVERTISING FEE: *None*
ADDRESS: *7950 E. Redfield #120, Scottsdale, AZ 85260*
TELEPHONE: *1-602-443-0432*
CONTACT PERSON: *Brook Carey*
INDUSTRY OVERVIEW
- *Service businesses are booming. The more specific the niche, the better your chances of succeeding in today's business environment. Mobile blind cleaning is a niche within a niche.*

BENEFIT OF THIS COMPANY
- *Although Shade Shower is young, it has grown appreciably due to its modest investment and novel concept.*

COMPANY HISTORY
- **IN BUSINESS SINCE:** *1989*
- **FRANCHISING SINCE:** *1990*
- **NUMBER OF FRANCHISE UNITS:** *14*

They're always there—dust bunnies that collect on venetian blinds. Most consumers have only two options: leave them and hope no one notices them, or hire Shade Shower to wash them away.

Shade Shower franchisees travel to hospitals, offices, and homes, anywhere a venetian blind, mini-blind or custom-made shade needs cleaning. The mobile service sponsors fourteen franchises and estimates that sixty franchises will be operating by 1995.

An easy-to-run franchise, Shade Shower has attracted franchisees from all walks of life. The franchise can be operated as a part-time business or as a full-service, full-time business.

The $8,500 franchise fee entitles a franchisee to a ten-year contract and covers the cost of the WashWagon, the lightweight portable cleaning machine that allows Shade Shower franchisees to clean blinds quickly and efficiently. Franchisees need another $1,000 for working capital.

Shade Shower doesn't charge a royalty or advertising fee, and with all services done on-site, there's no need for leasing office space. All Shade Shower franchisees presently operate from home.

Training covers two days of marketing and management, as well as hands-on cleaning techniques. All franchisees receive operations manuals and marketing, management, and job-bidding handbooks to use in the field. The company also sponsors an 800 number to handle franchisee concerns.

FORECAST AND ANALYSIS

Blind and shade cleaning are necessary services, but do they warrant a specialized business? This company takes niche marketing to the extreme. The two-day training program is very short compared to other franchise opportunities. However, the franchise may make an excellent add-on to an existing home-based cleaning business.

27. AEROWEST SANITATION SERVICES, INC.

■───■

FRANCHISE FEE: *$1,000*

TOTAL INITIAL INVESTMENT: *$9,600*

FINANCING AVAILABLE: *None*

ROYALTY FEE: *50 to 55 percent on customers contracted by franchisor; 35 to 40 percent on customers contracted by franchisee*

ADVERTISING FEE: *None*

ADDRESS: *25100 S. Normandie Avenue, Harbor City, CA 90710*

TELEPHONE: *1-213-539-6104*

CONTACT *Graham H. Emery*

INDUSTRY OVERVIEW

- *Public washroom sanitation is a needed service in which janitorial and commercial cleaning companies don't specialize.*

- *There's little competition in the industry. Only a handful of companies specialize in public restroom sanitation.*
- *Washroom sanitation lacks the image that other service companies enjoy.*

BENEFITS OF THIS COMPANY

- *AeroWest is an offshoot of an eighty-year-old company that revolutionized the environmental sanitation industry. The company has been the leading marketer of both sanitizing and deodorizing products and services.*
- *AeroWest has worked hard to improve the image of this industry. The franchise network stresses organization and professionalism.*

COMPANY HISTORY

- **IN BUSINESS SINCE:** *1983*
- **FRANCHISING SINCE:** *1984*
- **NUMBER OF FRANCHISE UNITS:** *24*

It's a dirty job, but someone has to do it. If you're going to do it, you may as well do it profitably. That's the theory behind AeroWest Sanitation Services, a unique franchise opportunity that specializes in public washroom sanitation and odor control.

Established in 1983, AeroWest is the offspring of eighty-year-old West Chemical Products, Inc., a pioneer in the washroom sanitation industry. Although viewed as a separate entity, AeroWest uses its parent company's exclusive odor neutralizing fluid and other sanitation products to take on the tasks of washroom maintenance.

West Chemical, with more than 2,000 employees and offices throughout the United States and Canada, provides AeroWest franchisees with ample product development and support. The AeroWest franchise organization also backs up franchisees with intensive training and abundant in-field assistance.

An investment of $9,600 assures franchisees a route with established clients. AeroWest doesn't allocate exclusive territories, and franchisees are encouraged to build and expand routes at their own speed. Since the bulk of the work is done on the road, AeroWest urges franchisees to operate the business from home.

Franchisees invest $8,000 to buy guaranteed first-year billings of $40,000. In addition, there is a $1,000 franchise fee. The remaining $600 of the $9,600 investment is for the purchase of equipment and supplies. Not included is the AeroWest royalty, which ranges from 50 to 55 percent and is payable weekly on revenue generated through franchisor-established contracts. There's a lower royalty of 35 to 40 percent for revenue earned on customers contracted by franchisees.

All training is conducted at the franchisee's location. AeroWest provides a maximum instruction period of two weeks. Most franchisees need less time to learn the cleaning, management, and sales techniques needed to run the business efficiently. AeroWest also provides in-field assistance on a regular basis for a franchisee's first three months of operation, plus ongoing in-field support as needed.

Although franchisees receive training in bookkeeping and contract procurement, AeroWest performs billing and collection chores for franchisees. The company secures new contracts for franchisees throughout the life of the franchise agreement, which runs five years and is automatically renewable at the franchisee's request.

FORECAST AND ANALYSIS

This isn't the most glamorous business in the world, but it's necessary. As fear of communicable disease increases, the need for public washroom sanitation grows. Franchisees need to have a positive sales attitude and a commitment to building route customers. The royalty is among the highest in franchising. Potential franchisees should carefully consider whether a royalty that ranges from 35 to 55 percent of gross sales is warranted.

28. SPR INTERNATIONAL, INC.

■━━■

FRANCHISE FEE: *$995 to $1,995*
TOTAL INITIAL INVESTMENT: *$995 to $1,995*
FINANCING AVAILABLE: *Yes*
ROYALTY FEE: *10 percent to 15 percent on all completed jobs*
ADVERTISING FEE: *None*
ADDRESS: *3398 Sanford Drive, Marietta, GA 30066*
TELEPHONE: *1-800-475-9271 or 1-404-429-0232*
CONTACT PERSON: *Franchise Information*
INDUSTRY OVERVIEW

- *The company franchises three different concepts: bathtub refinishing, roof and marble repair, and automotive detailing. Each industry faces its own set of marketing challenges.*

BENEFIT OF THIS COMPANY
- *Its diversification provides insights into many different industries.*

COMPANY HISTORY
- **IN BUSINESS SINCE:** *1973*
- **FRANCHISING SINCE:** *1974*
- **NUMBER OF FRANCHISE UNITS:** *50*

House repairs can quickly mount and leave a homeowner frustrated. But SPR International of Marietta, Georgia, works with homeowners to repair and clean their houses and possessions economically and efficiently. Offering various services which include bathtub refinishing and restoration, roof and marble restoration, and automobile detailing, this franchise network appeals to many service-oriented entrepreneurs.

Working under the umbrella organization SPR International, the company franchises three separate concepts. Although the products and services are different, the training and franchise packages are remarkably similar and geared toward entrepreneurs who have little investment capital. SPR includes fifty franchise locations throughout the United States and Canada, and the company projects it will add 100 franchises annually and expand into Europe and Asia.

Franchise fees for these businesses range from $990 for the bathroom restoration operation to $1,995 for the fixture refinishing systems. Most franchisees pay either a royalty fee ranging between ½ percent and 10 percent on gross revenue. Franchisees are required to use SPR products for their contracted work. The company does not assign exclusive territories, but franchisees can make them exclusive by purchasing the rights to all territories in the immediate geographic area.

SPR discourages franchisees from leasing professional office space. All work and sales calls are completed at the customer's site, and the business attracts no walk-in traffic. Equipment is minimal and easily stored. Franchisees need only a tool box and some specially designed sprayers for the refinishing and restoration process.

SPR requires all franchisees to complete a training course at the company's headquarters in Marietta, Georgia. There, franchisees learn to use and maintain equipment, and they receive marketing and sales instruction as well. SPR also provides ongoing support for franchisees with clearly designed marketing and sales plans, a telephone assistance program, and on-site personal help.

FORECAST AND ANALYSIS

The company is remarkably diversified for its size. Is this an advantage? It's difficult to tell. But SPR claims that each franchise division is carefully watched and supported. You might want to carefully investigate this franchise to determine whether it has the expertise and manpower to succeed in each of the industries it targets.

17

CLEANING, RESIDENTIAL

━━

29. THE MAIDS INTERNATIONAL, INC.

━━

FRANCHISE FEE: *$17,500*
TOTAL INITIAL INVESTMENT: *$31,500 to $49,000*
FINANCING AVAILABLE: *Yes*
ROYALTY FEE: *5 percent to 7 percent*
ADVERTISING FEE: *4 percent*
ADDRESS: *4820 Dodge Street, Omaha, NE 68132*
TELEPHONE: *1-800-THE-MAID or 1-402-558-5555*
CONTACT PERSON: *Ron Roth*
INDUSTRY OVERVIEW
- *Service industries are on the rise.*
- *Two-career families have little time for domestic cleaning.*
- *The advent of the residential cleaning industry has spurred competition and reduced prices, putting the cost in reach of many homeowners.*

COMPANY HISTORY
- **IN BUSINESS SINCE:** *1980*
- **FRANCHISING SINCE:** *1980*
- **NUMBER OF FRANCHISE UNITS:** *192*

━━

During its twelve-year history, The Maids has significantly altered the way people view domestic help. With 192 North American franchises, The Maids has secured its place in the $9 billion home-services industry, using the tested team-cleaning approach which relies on teams of workers to clean homes quickly. The Maids, which reported more than $18 million in networkwide revenue in 1990, is currently growing at a rate of 20 percent a year.

The Maids takes on all normal day-to-day household chores as well as any special tasks a customer may request. The uniformed team of cleaners travels to the consumer's home in a well-recognized company car embossed with The Maids logo. The average house takes about 1½ hours to clean thoroughly, and the team usually completes four to six houses per day.

Although franchisees oversee cleaning procedures and policies, they normally don't do the cleaning themselves. They focus on promoting The Maids service and managing employees.

With all work done at a customer's site, The Maids runs effectively as a home-based franchise. But a spurt in business volume may mean a move to an outside office.

One reason The Maids has achieved success is its affordability. A $17,500 up-front fee assures a franchisee of an exclusive territory for five years. The initial investment, depending on the size of the territory, costs between $31,500 and $41,900. Included in this price is the purchase of all equipment and materials needed to run the business efficiently. Franchisees pay a 5 to 7 percent royalty and a 4 percent advertising fee.

In turn, franchisees receive one of the industry's top support systems, beginning with a twelve-day training program at headquarters. Classroom work teaches franchisees the company's proprietary cleaning system and business management through The Maids' computer system, and proprietary marketing, sales, and advertising programs.

Ample back-up is available throughout the franchise relationship. Audio and video training tapes not only assist franchisees with problems but also provide motivational help. The company also sponsors regional meetings and prints newsletters that promote The Maids to customers in franchise areas.

FORECAST AND ANALYSIS

The Maids is a strong leader in the $9 billion home-services industry. With more dual-career families, The Maids offers a convenient way to make life easier. The Maids is competitive with local housecleaning services and the company's efficient team-cleaning concept makes domestic help more economical for consumers and more profitable for franchise owners.

30. CLASSY MAIDS USA, INC.

FRANCHISE FEE: *Ranges between $2,950 and $9,500 depending on type of territory purchased*

TOTAL INITIAL INVESTMENT: *$8,000 to $14,000*

ROYALTY FEE: *6 percent of gross sales*

ADVERTISING ROYALTY: *None*

ADDRESS: *P.O. Box 160879, Altamonte Springs, FL 32761-0879*

TELEPHONE: *1-800-445-5238 or 1-407-862-0493*

CONTACT PERSON: *William Olday*

INDUSTRY OVERVIEW

- *Households and small businesses tend to trust cleaning companies that have national or regional reputations.*
- *Poor economic conditions can force people to cut back on domestic cleaning services. Too much competition at lower prices could also affect a franchisee's profit margins.*

COMPANY HISTORY

- **IN BUSINESS SINCE:** *1980*
- **FRANCHISING SINCE:** *1984*
- **NUMBER OF FRANCHISE UNITS:** *12*

Good help is hard to find, and very few people have the time to find it. That fact is what brought Classy Maids to life. Founded in 1980, Classy Maids filled a gap in the lives of the growing population of two-income families: they could afford a house, but they could not find the time to clean it.

Today, the house-cleaning industry is expected to gross more than $9 billion, and Classy Maids franchisees are ready to claim their share of the market. Franchisees manage teams of cleaners who go into a customer's home and perform basic and special cleaning services. Customers can either ask for a one-time call or contract Classy Maids for ongoing cleaning services.

The company now supports twelve franchises throughout the United States, and it estimates that twenty will be operating by 1995. Classy Maids says slow expansion will allow it to remain in control of its franchise network. The company also contends that cautious growth will help it thrive as the industry becomes more competitive.

The Florida-based company uses a unique franchise structure for establishing its exclusive territories. The franchise fees range from $5,900 to $9,500, and the company attracts entrepreneurs with various financial capabilities. The least expensive fee purchases the rights to a community franchise, which contains a maximum population base of 50,000. Classy Maids also offers financing for 50 percent of the fee with the balance paid over four years at 10 percent interest. The metropolitan franchise territory costs a franchisee $9,500. Again the company is willing to finance half the fee at the same terms as the community territory. Finally, the company offers an area development program which grants metropolitan franchisees additional territories at a fraction of the price of their first territory. No matter what package a franchisee chooses, the company estimates that each franchisee will need an additional $4,000 in working capital for the purchase of the Classy Maids uniforms and the lease or purchase of a company vehicle.

The average Classy Maid franchisee has six to ten employees or cleaning personnel on call. The business generates no walk-in traffic and all cleaning crews go to the customer's site. Consequently, the business is well suited for home-based operation.

The company provides a week-long training session which teaches franchisees the managerial, communication, and marketing skills needed to recruit customers and personnel. Classy Maids follows up this training with workshops, seminars, and in-field assistance. First-year franchisees can expect financial support for their advertising expenses as well as an abundance of promotional and advertising copy.

FORECAST AND ANALYSIS

Classy Maids is organized and efficient. Households and businesses feel more comfortable with cleaners that have a national reputation. The household cleaning industry is still growing, and the more established companies command the majority of market share.

31. MAID TO PERFECTION

FRANCHISE FEE: *$18,500*
TOTAL INITIAL INVESTMENT: *$25,500 to $37,500*
FINANCING: *Assist in third-party financing up to 100 percent of costs*
ROYALTY FEE: *7 percent*
ADVERTISING FEE: *None*
ADDRESS: *Trolley Building, 134 Nunnery Lane, Baltimore, MD 21228*
TELEPHONE: *1-800-648-6243 or 1-301-747-0891*
CONTACT PERSON: *Michael Katzenberger*
INDUSTRY OVERVIEW
- *Dual-career families want to spend fewer hours on housework.*
- *The residential cleaning market is part of the larger $9 billion home-services industry, which is rapidly expanding in answer to customer demand.*

BENEFITS OF THIS COMPANY
- *Maid to Perfection uses a team-cleaning concept which provides efficient cleaning services at lower costs.*
- *This franchisor is new in comparison to others, which classifies it as a ground-floor opportunity.*

COMPANY HISTORY
- **IN BUSINESS SINCE:** *1991*
- **FRANCHISING SINCE:** *1991*
- **NUMBER OF FRANCHISE UNITS:** *8*

The home-cleaning industry is one of the most rapidly growing industries of this decade. Dual-career couples and the increase of women in the workforce have left many families looking to escape dreaded housecleaning chores which usurp precious recreational time.

Maid to Perfection, a residential housecleaning service, is another franchisor capitalizing on the hectic schedules of dual-income couples and affluent singles by providing the in-home cleaning busy families need and for which they'll pay.

Established in 1991, the company provides an assortment of cleaning services which range in price and are individually tailored to the customer's needs. Maid to Perfection uses mini-teams or individuals to complete the housework rather than four or five workers, which other franchisors use.

"With many cleaners in one house, some chores will be over-looked," says president Michael Katzenberger. "With a mini-team of two cleaners, the work has to be done and there is no passing the buck. Employees guarantee their work to franchisees and franchisees guarantee their work to customers."

Franchisees are responsible for managing the business and the workers who perform the actual service.

Franchisees are encouraged to work from the home at the begin-ning. As sales and staff increase, most franchisees move out of the home into commercial space.

Although the company has sold only six franchises in its first year of operation, Maid to Perfection has set aggressive expansion goals. The company estimates that 100 franchises will be in operation by 1995.

The franchisee looking to be part of a new, up-and-coming network would see Maid to Perfection as an interesting prospect. An $18,500 franchise fee purchases the rights to an exclusive territory for ten years. The package, which can total $37,500, includes all business, office, and initial cleaning supplies. Franchisees can purchase sup-plies from other sources, but supplies have to be approved by the Maid to Perfection home office.

Franchisees are also expected to lease or purchase a vehicle with the Maid to Perfection logo prominently displayed.

Training for franchisees consists of a five-day course at headquar-ters in Baltimore, where franchisees learn how to use the Maid to Perfection cleaning system and related cleaning products. The company also instructs franchisees in its tested management, book-keeping, marketing, and sales procedures.

The company operates a hotline for franchisees and holds annual meetings as well as regular seminars to update franchisees on prod-uct or marketing developments in the company and industry.

FORECAST AND ANALYSIS

Unlike other franchise companies, Maid to Perfection does not rely on the team-cleaning concept. Is this an advantage? It certainly differentiates the company from scores of competitors. In addition, the company's smaller size may offer franchise owners more individ-ualized service from the home office.

32. MAID BRIGADE, INC.

FRANCHISE FEE: *$16,900*

TOTAL INITIAL INVESTMENT: *Under $32,000*

FINANCING AVAILABLE: *Yes*

ROYALTY FEE: *7 percent but decreases as business grows*

ADVERTISING FEE: *2 percent*

ADDRESS: *850 Indian Trail, Atlanta, GA 30247*

TELEPHONE: *1-800-722-MAID or 1-404-564-2400*

CONTACT PERSON: *Don M. Hay*

INDUSTRY OVERVIEW

- *Home-service industries are on the rise along with the increase in two-career families.*
- *There is plenty of competition from other franchises as well as private housekeeping services.*

BENEFIT OF THIS COMPANY

- *Established since 1980, it is the largest team-cleaning maid service on the market today.*

COMPANY HISTORY

- **IN BUSINESS SINCE:** *1979*
- **FRANCHISING SINCE:** *1980*
- **NUMBER OF FRANCHISE UNITS:** *225*

Changing family roles and two-career families have made an outside cleaning service a necessity in many homes. The Maid Brigade, which includes 225 franchises across North America and networkwide revenues nearing $18 million, fills that need.

Maid Brigade franchisees employ a highly systematized housecleaning strategy. Supervised, four-member teams arrive at a household together and provide basic and specially requested cleaning chores. No owners need to be present, and the work is accomplished usually within two hours depending on a house's size. Franchisees are managers and are discouraged from participating in the housecleaning duties.

For a $16,900 fee, a franchisee purchases the rights to an exclusive territory for ten years, which contains a minimum of 10,000 homes that have an average income in excess of $50,000. Maid Brigade estimates that franchisees need another $15,000 to start the franchise properly. However, the company has recently developed a program which grants up to $8,500 in financing to qualified franchisees. Maid Brigade permits franchisees and their employees to use personal cars to get to a customer's home. The company dropped its requirement of a leased vehicle in an effort to keep down franchisees' costs to a minimum.

"The use of personal cars cuts down on insurance, repair, and gasoline costs, making the franchise more affordable and appealing to entrepreneurs," says Don Hay of Maid Brigade. "We know there is competition in the residential cleaning market, and we want to stand out as the best opportunity."

The average franchisee employs four to six maids, but Maid Brigade is still predominantly a home-based business. More than 60 percent of franchisees are women, who seem attracted to the franchise's management-from-home system.

Maid Brigade requires franchisees to attend a week-long training program in Atlanta. Owners learn company-tested practices in customer development, personnel training, and in-field operations. Training does not end with the grand opening. The company maintains close support through its nine regional offices. An 800 hotline puts franchisee and franchisor in immediate contact for emergencies or questions, and the company provides a buddy-system support team for franchisees as well.

FORECAST AND ANALYSIS

Maid Brigade is an international organization. Competition has been successful in the market as well, but Maid Brigade has amended franchising policies, such as forgoing the need for a company van, to make its opportunity more appealing. The home-services industry generates more than $9 billion annually. Many companies can exist in this market profitably.

33. SERVPRO INDUSTRIES, INC.

FRANCHISE FEE: *$17,800*
TOTAL INITIAL INVESTMENT: *$34,500*
FINANCING AVAILABLE: *Yes*

ROYALTY FEE: *10 percent decreasing to 3 percent*
ADVERTISING FEE: *3 percent (not implemented)*
ADDRESS: *575 Airport Boulevard, Gallatin, TN 37066*
TELEPHONE: *1-800-826-9586 or 1-615-451-0200*
CONTACT PERSON: *Richard Isaacson*

INDUSTRY OVERVIEW

- *The $9 billion home-service industry is large enough to accommodate many companies profitably. However, businesses that operate their companies inefficiently or have poor marketing strategies tend to get lost in the shuffle.*

BENEFITS OF THIS COMPANY

- *ServPro is franchisee-oriented. Technical and financial support make this company an interesting possibility as an investment opportunity.*
- *The company works in both the residential and commercial markets, but busy franchisees sometimes must forgo commercial janitorial work in order to concentrate on residential work. For this reason, ServPro has also launched a separate commercial janitorial franchise, Building Service and Maintenance (BSM), which is available in all areas of the United States. BSM franchisees aren't permitted to do residential cleaning or restoration work, and they can only co-exist in areas where ServPro franchisees have opted not to do commercial cleaning.*

COMPANY HISTORY

- **IN BUSINESS SINCE:** *1967*
- **FRANCHISING SINCE:** *1969*
- **NUMBER OF FRANCHISE UNITS:** *803*

Scores of copy-cat residential cleaning franchises offer similar services, but ServPro Industries went beyond the residential cleaning niche to find new opportunities for its franchise owners.

Established in 1967, ServPro is a full-service residential and commercial cleaning company, which performs all types of residential cleaning chores, a la Merry Maids, Molly Maids, and The Maid Brigade. But where ServPro differs from the rest is in the fire restoration and cleaning work that the company also targets. According to company president Richard Isaacson:

"We researched the residential cleaning business and discovered that the competition from franchises and small 'mom-and-pop' cleaning service was fierce. We wanted to profitably differentiate ourselves. Fire and water restoration was attractive because it allowed franchise owners to become proactive.

"Unlike the carpet-cleaning business, fire restoration allows our owners to go out and sell and market the service year-round. They don't have to sit around waiting for the season to change and the telephone to start ringing."

The strategy paid off in terms of franchise sales. With 803 franchises operating throughout the United States, ServPro is now a recognized leader in the $9 billion home-services industry. Franchisees are responsible for managing their businesses and the cleaners they hire to perform the work. The company allows franchisees to start as cleaners, but it expects owners to outgrow this role in six to nine months as they assume more management and administrative functions.

This evolution is one of the keys to expanding the business. Scores of cleaning companies never evolve because the ownership is too involved in low-paying cleaning work and not available to pursue contracts and additional sales.

ServPro tries to overcome this challenge by providing full training in management and marketing. The company also believes that the fire and restoration work, which typically requires franchisees to sell to insurance adjustors and brokers, forces many new franchisees to become more professional and business-oriented.

ServPro networkwide revenue totaled more than $100 million in 1991. The company plans to have 2,000 franchises in existence by the year 2000.

The company's support system is built around a pyramid structure that links franchisees to regional trainers to state directors and finally to the corporate headquarters itself.

ServPro will finance almost half of the total $34,500 franchise package. Franchisees are expected to have at least $15,000 as a down payment, which covers most of the $17,800 franchise fee, to purchase the rights to a non-exclusive area and the use of the ServPro name and products for a minimum of five years.

Although the territories aren't exclusive, the company makes every effort not to dovetail areas and will only do so if an area isn't being marketed or developed correctly. The remainder of the costs, which is financed over a seven-year period, purchases equipment and cleaning products.

Franchisees don't have to purchase products from ServPro, but most supplies are manufactured "in-house" and are available to all franchisees at a relatively low cost. One additional expense that isn't figured into the franchise package is the purchase or lease of a truck which will be needed to carry equipment from job to job.

ServPro encourages all new franchisees to start their franchise as a home-based business. Presently, 33 percent of ServPro franchisees maintain a home office, and the company predicts that more than 90 percent of these franchisees will move to commercial space after their sales volumes reach the $250,000 mark. This figure usually spurs franchisees to hire clerical and cleaning employees who require more working space than a home office allows.

Along with the up-front fees, franchisees pay an ongoing royalty, which starts at 10 percent and decreases to 3 percent as business volume grows. There is a provision in the franchise agreement for a 3 percent advertising fee, but that charge has yet to be implemented.

Franchisee training for ServPro encompasses four distinct phases, which include in-field observation of an operating ServPro franchise; a two-week home study course with manuals and workbooks; an on-the-job training course conducted at an operating franchise; and a week-long classroom training course conducted at the home office.

FORECAST AND ANALYSIS

ServPro is a company that is supportive and conscious of its franchisees. Its goal of 2,000 franchises is extremely ambitious, but the company has a large current foundation of franchisees and has a proven track record of supporting many franchise owners. The company offers franchisees incentives for success, such as an annual 10 percent rebate on their royalty payments. This is a rare offer in franchising and one that demonstrates a commitment to franchisee success over home-office profitability.

18

CLEANING AND DYEING, CARPET

34. COLOR YOUR CARPET

FRANCHISE FEE: *$20,000 to $30,000*
TOTAL INITIAL INVESTMENT: *Under $50,000*
ROYALTY FEE: *3 percent of gross monthly sales*
ADVERTISING FEE: *None*
ADDRESS: *2465 Ridge Crest Avenue, Orange Park, FL 32065*
TELEPHONE: *1-800-321-6567 or 1-904-272-6567*
CONTACT PERSON: *Connie D'Imperio*

INDUSTRY OVERVIEW

- *Consumers are looking for ways to maintain the value of their homes. Redecorating is one such way. Homeowners can achieve a "new look" in a house by reupholstering furniture or dyeing carpets.*
- *Consumers do not have as much discretionary cash as in the past, so homeowners are looking for services that can save them money over the long term.*

BENEFITS OF THIS COMPANY

- *Color Your Carpet has an aggressive franchising expansion and marketing plan.*
- *The company prides itself on both its franchise support systems as well as its training programs.*

COMPANY HISTORY

- **IN BUSINESS SINCE:** *1987*

- **FRANCHISING SINCE:** *1988*
- **NUMBER OF FRANCHISE UNITS:** *72*

Redecorating a house is an expensive proposition, with the largest cost going to the installation of new carpet. A Florida-based franchise company claims it can reduce the price of home redecorating with its unique service that revitalizes, tints, or dyes a carpet to a customer's specifications.

Color Your Carpet franchisees charge customers between 40¢ and $1 per square foot to revamp their carpets. Franchisees also offer furniture reupholstering and cleaning services. The company estimates that its dyeing and tinting process saves consumers thousands of dollars associated with carpet replacement.

First franchised in 1988, Color Your Carpet now has fourteen franchises in operation. However, that number doesn't reveal the full extent of the franchise's development since those franchisees have also bought rights to develop seventy-four surrounding areas within the next two years. As in many home-based service businesses, Color Your Carpet's success depends on the tenacity of franchisees to promote their product. Hotel chains, retail outlets, apartment and office complexes, as well as residential consumers comprise the customer target list for every franchisee.

With Color Your Carpet's emphasis on local promotion and marketing, the company encourages former managers or sales people to become franchisees. An initial investment fee of $15,000 purchases an exclusive territory with a minimum population of 100,000 people and a guaranteed lock-in on neighboring territories as well. Franchisees will need to invest an additional $5,000 to $15,000 to cover the costs of equipment, promotional material, brochures, stationery, and a lease agreement on the bright purple van that has become Color Your Carpet's trademark. Although the company charges no advertising fee, it does charge a 3 percent royalty fee.

Color Your Carpet requires franchisees to spend one week at the home office learning technical, marketing, and communication skills. In-field assistance, especially public relations and advertising counseling, is available to all franchisees, especially during the first two years of operation.

FORECAST AND ANALYSIS

This franchise has potential as long as it is marketed as a redecorating service. The franchise needs no space to operate effectively. All service calls are done at the customer's premises, including estimates and consultations. Although franchisees are not discouraged from branching out into commercial office space, the move is not necessary.

35. RAINBOW INTERNATIONAL CARPET DYEING AND CLEANING CO.

FRANCHISE FEE: *$15,000*
TOTAL INITIAL INVESTMENT: *$40,000*
FINANCING AVAILABLE: *Yes*
ROYALTY FEE: *7 percent*
ADVERTISING FEE: *None*
ADDRESS: *P.O. Box 3146, Waco, TX 76707*
TELEPHONE: *1-817-756-2122*
CONTACT PERSON: *Don Dwyer*

INDUSTRY OVERVIEW

- *Consumers are looking for ways to improve the carpet and furniture they already possess rather than investing in new items.*
- *There's a great deal of competition in this industry. Many companies sport exclusive methods and claim to be better than others.*

BENEFITS OF THIS COMPANY

- *Rainbow offers customers a broad range of services, from carpet cleaning and restoration to carpet dyeing. The company is one of the recognized leaders in the industry, and its franchise system is one of the most extensive of any organization in the world.*
- *Rainbow International is the cornerstone company in a franchising conglomerate that includes five companies, including Worldwide Refinishing Systems and Mr. Rooter.*

COMPANY HISTORY

- **IN BUSINESS SINCE:** *1981*
- **FRANCHISING SINCE:** *1981*
- **NUMBER OF FRANCHISING UNITS:** *over 2000*

If any company can boast about its success with franchising, it's Rainbow International Carpet Dyeing and Cleaning Co. With more than 2,000 franchises worldwide and $60 million in total revenue, Rainbow is the cornerstone of a franchise network that includes five individual service companies—all run under the direction of Rainbow founder Don Dwyer.

Established in 1981, Rainbow offers customers custom-dyed carpets that give new life to dirty and damaged carpeting. Using its exclusive dyeing process, Rainbow franchisees provide service quickly and efficiently without relying on high-priced labor, which was once a prerequisite for custom carpet work. A Rainbow franchisee performs most of the work, along with a small crew.

What attracts a franchisee to this opportunity? Rainbow is a complete, professional package. The investment is a reasonable $40,000, and the company's long history of success indicates an ability to spawn successful franchisees. Included in the investment is a $15,000 fee that buys the rights to an exclusive territory based on a population of 50,000 residences for ten years.

Franchisees who wish to buy more than one territory are allowed to do so. They pay another $300 for every 1,000 people in their areas. The company charges no advertising fee. Franchisees pay a 7 percent royalty on gross revenue.

Rainbow also provides cleaning, deodorizing, and restoration services for carpets and upholstery and offers financing for qualified applicants. Total initial investment, which includes equipment (cleaning and dyeing machines) and supplies is $40,000.

Since all work is done at the customer's site, most franchisees opt to start the franchise at home. As volume expands, many franchisees add more vans, staff, and equipment, forcing some of them to lease commercial space.

Rainbow provides franchisees with ample training. Franchisees spend approximately one week at the training center in Texas, where they learn dyeing and cleaning processes and receive marketing, management, and personnel recruitment instruction. Post-training support is also a major part of this franchise's tradition, coming in the form of daily telephone contact as needed, personal in-field assistance, seminars, and conventions.

FORECAST AND ANALYSIS

The Dwyer empire provides a solid foundation for Rainbow franchisees. Rainbow and its sister franchises frequently refer business and share business ideas and practices. There is one concern: the company's reported networkwide income of $60 million translates into average franchisee (2,000 of them) annual gross sales of only $30,000 a year. That's a modest return and one not likely to yield much of a profit once expenses are subtracted.

36. CHEM-DRY CARPET CLEANING (HARRIS RESEARCH, INC.)

FRANCHISE FEE: *$9,950*

TOTAL INITIAL INVESTMENT: *$9,950*

FINANCING AVAILABLE: *Yes, with $3,950 down; zero percent interest for sixty months at $99 per month*

ROYALTY FEE: *$175 per month*

ADVERTISING FEE: *None*

ADDRESS: *3330 Cameron Park Drive, Suite 700, Cameron Park, CA 95682*

TELEPHONE: *1-800-841-6583 (1-800-CHEM-DRY) or 1-916-677-0231*

CONTACT PERSON: *Raymond Moors or Michael Mastous*

INDUSTRY OVERVIEW
- *The carpet and upholstery cleaning markets are extremely competitive. Successful firms rely on marketing and repeat customers.*

BENEFIT OF THIS COMPANY
- *Chem-Dry is a widely recognized name in the industry. Carpet and upholstery manufacturers such as Monsanto and DuPont approve Chem-Dry services for their products.*

COMPANY HISTORY
- **IN BUSINESS SINCE:** *1976*
- **FRANCHISING SINCE:** *1976*
- **NUMBER OF FRANCHISE UNITS:** *2,048*

Carpet cleaning companies are everywhere, cleaning and steaming rugs and upholstery in homes and businesses throughout the country. But only a few have achieved the same recognition as Chem-Dry. Once just one of the crowd, the California-based company took its unusual dry-cleaning process and parlayed it into a multinational network of more than 2,000 franchises in twenty countries. The company's great competitive advantage is its patented non-toxic cleaners and dyes that dry in less than one hour. For an initial $9,950 investment, franchisees purchase the rights to an exclusive territory for five years and all equipment needed to perform the Chem-Dry cleaning process. Most franchisees start their businesses by doing the cleaning themselves, but most evolve into managers and hire staff to do the cleaning. Along with the initial investment, the company also charges franchisees a $175-per-month royalty fee.

Chem-Dry makes it easy for entrepreneurs to invest in the franchise. For undercapitalized franchisees, the company finances $6,000 of the initial fee for five years at zero percent interest, which amounts to $99 per month. The company also encourages its franchisees to work from home, which eliminates the cost of rental space. At present, 95 percent of all franchisees operate their Chem-Dry franchises from their homes.

Chem-Dry works to stay ahead of competition by developing new products for its franchisees to sell. Through its parent company, Harris Research, Inc., Chem-Dry continues to investigate and research new products and services.

Chem-Dry requires franchisees to attend a four-day training class. During this course, franchisees are instructed in the technical aspects, promotion, and marketing of the business. Conventions, training seminars, and regional and local meetings are also held annually to keep franchisees up-to-date on new research and product development. Chem-Dry produces training videos and publishes a newsletter for the benefit of the franchise network.

FORECAST AND ANALYSIS

Chem-Dry offers well-known, high-quality products and processes, and an outstanding training program. The company's support of its franchise owners and its ability to draw on the experience of thousands of franchisees gives it high marks in the carpet and upholstery-cleaning business.

37. AMERICLEAN

FRANCHISE FEE: *$15,000 to $45,000 depending on size of territory*
TOTAL INITIAL INVESTMENT: *$28,000 to $124,000*

FINANCING AVAILABLE: *Yes (for larger territories)*
ROYALTY FEE: *8½ percent decreasing to 1 percent*
ADVERTISING FEE: *None*
ADDRESS: *6602 S. Frontage Road, Billings, MT 59101*
TELEPHONE: *1-800-827-9111 or 1-406-652-1960*
CONTACT PERSON: *Jim Pearson*

INDUSTRY OVERVIEW
- *Residential cleaning services is a $9 billion industry.*
- *Fire and water restoration services are constantly in demand due to home fires and flooding.*

BENEFITS OF THIS COMPANY
- *By combining carpet cleaning with fire restoration, AmeriClean provides its franchisees with services that can be marketed throughout the year (carpet cleaning is typically seasonal with demand greatest in the fall and spring).*
- *The company offers ample support in the form of field and telephone contact. It also has on staff a certified restorer, one of only 100 such professionals in the country.*

COMPANY HISTORY
- **IN BUSINESS SINCE:** *1979*
- **FRANCHISING SINCE:** *1981*
- **NUMBER OF FRANCHISE UNITS:** *85*

Making adjustments is often the telltale sign of an effective franchisor.

When the Pearson family bought AmeriClean in 1979, the business concentrated on carpet and upholstery cleaning. The Pearsons quickly discovered a problem: carpet and upholstery cleaning is a seasonal business with the bulk of the work occurring in fall and spring.

AmeriClean needed a way to beef up sales during other times of the year. The solution came when the Pearsons added a fire and water restoration component to the business. The move differentiated the company from thousands of other carpet and upholstery cleaners and provided the impetus to start franchising in 1981.

Today, AmeriClean sponsors eighty-five franchisees throughout the United States, most of whom perform carpet and upholstery cleaning as a sideline to their more profitable fire and water restoration businesses. The company has gained national recognition for its work and keeps on staff a restoration specialist, one of only 100 certified restorers in the United States today.

AmeriClean expects its growth to continue and predicts that at least 100 franchises will exist by the mid-1990s.

Typically, franchisees start their business performing most of the cleaning and restoration work themselves. As the business grows, some franchisees choose to remain small and focus on the work. Other franchisees hire crews and move on to managing and marketing the business.

Franchisees invest between $28,000 and $124,000 to open their businesses. The franchise fee of $15,000 to $45,000 secures an exclusive territory with a population ranging between 30,000 and 500,000. The agreement runs for ten years, and franchisees can automatically renew it for five years without paying an additional charge.

The company offers financing to select candidates, and works with franchisees to obtain the most affordable leases on equipment and supplies. In addition, it will direct franchisees to reputable third-party lenders.

Franchisees pay AmeriClean an ongoing monthly royalty, which begins at 8.5 percent and decreases to 1 percent as volume grows. Initially, no capital is needed for rental of office space. AmeriClean encourages new franchisees to operate their businesses from home.

Training includes a home study course complete with operations manuals and videotapes and a one-week classroom and in-field instruction course at headquarters. An AmeriClean representative assists new franchisees in the start-up, marketing, and sales of the new business.

The company also holds an annual convention, which all franchisees are required to attend. There are also regional meetings and three 800 hotlines for franchisees needing help.

FORECAST AND ANALYSIS

AmeriClean isn't a carpet-cleaning company that accidentally fell into restoration. During the early 1980s, the company spent a great deal of money analyzing its structure and services. It saw restoration as the perfect market to overcome the seasonal nature of carpet and upholstery cleaning.

38. PROFESSIONAL CARPET SYSTEMS

FRANCHISE FEE: *$5,000 for a 50,000 population territory*
TOTAL INITIAL INVESTMENT: *$13,500*
FINANCING AVAILABLE: *Yes*
ROYALTY FEE: *6 percent*
ADVERTISING FEE: *None*
ADDRESS: *5182 Old Dixie Highway, Forest Park, GA 30050*
TELEPHONE: *1-800-925-5055 or 1-404-362-2300*
CONTACT PERSON: *Investment Counselor*
INDUSTRY OVERVIEW

- *Carpet dyeing is increasing in popularity as more consumers seek cost-effective alternatives to replacing carpets.*

BENEFIT OF THIS COMPANY

- *With more than 450 franchises, Professional Carpet is known throughout the United States and has a reputation for being solid and profitable.*

COMPANY HISTORY

- **IN BUSINESS SINCE:** *1978*
- **FRANCHISING SINCE:** *1980*
- **NUMBER OF FRANCHISE UNITS:** *491*

For the cost of installing wall-to-wall carpeting, most people could take a cruise, buy a new car, or put a down payment on a house. And it was the size of this investment that put Professional Carpet in business.

When the company entered the carpet and upholstery-cleaning industry thirteen years ago, it went to battle against those who claimed a soiled carpet meant a spoiled carpet. Aided by an in-house laboratory and its own line of dyes and cleaners, Professional Carpet proved it could not only revitalize soiled rugs but also tint, dye, and deodorize them at a price averaging 80 percent less than replacement cost.

The technical approach paid off, and the company, which has 491 franchises, is now recognized as an industry leader. International expansion is on the horizon, and Professional Carpet estimates that 1,000 franchises will exist by 1995.

Although the expansion plan is exhaustive, the capital needed to become part of the franchise network isn't. An initial $5,000 franchise fee, which the company finances, acquires the rights to an exclusive territory of 50,000 people for ten years. Territories can be enlarged at any time, and the additional coverage rights, which may also be financed, cost about $100 for every 1,000 people in the area.

Franchisees pay an ongoing 6 percent royalty and total initial investment is $13,500. The figure covers the cost of all equipment and marketing and training materials, plus the right to use any new products and services developed in the company's laboratory.

The low overhead and mobile in-home service combine to make a Professional Carpet Systems franchise a suitable home-based franchise. The company encourages franchisees to work from home and emphasizes that 100 percent of the franchisees opt for this set-up initially. However, the company has a strong record of rapid growth. With that growth often comes a need for more working space. According to the company, 40 percent of its franchisees eventually move to a commercial environment.

Although a franchise requires some technical know-how, no previous experience is required. The company offers two weeks of training that focus on dyeing and cleaning, as well as marketing and management.

To new franchisees, the company provides grand opening advertising and public relations support. In-field programs include training videos, workshops, and an 800 hotline if assistance is needed. The company holds bi-annual conventions to introduce new product lines and services to franchisees and publishes a monthly newsletter, *Dyegest,* which details franchisee successes and evaluations.

FORECAST AND ANALYSIS

Carpet dyeing provides a cost-effective way for consumers to beautify their homes. Franchisees benefit from the security of a large company while enjoying self-employment. Professional Carpet is an industry leader and one of the largest players in the market.

39. HEAVEN'S BEST CARPET AND UPHOLSTERY CLEANING

FRANCHISE FEE: *$9,500*

TOTAL INITIAL INVESTMENT: *$9,500 to $25,000 depending on size of territory and amount of equipment purchased*

FINANCING AVAILABLE: *No*
ROYALTY FEE: *$40 per month*
ADVERTISING FEE: *None*
ADDRESS: *P.O. Box 607, Rexburg, ID 83440*
TELEPHONE: *1-800-359-2095 or 1-208-356-8765*
CONTACT PERSON: *Cody Howard*

INDUSTRY OVERVIEW
- *New carpeting is a major expense. Consumers need to save money and maintain their carpets as long as possible.*
- *The carpet cleaning industry is heavily competitive. The more successful companies promote their products extensively and develop new techniques to attract customers.*

BENEFITS OF THIS COMPANY
- *Heaven's Best has a history of success in this industry.*
- *The company also works to assure franchisees profitable territories. It offers ample support and service to franchisees.*

COMPANY HISTORY
- **IN BUSINESS SINCE:** *1983*
- **FRANCHISING SINCE:** *1983*
- **NUMBER OF FRANCHISE UNITS:** *80*

The carpet cleaning industry is not an industry light in competition. For a company to succeed, its product and service must somehow rise above the rest. Heaven's Best of Rexburg, Idaho, believes its unique system of carpet cleaning and maintenance gives it that competitive edge.

Established in 1983, Heaven's Best uses an exclusive non-toxic chemical solution to clean soiled carpets and upholstery. The chemical solution, which dries in under two hours, prevents the build-up of mildew and dirt, which is a recurring problem with steam or water-saturation cleaning methods.

Heaven's Best, which grossed more than $1.5 million in networkwide revenues in 1991, attracts a wide variety of franchisees, including part-time entrepreneurs as well as well-heeled master franchisees. Master franchisees buy and control large territories and are responsible for marketing the franchise opportunity and supporting and training smaller "subfranchisees."

The company, which estimates supporting 400 franchisees by 1995, prides itself in offering a flexible and affordable franchise. A $9,500 initial investment purchases the right to an exclusive, five-year territory, which is based on population. Equipment and training is also included in the investment. Franchisees also pay a $40-per-month royalty fee.

Franchisees who plan on pursuing a full-time career in the carpet-cleaning business have the option to purchase more equipment, but it is not essential.

A Heaven's Best franchisee needs only about 200 square feet to operate the business effectively. For this reason, 100 percent of all franchisees choose to run their Heaven's Best franchises from their homes.

Heaven's Best requires all franchisees to attend a week-long training seminar before they open their businesses. Along with instruction on how to perform the carpet-cleaning services, mix chemicals, and maintain equipment, franchisees also learn the basics of advertising, customer relations, and bookkeeping.

After the initial training period, Heaven's Best is available to answer franchisees' questions through its 800 hotline. The company also hosts regional training seminars, and in-field support is available to franchisees either from the home office or from their master franchisees.

FORECAST AND ANALYSIS

Although there is a great deal of competition in the carpet-cleaning industry, Heaven's Best's proprietary cleaning methods may provide franchisees with a competitive advantage. The company still must contend with small "mom-and-pop" companies who offer services at rock-bottom prices as well as large retailers who offer similar services.

Heaven's Best's flexible franchise program, which can be tailored to a part-time, full-time, or master franchise opportunity, offers a range of investment levels for potential franchisees.

40. CLEANWAY INDUSTRIES

FRANCHISE FEE: *$23,500*
TOTAL INITIAL INVESTMENT: *Under $50,000*

ROYALTY FEE: *12 percent of total gross*
ADVERTISING FEE: *None*
ADDRESS: *Box 6, Westhampton Beach, NY 11978*
TELEPHONE: *1-800-332-6996 or 1-516-288-6300*
CONTACT PERSON: *Bill Harding*

INDUSTRY OVERVIEW
- *Commercial office space increased dramatically during the 1980s, and with that came the demand for office maintenance.*
- *The entry of many companies into this competitive industry may cause a maintenance glut in the future. Companies must find a specialty in order to thrive.*

BENEFITS OF THIS COMPANY
- *Cleanway distinguishes itself among the competition by being experts in the upholstery, fabric, and non-wood floor maintenance field. The company markets its service to the health- and environment-conscious business owner who wants to eliminate internal contaminants from the office space.*
- *Cleanway has been a profitable enterprise for more than seventeen years. The company waited to perfect its system of operation before franchising less than two years ago.*

COMPANY HISTORY
- **IN BUSINESS SINCE:** *1974*
- **FRANCHISING SINCE:** *1989*
- **NUMBER OF FRANCHISE UNITS:** *2*

Competition in the building- and office-maintenance industry is fierce, but one company has managed to sidestep its adversaries by carving a specialized niche for itself. Cleanway Industries decided to concentrate its cleaning practices on upholstery, fabric, and non-wood flooring. Marketing Cleanway services to national and regional retail chains and offices, franchisees negotiate long-term contracts with customers who wish to have their furniture and fabrics cleaned on a regular and specific basis.

Cleanway is an experienced service company that began operation in 1974. In 1989, father-and-son owners, Richard and Bill Harding, decided to franchise the company to attract national clients. Presently, there are only two franchise operations, but the company claims that 95 to 120 franchises will exist by 1995.

Cleanway's optimism for its success stems from its unique management and operational system. All franchise outlets can be run from home. No special equipment or inventory is needed, but most importantly, no employees are essential. All cleaning crews are independent contractors previously screened and interviewed by the home office or regional franchisee. Franchisees make the business contact, formalize the contract, and subcontract work to the cleaning crew. Franchisees are encouraged to pursue contracts on both the local and national scale. Any contracts that are out of a franchisee's territory will be serviced by the home office, and Cleanway will pay that franchisee a commission on the contract.

An initial $23,500 fee guarantees a Cleanway franchisee a territory with a minimum corporate and business population of 250,000. The company estimates franchisees will need a maximum total investment of $50,000, which covers the costs of equipment, promotional material, and working capital.

The Cleanway franchisee should be a savvy marketer and communicator. The company sponsors a training class which teaches the basics of contract negotiation. In addition, all franchisees are required to undergo at least two weeks of in-field training. The home office monitors contracts and services to assure customers of quality work.

FORECAST AND ANALYSIS

Office and retail environments are getting a great deal of attention from the federal government. The proposed Indoor Air Quality Act is before Congress now, and the EPA is lobbying for its enactment. Under this bill, offices will have to take special precautions to ensure a healthy work environment, which includes the monitoring of air, water, and any other environmental hazard. Upholstery, carpet and fabric wall coverings are among the EPA's targets since they act as collection basins for bacteria and germs.

19

DIRECT MAIL

---

41. MONEY MAILER, INC.

FRANCHISE FEE: *$15,000 for first 30,000 homes in territory and $4,000 for each additional 10,000 homes; fee may be reduced or waived at choice of franchisor*

TOTAL INITIAL INVESTMENT: *$20,000 and up, depending on franchise fee agreement*

ROYALTY FEE: *10 percent*

ADVERTISING FEE: *None*

FINANCING AVAILABLE: *Yes*

ADDRESS: *14271 Corporate Drive, Garden Grove, CA 92643*

TELEPHONE: *1-800-624-5371 (1-800-MAILER-1)*

CONTACT PERSON: *Kris O. Friedrich or Franchise Sales Department*

INDUSTRY OVERVIEW

- *Direct mail advertising is an effective form of advertising that gives advertisers the ability to directly measure effectiveness. This form of advertising appeals to companies who are looking for ways to reach consumers cost-effectively.*

BENEFIT OF THE COMPANY

- *Money Mailer is a well-organized veteran in the direct mail industry. Its track record and repeat customers shows that the direct mail concept works.*

COMPANY HISTORY

- **IN BUSINESS SINCE:** *1979*
- **FRANCHISING SINCE:** *1980*
- **NUMBER OF FRANCHISE UNITS:** *328*

The impact of direct mail advertising on a business's sales can be significant. Marketing research estimates that 83 percent of women and 57 percent of men redeem coupons—especially those that come directly to their mailboxes. Money Mailer, Inc., of Garden Grove, California, banks on consumers in search of a bargain. The company's direct mail franchise network includes 328 franchises across the country and generates networkwide revenues in excess of $32 million.

The concept behind a Money Mailer franchise is simple. Franchisees contact local and national businesses and sell them space in Money Mailer advertising circulars. Businesses participate in coupon offers, brochures, direct mail orders, or catalogues without the expense of conducting a direct mail campaign themselves. Franchisees either design and lay out the advertisement as part of their services, or they call upon the home office to perform these functions. All printing is completed by an outside company approved by Money Mailer. Franchisees send out the completed circular to a minimum of 30,000 homes in their area, usually on a bi-monthly basis.

A $15,000 fee assures a franchisee of an exclusive territory of 30,000 homes for five years. For an additional $4,000, a franchisee can increase a territory by 10,000 homes. Since Money Mailer is willing to finance qualified franchisees, the average entrepreneur needs only a fraction of the $25,000 in start-up costs to get the franchise in operation. Money Mailer does not require franchisees to lease commercial office space. Most sales and inquiries are accomplished by telephone, and franchisees need only a computer, copier, and separate telephone line to run the business efficiently. To keep overhead costs to a minimum, most Money Mailer franchisees operate their business from home.

Money Mailer requires three weeks of training for franchisees. Each owner is instructed in sales, management, and communications techniques. The company offers its franchisees continued support through ongoing regional training programs and aggressive advertising and promotional campaigns.

FORECAST AND ANALYSIS

Convenience and price are increasingly important to consumers. Direct mail gives consumers an easy and convenient way to take advantage of discounts and other incentives to buy products and services. Money Mailer runs an organized and professional franchise company and offers ample support to help franchisees overcome most business and sales obstacles.

42. SUPER COUPS COOPERATIVE DIRECT MAIL

■——■

FRANCHISE FEE: *$22,000*
TOTAL INITIAL INVESTMENT: *$22,000*
FINANCING AVAILABLE: *No*
ROYALTY FEE: *$148 per mailing*
ADVERTISING FEE: *None*
ADDRESS: *180 Bodwell Street, Avon Industrial Park, Avon, MA 02322*
TELEPHONE: *1-800-626-2620 or 1-508-580-4340*
CONTACT PERSON: *David Siersdale*
INDUSTRY OVERVIEW

- *Direct mail is recognized as an effective form of advertising for a wide variety of companies.*
- *Many consumers appreciate the value direct mail coupons provide. Relatively few consumers consider the product junk mail.*
- *More and more direct mail coupon franchises are entering the market. Too many companies competing within one region can saturate markets and cause price wars that cut profit margins for franchisees.*

BENEFIT OF THIS COMPANY

- *Super Coups is a well-established company which enjoys a record of success and growth. Consumers and advertisers know the Super Coups trademark, and respond enthusiastically to the company's mailings.*

COMPANY HISTORY

- **IN BUSINESS SINCE:** *1983*
- **FRANCHISING SINCE:** *1984*
- **NUMBER OF FRANCHISE UNITS:** *96*

■——■

Direct mail coupons are a marketing technique with a high rate of consumer response. More than 70 percent of all redeemed coupons come from direct mail advertising. This statistic is what launched Super Coups, the Avon, Massachusetts–based direct mail service. In

1983, Super Coups began sending consumers packages filled with coupons, brochures, and mail-order catalogues from a variety of vendors. The Super Coups franchise network now includes ninety-six franchises and twelve company outlets in the United States. The company estimates that more than 180 franchises will exist by 1995.

For an initial investment of $22,000, franchisees purchase the rights to an exclusive territory based on a population of 60,000 homes. The contract lasts for ten years. Franchisees make money by selling advertising space to local and national businesses. The firms that buy the space decide what type of insert will be most effective for their products and services, and franchisees design the layout and write the copy for the ads. If franchisees are uncomfortable with the layout and copywriting aspects of the Super Coups business, the franchisor will assist in composing artwork and copy. Franchisees use local printers approved by Super Coups. Super Coups charges franchisees $148 per mailing as part of their franchise agreement.

Franchisees should also have in reserve an additional $1,000 to $2,000 for the purchase of basic office equipment. Recommended equipment includes a typewriter or computer, a copier, and, most importantly, a telephone line dedicated to the franchise operation. The Super Coups franchise generates very little walk-in traffic, and almost all advertising contracts are secured through telephone sales. This franchise requires minimal space for operation, and Super Coups advises franchisees to forgo the overhead expense of a professional office and run their businesses from home.

Franchisees attend a two-week training class which focuses on sales and marketing skills. Super Coups also provides post-training support such as in-field assistance, seminars, workshops, and conventions on the regional and national level. The home office also provides an 800-number hotline to support its franchisees.

FORECAST AND ANALYSIS

Super Coups is a recognized player in the direct mail industry. The company has developed a series of sales programs that franchisees can rely on to help them attract more advertisers. According to the company, 92 percent of consumers who receive Super Coups mailers use the coupons or discount materials in the package. That's well above the industry average.

43. TRIMARK, INC.

FRANCHISE FEE: *$5,000*
TOTAL INITIAL INVESTMENT: *$10,000*
FINANCING AVAILABLE: *None*
ROYALTY FEE: *None*
ADVERTISING FEE: *None*
ADDRESS: *184 Quigley Boulevard, New Castle, DE 19720*
TELEPHONE: *1-800-874-6275 or 1-302-322-2143*
CONTACT PERSON: *Gilbert Kinch*

INDUSTRY OVERVIEW
- *Direct mail coupon advertising works. Seventy percent of all coupons redeemed come from direct mailings to consumers.*
- *Local merchants like the idea of direct mail because they can track the response by counting the number of redeemed coupons.*

BENEFITS OF THIS COMPANY
- *Despite its financial woes of late, TriMark still possesses the experience and know-how which once made the company great.*
- *TriMark has been candid about its financial problems and its Chapter 11 filing. The company has struck some surprisingly generous deals with recent franchisees to bring them into the network at franchise fees that are significantly discounted.*

COMPANY HISTORY
- **IN BUSINESS SINCE:** *1972*
- **FRANCHISING SINCE:** *1978*
- **NUMBER OF FRANCHISE UNITS:** *29*

In the last five years, TriMark has experienced its fair share of financial turbulence. At its peak in 1985, the company boasted a network of more than ninety-two franchises, but dissension among franchisees and a damaging legal battle over sales practices reduced it to twenty-nine surviving franchisees. In an effort to protect itself and its remaining franchisees, TriMark filed Chapter 11 in October 1989.

Why write about a company that is struggling to survive? Because TriMark is slated to emerge from bankruptcy soon. As part of its restructuring plan, the company has slashed franchise fees and promised an inordinate amount of support to any franchisee willing to gamble on it.

The company, which solicits advertising from local merchants and mails coupons and brochures to consumers' homes, has also instituted a number of new national marketing and financing programs.

Is it a risk? You bet. TriMark is not the only fish in the direct mail sea, and there are other companies in better financial shape. Still, TriMark is one of the oldest and most respected direct mail franchisors, and in franchising, experience means everything.

For bargain-hunting franchisees, TriMark may be worth investigating. The company is willing to reduce and even waive initial franchise fees to get the company rolling again.

Presently, a $5,000 franchise fee buys an exclusive territory consisting of 150,000 mailable homes. A TriMark contract is indefinite and the territory can be extended at the request of a franchisee for a fee of $100 per 1,000 households.

Trimark estimates that a franchisee should have in reserve an additional $5,000 to cover other expenses including office equipment, marketing materials, postal permits, and living expenses. TriMark does not require a computer system or a fax, but highly recommends their use. To run a franchise effectively, little room or equipment is needed. All sales calls are accomplished by telephone, and a TriMark franchise generates no walk-in traffic. For this reason, 85 percent of TriMark franchisees choose to operate from home.

Sales is the primary responsibility of TriMark franchisees. To make it in direct mail, you have to know how to convince local merchants to part with their hard-earned money.

TriMark provides one week of classroom instruction and one week of in-field practice to familiarize franchisees with sales techniques, ad layout, and business management. The home office also maintains a specially trained staff to answer all franchisee questions and concerns as they arise.

FORECAST AND ANALYSIS

TriMark has certainly seen dark days, and there is no doubt that an investment is risky. It's important to note that TriMark did not lose financial ground due to overexpansion or faulty business decisions. The majority of the company's problems lay in a harsh legal battle over the previous sales practices.

20

ENVIRONMENTAL SERVICES

---

44. STEAMATIC, INC.

FRANCHISE FEE: *$18,000 to $35,000*

TOTAL INITIAL INVESTMENT: *$48,000 to $75,000*

FINANCING AVAILABLE: *Yes*

ROYALTY FEE: *8 percent decreasing to 5 percent as volume grows*

ADVERTISING FEE: *None*

ADDRESS: *1320 S. University Drive, Suite 400, University Center, Fort Worth, TX 76107*

TELEPHONE: *1-800-527-1295 or 1-817-332-1575*

CONTACT PERSON: *Bob Phillips*

INDUSTRY OVERVIEW

- *The EPA has identified indoor air pollution as a major environmental threat. At the same time, more consumers, hospitals, restaurants, hotels, and health-care facilities are becoming aware of the health hazards posed by indoor pollutants.*

BENEFIT OF THIS COMPANY

- *Steamatic enjoys national recognition for its indoor pollution control methods. The company has been in existence for almost thirty years, and has been at the forefront of industry changes and developments.*

COMPANY HISTORY

- **IN BUSINESS SINCE:** *1968*
- **FRANCHISING SINCE:** *1969*
- **NUMBER OF FRANCHISE UNITS:** *198*

The energy crisis of the 1970s and 1980s inspired a new trend in construction—energy-efficient buildings. While new structures locked out energy waste, they locked in bacteria, viruses, fungi, and other health hazards. Steamatic uses its specially designed proprietary equipment to rid air ducts, condenser coils, filters, furniture, and floors of substances that can cause environmental damage or ill health.

With total revenues exceeding $5 million, Steamatic is a recognized leader in the indoor pollution-control industry. The company, which now includes 198 franchises and 10 company-owned outlets, plans to support 425 franchises by 1995.

Most Steamatic franchisees perform the majority of the cleaning themselves. Some franchisees hire multiple crews and focus their time and energy on marketing and managing the business.

Target markets for franchisees include restaurants, hospitals, and office buildings. In addition to air duct cleaning, franchisees also clean carpets, although the company downplays this component of the business.

Franchisees invest about $30,000 to open and outfit their businesses. This includes a $18,000 franchise fee.

Steamatic offers financing but only on equipment. Steamatic also recommends that franchisees purchase or lease a van and standard office equipment, including a personal computer.

Since all work is completed at the customers' site, Steamatic doesn't require franchisees to lease office space. More than 50 percent of franchisees elect to begin at home. Many franchisees move to commercial space as the need for warehouse and parking spaces becomes necessary.

The company charges franchisees an 8 percent royalty on gross receipts initially. As volume grows, Steamatic decreases the royalty to a minimum 5 percent.

Steamatic requires two weeks of training for all franchisees. The first week concentrates on the various cleaning methods and products. New franchisees learn how to handle all equipment, cleaners, and chemicals. In the second week, training focuses on the business end of the operation, with emphasis on management, marketing, and financial techniques.

After the two weeks, franchisees receive training in sales, promotions, and personnel development. Steamatic also offers a specialized program for struggling franchisees. Telephone and in-field support are also available.

FORECAST AND ANALYSIS

Steamatic markets not only to the consumer but also to the insurance and commercial markets. The multilevel marketing works to assure franchisees exposure to several key target audiences. The company traces its roots to the carpet-cleaning industry. Its recent foray into indoor air pollution might confuse some consumers. In fact, the company's name still reflects its carpet-cleaning roots.

Although high on the list of EPA priorities, the agency has yet to license or regulate indoor air-pollution or duct-cleaning businesses. Regulation would seem likely as more companies claim they know how to prevent indoor air pollution. Before investing in any indoor air-pollution franchise, investigate the processes and products the company uses to improve air quality.

Have they been tested and certified effective and safe? If Steamatic's products perform as the company claims, the company could become a powerhouse—roughly analogous to the weight-loss franchises that exploded in the 1980s. If the products aren't proven, franchisees could be saddled with tremendous liability if their efforts fail to provide promised environmental and health benefits.

45. ARMOR SHIELD

■━━━━━━━━━━━━━━━━━━━━━━━━━━━━━━━■

FRANCHISE FEE: *$6,500*
TOTAL INITIAL INVESTMENT: *$38,000 to $138,000*
FINANCING AVAILABLE: *No, but the company works with leasing companies to acquire best financing arrangement on equipment*
ROYALTY FEE: *7½ percent*
ADVERTISING FEE: *Yes, but not yet implemented*
ADDRESS: *7685 Field Ertel Road, Cincinnati, OH 45241*
TELEPHONE: *1-800-543-1838 or 1-513-530-5455*
CONTACT PERSON: *Michelle Phillips*
INDUSTRY OVERVIEW
- *Newly established federal and state environmental laws are requiring businesses with underground tanks to do a better job securing their toxic contents.*

- *The industry is highly regulated by all levels of government. Businesses that secure, line, test, or install underground storage tanks need to know how to cut through the red tape and comply with reams of regulation.*

BENEFIT OF THIS COMPANY

- *Armor Shield's processes are exclusive. The company maintains the highest safety standards, which have often become industry safety standards. The home office stays abreast of regulations and communicates changes in the law and circumstances to franchise owners.*

COMPANY HISTORY

- **IN BUSINESS SINCE:** *1967*
- **FRANCHISING SINCE:** *1975*
- **NUMBER OF FRANCHISE UNITS:** *26*

___

Concern over our environment has forced many industries to re-evaluate their methods of underground storage. Strict federal and state regulations requiring upgraded storage tanks have also sent companies searching for ways to protect their tanks against corrosion and rust without the expense of replacement.

Armor Shield works with service stations, fuel companies, and anyone else who stores materials in underground tanks to secure tanks and prevent breakdowns and leaks that can damage the surrounding soil and water supply.

Established in 1967, Armor Shield has set industry standards with an exclusive lining system that reduces internal tank corrosion. The company's lining systems, which are guaranteed for ten years, cost approximately one-fifth the cost of tank replacement.

Franchisees are responsible for marketing their services and performing the relining work on storage tanks that hold everything from crude oil to molasses. The work is strenuous and performed in tight areas (franchise owners must enter the tanks to inspect and line them).

Armor Shield is one of the few heavily industrial franchise opportunities available. Franchisees work with other businesses in the chemical, petroleum, and food products industries to secure contracts and safeguard the environment against tank leaks.

Franchisees who have previous experience in any of these industries and who enjoy physical labor are likely to fare best in this area. The initial investment, which ranges from $38,000 to $138,000 and includes a $6,500 franchise fee, buys all the equipment, inventory, safety gear, and related assets needed to operate the business.

Armor Shield doesn't directly finance franchisees, but works with leasing companies to arrange terms for the purchasing or leasing of a truck and equipment.

Armor Shield charges a monthly 7½ percent royalty and an advertising fee, which has yet to be implemented.

Although the administrative work may be done from a home office, all franchisees will need a space to park a tractor trailer which contains the compressors, spray systems, and safety equipment needed to perform tank rehabilitation. Most Armor Shield franchisees begin operation from their homes and rent storage space for the truck. Eventually, most franchise owners move to an outside office with garage space to accommodate the growth in business.

Training costs franchisees $1,500 and can take place either at the franchisor's or franchisee's site. If training is done at the franchisee's location, the operator is responsible for paying the expenses of the company trainer.

After initial training, franchisees receive support from the home office through the company's technical support line. Armor Shield also conducts yearly franchise meetings and safety seminars. The company will also train additional crews hired by the franchisee.

FORECAST AND ANALYSIS

Leaking underground storage tanks have become a major environmental concern—particularly in light of recently enacted clean water and air legislation.

With twenty-six Armor Shield franchises in the United States, the company is positioned as a major player in this evolving market. There is competition from regional and even national firms that provide similar services to storage-tank owners. Still, the market is expected to keep growing with above-ground storage tanks now on the EPA and OSHA "hit" lists.

This is a technical business with lots of liability. As part of a franchise, Armor Shield franchisees benefit from training, support, and networking that takes place within a franchise.

46. ENVIROBATE SERVICES

FRANCHISE FEE: *$25,000*

INITIAL INVESTMENT: *$75,000*

FINANCING AVAILABLE: *None*

ROYALTY FEE: *6 percent*

ADVERTISING FEE: *None*

ADDRESS: *500 E. 36th Street, Minneapolis, MN 55408*

TELEPHONE: *1-612-825-6878*

CONTACT PERSON: *Jeff Anlauf*

INDUSTRY OVERVIEW

- *Increased environmental awareness has spurred the need for asbestos and lead abatement services. Abatement of hazardous materials are mandated by law in most communities throughout the United States.*
- *Asbestos is slowly being eliminated from the environment, which means that eventually asbestos abatement firms will find themselves out of work. EnviroBate is already researching other areas of environmental concern and recently added lead abatement to its portfolio of services.*

BENEFIT OF THIS COMPANY

- *EnviroBate adheres strictly to all federal and state laws which dictate procedures and policies of asbestos and lead removal. The company, which is licensed in forty-three states, has officers experienced in business, medicine, and law.*

COMPANY HISTORY

- **IN BUSINESS SINCE:** *1988*
- **FRANCHISING SINCE:** *1991*
- **NUMBER OF FRANCHISE UNITS:** *1*

Very few health hazards have caused such widespread alarm as asbestos. Once considered the perfect economical, multiuse product, asbestos is now viewed as a villain in the fight against cancer and other progressive diseases.

EnviroBate is a Minnesota-based company that detects and eliminates the contaminating fibers asbestos emits. EnviroBate uses state-of-the-art equipment to detect, inspect, evaluate, remove, or encapsulate asbestos before the substance's fibers have a chance to break down and infiltrate the environment.

The company's asbestos abatement service has existed since 1988, but EnviroBate only recently elected to expand its services to provide lead testing and elimination for homes and businesses. The new direction spurred the company's move into franchising. The company estimates that thirty-eight franchises will be in operation by 1995.

Franchisees are expected to perform inspections on houses and commercial buildings. After the initial analysis, the EnviroBate franchisee recommends and completes a course of action which removes or encapsulates asbestos or other environmental toxins.

An initial fee of $25,000 secures an exclusive territory for ten years. Franchisees should expect to invest an additional $50,000 which purchases toxin abatement equipment, protective gear, uniforms, and promotional and marketing materials. Franchisees market the EnviroBate services to consumers and businesses through direct mail campaigns and telemarketing. The company also receives referrals from insurance companies and law firms which specialize in environmental litigation.

EnviroBate requires franchisees to attend an EPA- approved training school. The company expects franchisees to complete an in-house training course which teaches abatement and removal techniques plus toxin recognition, testing, danger analysis, and treatment. Franchisees receive instruction in estimating costs associated with an abatement project and personnel recruitment. Most EnviroBate franchisees run their businesses from home. The company encourages this practice as long as some storage space is reserved in the house for equipment.

FORECAST AND ANALYSIS

EnviroBate is positioned to be a leader in the elimination of asbestos. However, the life cycle of asbestos clean-up is quickly coming to an end. With a new emphasis on lead abatement, the company is now positioning itself to address a new environmental threat. The company has a safety record with its customers and, more importantly, government agencies such as OSHA and the EPA.

47. ADVANTAGE RADON CONTROL CENTERS

FRANCHISE FEE: *$17,500*

TOTAL INITIAL INVESTMENT: *$25,000*

FINANCING AVAILABLE: *Not now but will implement loan programs in near future*

ROYALTY FEE: *8 percent*

ADVERTISING FEE: *1 percent*

ADDRESS: *804 Second Street Pike, Southampton, PA 18966*

TELEPHONE: *1-800-535-TEST or 1-215-953-9200*

CONTACT PERSON: *Perry Ecksel*

INDUSTRY OVERVIEW

- *Many environmental hazards are now known to exist in homes, schools, hospitals, and businesses. Even state- of-the-art facilities are susceptible to environmental toxins.*
- *Environmental testing will become more government-regulated, especially in terms of licensing, testing, and abatement procedures. Companies that already follow strict methods of testing and abatement will fare the best under new regulations.*

BENEFIT OF THIS COMPANY

- *Advantage Radon Control handles many environmental toxins, not just radon as the name implies. The company owns a large testing laboratory and is recognized by government agencies, insurance companies, and mortgage lenders.*

COMPANY HISTORY

- **IN BUSINESS SINCE:** *1985*
- **FRANCHISING SINCE:** *1991*
- **NUMBER OF FRANCHISE UNITS:** 7

Environmental toxins such as asbestos, radon, and lead can exist anywhere. Very few homes or buildings are immune from their effects. Companies such as Advantage Radon Control Centers evaluate and eradicate the toxins from the environment, safely and effectively.

Advantage Radon uses government-approved equipment and methods to test homes and businesses for the presence of toxins within walls, foundations, and pipes.

The company supports seven franchises in the United States and

Canada. The franchise typically appeals to environmentally concerned entrepreneurs who enjoy working with their hands and solving problems. The franchise fee is $17,500 and the exclusive contract, which is based on county lines, runs for fifteen years.

Due to the technical nature of the business, specialized inspection and abatement equipment is required. To reduce initial costs, many franchisees choose to lease equipment.

In addition to the up-front investment, Advantage Radon charges franchisees an 8 percent monthly royalty and a 1 percent advertising fee.

The business requires little room to operate efficiently: a telephone, desk, and fax machine are all the office equipment needed by the franchisee. Currently, all franchisees work from their homes. Sales calls and inspections are done at the customer's location, which also eliminates the need for an outside office.

Attorneys, realtors, mortgage companies, as well as consumers comprise Advantage Radon's primary market. Franchisees are required to attend and pass the three-week training class and acquire all local, state, and federal testing certifications. Along with technical training, franchisees receive marketing and sales instruction. After that, each franchisee is required to receive an additional eighteen hours of training annually.

Company representatives are available for in- field assistance, and franchisees have access to an 800 hotline if they encounter problems.

FORECAST AND ANALYSIS

Radon, asbestos, formaldehyde, and lead all pose serious health hazards to Americans. Advantage Radon is rolling out its franchise program at a time when environmental awareness is at a high. The company's knowledge of the industry offers franchisees an advantage in an emerging market.

21

FINANCIAL SERVICES

━━━

48. THE LOAN SOURCE

━━━

FRANCHISE FEE: *$9,950 to $11,950*
TOTAL INITIAL INVESTMENT: *$13,000 to $16,000*
FINANCING AVAILABLE: *None*
ROYALTY FEE: *None*
ADVERTISING FEE: *None*
ADDRESS: *3841 N. Freeway Boulevard., #145, Sacramento, CA 95834*
TELEPHONE: *1-800-683-LOAN or 1-916-648-7100*
CONTACT PERSON: *Tim Dyckman*
INDUSTRY OVERVIEW

- *Second mortgages and home equity loans have gained popularity with many consumers, especially those trying to consolidate debts.*
- *States are requiring more regulation regarding money brokering. Regulation will separate fly-by-night brokers from legitimate lenders who can help consumers find necessary financing.*

BENEFITS OF THIS COMPANY

- *The Loan Source uses a network of banks and other lending institutions to make as many loans as possible.*
- *Franchisees aren't allowed to charge consumers up-front fees. The points or fees are collected only at the settlement of the loan. This policy gains consumers' trust and patronage.*
- *The Loan Source requires franchisees to meet state regulations and qualifications before they can operate their Loan Source franchise.*

COMPANY HISTORY

- **IN BUSINESS SINCE:** *1990*

- **FRANCHISING SINCE:** *1990*
- **NUMBER OF FRANCHISE UNITS:** *120*

Second mortgages aren't as easy to obtain as consumers may think, especially in a tight economy when banks are reluctant to lend money. The Loan Source uses a network of financial institutions to obtain loans for the average homeowner.

Started in 1990, The Loan Source now has 120 franchises across the United States. Expansion of the brokerage company is expected to continue, and The Loan Source estimates that nearly 200 franchises will be in operation by 1995.

Franchisees are considered loan originators and take only the initial information from an applicant. The Loan Source's main office handles all processing, approval, and closing arrangements.

A telephone, fax, and computer system are the only equipment needed to run the franchise. That makes this franchise a perfect home-based business. The company has also attracted many attorneys, accountants, realtors, and financial planners, who have discovered that The Loan Source adds an interesting profit center to their businesses.

A franchise fee of $11,500 covers the expenses of opening a franchise territory which covers a population of 100,000 or more. Territories aren't exclusive, but The Loan Source takes great pains not to put two franchisees in the same area.

The franchise fee also covers the cost of grand opening marketing and advertising and the purchase of a computer system and modem. Franchisees don't have to buy the computer or office equipment from The Loan Source. If they already own a system or plan to purchase it elsewhere, $2,000 is deducted from the franchise fee.

Franchisees don't pay a monthly royalty or advertising fee. The Loan Source earns its money by charging the franchisee a fee of less than $350 per loan.

Training is brief. A two-day seminar at offices in Florida or California introduces franchisees to the world of loan origination. After initial training, franchisees are given videotapes to hone sales and financial skills. The company's hands-on participation in each loan makes sure that loans are processed quickly and professionally.

FORECAST AND ANALYSIS

Consumers always need money, and second mortgages and home refinancing are popular sources of cash. More people are taking advantage of this type of financing, which is spurring demand for franchises such as The Loan Source. The initial training is short compared with most franchises, even though increased regulation could require higher competency on the part of mortgage professionals.

49. CREATIVE ASSET MANAGEMENT

FRANCHISE FEE: *$12,500 to $17,500*
TOTAL INITIAL INVESTMENT: *$14,500 to $19,500*
FINANCING AVAILABLE: *Yes*
ROYALTY FEE: *$300 per month*
ADVERTISING FEE: *None*
ADDRESS: *170 Wood Avenue S., Suite 300, Iselin, NJ 08830*
TELEPHONE: *1-800-245-0530 or 1-908-549-1011*
CONTACT PERSON: *Rich Rodman*
INDUSTRY OVERVIEW

- *Americans are becoming increasingly concerned about saving for their children's college tuition or their retirement.*
- *Tax law changes affect many Americans, and investment advice may be the key to minimizing the tax burden.*

BENEFIT OF THIS COMPANY

- *Creative Asset Management shows clients how they can embark on a long-term savings and investment plan. The company also teaches consumers how to use long-term investment strategies to minimize risk.*

COMPANY HISTORY

- **IN BUSINESS SINCE:** *1982*
- **FRANCHISING SINCE:** *1988*
- **NUMBER OF FRANCHISE UNITS:** *40*

The rising cost of education, health care, and everyday living has caused many consumers to worry about their financial futures. Creative Asset Management turns that concern into long-term investment programs for consumers.

Started in 1982, the company uses its exclusive START NOW program to help individuals and businesses manage their assets, especially income, efficiently and profitably. The company targets middle-class America, typically the people most in need of financial planning. The franchise hopes that niche will propel its growth to 200 franchises by 1995.

Although no previous financial experience is required, all franchisees must pass industry and state examinations to act as licensed investment counselors. Once the testing is complete, the franchisee can begin operations.

For a fee of $12,500 to $17,500, franchisees acquire the rights to a fifteen-year contract entitling them to use Creative Asset Management's name and START NOW program. Franchisees pay a monthly $300 royalty to the franchisor, regardless of gross income.

There are virtually no other start-up expenses unless a franchisee chooses to rent an outside office or conference room space. Few Creative Asset franchisees take this route, and more than 80 percent run the franchise from home.

Territories aren't exclusive because business growth relies on personal referrals, not walk-in traffic.

Franchise training differs from individual to individual. For those already in the tax, insurance, or financial-planning fields, instruction is neither intensive nor extensive. For the inexperienced, Creative Asset offers classes in all aspects of financial and tax planning. The company also sponsors seminars and workshops and produces newsletters and videotapes to keep franchisees up-to-date.

FORECAST AND ANALYSIS

After the hard lessons of the frivolous 1980s, America is becoming a nation of savers. Consumers are looking for ways to save on a long-term basis. Most financial planning is geared toward upper-class consumers who have the extra disposable income to invest as opportunities arise. But Creative Asset Management works with middle-class Americans to find profitable, growth-oriented investments. This niche is likely to grow as baby-boomers mature and begin thinking about their futures.

50. TRIPLE CHECK INCOME TAX SERVICES, INC.

FRANCHISE FEE: *$1,500 to $3,000 based on gross revenue in current practice*

TOTAL INITIAL INVESTMENT: *$1,500 to $3,000*

FINANCING AVAILABLE: *None*

ROYALTY FEE: *Depends on new income generated from franchise work and decreases as volume builds*

ADVERTISING FEE: *$700 per year*

ADDRESS: *727 S. Main Street, Burbank, CA 91506*

TELEPHONE: *1-800-733-1040 or 1-213-849-3100*

CONTACT PERSON: *David W. Lieberman*

INDUSTRY OVERVIEW

- *A large percentage of Americans rely on professional help to prepare and file their income-tax returns.*
- *Those Americans who prepare their tax returns themselves typically miss many deductions that could save them money.*

BENEFITS OF THIS COMPANY

- *Triple Check provides the training and professional image that generates consumer confidence—an important benefit for the professional tax preparer.*
- *In addition to tax-preparation services, Triple Check franchise owners offer additional financial services that generate revenue throughout the year, not just during tax season.*
- *Triple Check has fifty years of experience in the tax-preparation business. The company is the second largest tax-preparation franchise.*

COMPANY HISTORY

- **IN BUSINESS SINCE:** *1941*
- **FRANCHISING SINCE:** *1961*
- **NUMBER OF FRANCHISE UNITS:** *350*

If death and taxes are the only certainties in life, then an income-tax–preparation service shouldn't have to worry about demand.

Still, no business is a sure thing. The biggest challenge facing income-tax preparers is the seasonal nature of the business. Sure, there's lots of business in March and April, but July and August can be lonely.

Triple Check, one of the nation's oldest and largest tax-preparation services, overcomes some industry limitations by providing a range of financial-planning products in addition to traditional tax-preparation services.

"Many tax-preparation businesses actually close their doors during the off months, leaving their clients high and dry," says David Lieberman, president. "But taxes have become so complex, consumers need year-round service. That's how we have managed to win confidence and add products."

Founded fifty years ago, Triple Check has helped millions of Americans handle their tax burdens. Networkwide sales topped $85 million in 1991.

The demand for financial planning has driven the company's recent growth. Triple Check estimates that the 350-franchise chain will grow to 500 locations by 1995.

Triple Check franchisees are typically accountants, bookkeepers, or financial planners who convert to the Triple Check system to benefit from a known name and proven operating system. Because Triple Check doesn't require franchisees to operate from professional office space, many franchisees work at home. Home-based Triple Check franchisees must reserve at least one room in their house to conduct business.

Headquarters provides an array of marketing and promotional programs, including a national advertising program financed by a flat fee of $700 charged to each franchisee annually. In addition, the company sponsors a tax research department that franchisees can call for answers to any tax-related or financial service questions.

The franchise fee is a reasonable $1,500 and $3,000 for a territory that covers an eight- to ten-mile radius. The territories aren't exclusive, but Triple Check tries not to locate two franchisees in close proximity.

Before franchisees take the Triple Check name, they're required to complete thirty-eight to ninety-six hours of training, most of which is performed through home study. They're required to carefully follow company operating procedures to ensure standards and quality service throughout the network.

Along with the initial training, franchisees attend an annual professional conference and a yearly seminar on tax-related laws and regulations.

Triple Check franchisees are plugged into headquarters via a hot-line that places them in direct contact with home-office tax specialists.

FORECAST AND ANALYSIS

It's doubtful whether the demand for tax preparation will ever wane. H&R Block continues to dominate the industry, but there's certainly room for many competitors in the income-tax–preparation business. One warning: "mom-and-poppers" often undercut prices in order to win new customers. However, most consumers want quality representation when it comes to tax preparation.

Triple Check has a solid reputation and record for supporting franchisees and providing quality consulting to consumers. Its year-round schedule and a product line that includes financial services makes it a well-positioned player in the tax preparation market of the 1990s.

51. CLAIM-IT

■━━■

FRANCHISE FEE: *$5,250*
TOTAL INITIAL INVESTMENT: *$6,500*
FINANCING AVAILABLE: *None*
ROYALTY FEE: *4 percent*
ADVERTISING FEE: *None*
ADDRESS: *P.O. Box 4584, Greensboro, NC 27404*
TELEPHONE: *1-919-292-0094*
CONTACT PERSON: *Debbie Miller or G. Elaine Huddy*

INDUSTRY OVERVIEW

- *A service that can decipher and complete insurance medical forms is a necessity, especially for the elderly or disabled.*
- *There is not a great deal of competition in the industry yet. The service is specialized and affordable, which can attract individuals as well as senior citizen groups or organizations that help the disabled.*

BENEFITS OF THIS COMPANY

- *Claim-It was started as a result of a personal experience with medical forms. The procedures have been tried and tested by the franchise company.*
- *As the senior citizen population grows, so do health insurance prob-*

lems. Claim-It relieves seniors of the burden of insurance claims filing.

COMPANY HISTORY

- ● **IN BUSINESS SINCE:** *1983*
- ● **FRANCHISING SINCE:** *1991*
- ● **NUMBER OF FRANCHISE UNITS:** *4*

Family concerns mount when an elderly person needs hospitalization. Children or other "caretaking" family members must sort through mountains of insurance forms and related paperwork. Claim-It relieves this burden.

The company analyzes insurance policies, files appropriate paperwork, and monitors the progress of claims until the bills are paid. For those who request it, Claim-It will consult with them on insurance coverage and available options.

Potential franchisees need no previous insurance or accounting experience. The company seeks detail-oriented individuals who can deliver professionalism both in person and over the telephone.

Word of mouth is a key success factor in marketing the business. Franchisees must be prepared to go to hospitals, nursing homes, or rehabilitation centers to promote the service. Professionalism and sales ability are critical.

Established in 1983 by G. Elaine Huddy, a legal secretary, Claim-It offered its first franchise in 1991. Based in Greensboro, North Carolina, it now supports four franchises throughout the United States.

A $5,250 franchise fee purchases the rights to use the Claim-It name and an exclusive territory consisting of a minimum population of 250,000 residents. Franchisees also receive all forms needed to start the business as well as marketing and promotional material. The contract expires after one year, but the company will automatically renew it if a franchisee is developing the area properly.

Franchisees attend a four-day training course at the company's home base in North Carolina. During this training class, franchisees are taught to file insurance claims using the Claim-It system. The company also instructs franchisees on marketing strategies as well as management and bookkeeping procedures.

Claim-It suggests that franchisees keep in reserve an additional $1,000 to $1,500 for the lease of a copy machine plus the purchase of stationery, a typewriter, and an answering machine. There is no special equipment or minimum space requirement for this enterprise, and Claim-It encourages franchisees to operate the business from home.

FORECAST AND ANALYSIS

Claim-It provides a needed service in this day of increased paperwork and insurance red tape. As America moves to cut health care costs, paperwork, which accounts for one third the cost of U.S. healthcare, will become a prime target. Services that simplify the medical insurance filing process have the potential to find a ready market. The franchise concept is simple to operate and market, which makes it a viable home-based option.

22

HOME REPAIR, CONSTRUCTION, CONTRACTING, AND APPRAISING

---

52. KITCHEN TUNE-UP

FRANCHISE FEE: *$9,995*
TOTAL INITIAL INVESTMENT: *$11,495 to $11,995*
ROYALTY FEE: *7 percent*
ADVERTISING ROYALTY: *None*
ADDRESS: *131 N. Roosevelt, Aberdeen, SD 57401*
TELEPHONE: *1-800-333-6385 or 1-605-225-4049*
CONTACT PERSON: *Tony Haglund*
INDUSTRY OVERVIEW
- *This is an affordable service in a market that is not saturated. The service is also simple to understand, which attracts consumers easily. There is a drawback in that do-it-yourself consumers may bypass having the service done and learn the process on their own.*
BENEFITS OF THIS COMPANY
- *This company pioneered the cabinet refacing industry.*
- *Kitchen Tune-Up is a fast-growing business. It is only two years old, but it has achieved more success than companies three or four times its age.*

COMPANY HISTORY
- **IN BUSINESS SINCE:** *1986*
- **FRANCHISING SINCE:** *1989*
- **NUMBER OF FRANCHISE UNITS:** *121*

Kitchen Tune-Up, a South Dakota–based franchise, has found a way around the cost of kitchen remodeling. With a tried and tested nine-step cleaning process, Kitchen Tune-Up franchisees rejuvenate and revitalize wood surfaces, making them appear new. The cost for the service averages $200 to $300, a fraction of what it would take to replace cabinets.

New to the world of franchising, Kitchen Tune-Up is growing at a rapid rate. It sold its first franchise territory less than two years ago, and the company now has 121 franchise units across the United States and Canada. Kitchen Tune-Up estimates that more than 500 franchises will exist by 1995.

What is the secret behind the company's success? It simply filled a consumer void. Homeowners know that cabinets and all woodwork need tender loving care, but few have the expertise or patience to provide that attention.

For an initial $9,995 fee, franchisees purchase an eight-year contract which entitles them to an exclusive territory with a minimum population of 100,000 people. The Kitchen Tune-Up home office estimates that an additional $4,000 will be needed to cover other miscellaneous business expenses such as office equipment and telephone lines. There is no special equipment or inventory associated with this franchise, and all sales calls and work is completed at the customer's home. With this in mind, 100 percent of Kitchen Tune-Up franchisees elect to run their businesses from home. The company attracts both men and women as franchisees. Presently 36 percent of franchisees are women, and Kitchen Tune-Up expects that number to increase dramatically.

Kitchen Tune-Up conducts a five-day training seminar at its home office, and franchisees are taught marketing skills as well as the nine-step cleaning process. The home office provides in-field support and aids in national advertising and promotion programs. Each franchisee is also assigned an account representative who assists with problems and questions.

FORECAST AND ANALYSIS

Kitchen Tune-Up is a service designed for the customer who is trying to save money. Many consumers can't afford major kitchen remodeling. Hence the demand for Kitchen Tune-Up services.

53. KITCHEN SOLVERS, INC.

FRANCHISE FEE: *$7,500 to $12,500 depending on size of franchise territory*
TOTAL INITIAL INVESTMENT: *$15,000 to $20,000*
FINANCING AVAILABLE: *No*
ROYALTY FEE: *5 percent*
ADVERTISING FEE: *None*
ADDRESS: *401 Jay Street, La Crosse, WI 54601*
TELEPHONE: *1-800-845-6779 or 1-608-784-2855*
CONTACT PERSON: *David J. Woggon*

INDUSTRY OVERVIEW

- *Cabinet refacing has grown tremendously in the last decade as a cost-effective alternative to cabinet replacement.*
- *Competition from larger companies, such as Sears, has heated up the market. But franchise owners often support less overhead and can usually beat the prices of larger competitors.*

BENEFITS OF THIS COMPANY

- *Although the company officially started in 1982, Kitchen Solvers has more than fifty years of experience in the remodeling industry through company owners Gerald and Betty Baldner.*
- *Various size territories make the opportunity affordable to those who do not have a great deal of cash on hand. As a franchisee's business grows, franchisees can buy more territory.*

COMPANY HISTORY

- **IN BUSINESS SINCE:** *1982*
- **FRANCHISING SINCE:** *1984*
- **NUMBER OF FRANCHISE UNITS:** *19*

It used to be that a remodeled kitchen cost almost as much as a new house. Now, with companies like Kitchen Solvers, consumers can refurbish a kitchen without remortgaging the house.

Based in La Crosse, Wisconsin, Kitchen Solvers offers consumers an alternative to remodeling. Instead of replacing the entire cupboard unit, Kitchen Solvers performs a "facelift" on the cabinetry by replacing a cabinet's worn framework, doors, and drawers with updated wood or materials.

Established in 1982, the company decided to expand via franchising in 1984. Today, nineteen franchises exist throughout the United

States, but the company, which had networkwide revenue of $1.65 million in 1991, expects fifty-six franchises to be in operation by 1995.

For entrepreneurs who like carpentry and physical labor, Kitchen Solvers may be worth investigating. The franchise fee, which ranges between $7,500 and $12,500, purchases the rights to an exclusive area which is determined mostly by county lines. Kitchen Solvers estimates that working capital and the purchase of equipment may cost an additional $7,000 to $8,000, bringing the total investment to between $15,000 and $20,000. The company receives a 5 percent monthly royalty from all franchisees.

Since sales calls and work are conducted at the customer's location, little office space is needed to conduct the business properly. For this reason, 85 percent of all Kitchen Solvers franchisees operate their businesses from home. The franchisor does caution that the growth of business, including the addition of full-kitchen remodeling services, will require the hiring of more personnel, which may lead franchisees to open outside office and shop space.

The company's five-day training program teaches franchisees how to sell and install the cabinet facelifts. The training session also teaches new entrepreneurs the methods Kitchen Solvers uses to maintain and promote the company to customers throughout the country. After the initial training period, Kitchen Solvers provides back-up support to its franchisees with a telephone hotline manned by the company's own cabinet installers.

FORECAST AND ANALYSIS

Consumers are becoming more wary about spending thousands of dollars on home remodeling. At the same time, there is a trend to forgo new houses and fix up present ones.

Kitchen Solvers faces competition from local contractors and carpenters as well as large retailers such as Sears. But Kitchen Solvers offers a competitive product at a competitive price. The 1990s are being touted as the decade of the homebody. Demand for home renovation services is likely to remain strong.

54. ADD-VENTURES

■───■

FRANCHISE FEE: *$5,000*
TOTAL INITIAL INVESTMENT: *$5,000*
FINANCING AVAILABLE: *None*
ROYALTY FEE: *3 percent*
ADVERTISING FEE: *3 percent*
ADDRESS: *38 Park Street Station, Medfield, MA 02052*
TELEPHONE: *1-617-499-7972*
CONTACT PERSON: *Tom Sullivan or Franchise Sales*

INDUSTRY OVERVIEW

- *Today's homeowners are looking to improve their existing homes instead of purchasing new ones. In a sluggish economy, people would rather hold on to their present homes than invest in new ones.*
- *In a booming economy, the home-improvement industry also thrives because people have the money to finance major repairs and remodeling.*

BENEFIT OF THIS COMPANY

- *Add-Ventures provides existing contractors with national recognition and exposure. It trains these contractors in the proper methods of management, marketing, and salesmanship.*

COMPANY HISTORY

- **IN BUSINESS SINCE:** *1977*
- **FRANCHISING SINCE:** *1985*
- **NUMBER OF FRANCHISE UNITS:** *12*

■───■

One of franchising's greatest attributes is its ability to take unorganized mom-and-pop industries and transform them into cohesive, professional businesses. Howard Johnson did it with hotels; Ray Kroc applied the principle to hamburger stands; Century 21 did the same thing in real estate.

Today, there are still hundreds of industries in need of professional marketing and management. Residential contracting is a perfect example. Thousands of small contractors make modest livings plying their craft. Many of them could benefit from the power of a franchise and all it brings to the marketing of a business.

That need is the basis of Add-Venture, a franchise that converts operating contractors to Add-Venture franchise owners. Started in 1977, Add-Ventures worked eight years perfecting its strategies of marketing, management, and bidding. In 1985, the company offered its first franchise in Boston when the economy was struggling. That initial success has attracted other contractors; now twelve Add-Venture franchises exist throughout the United States.

Add-Venture franchisees are hands-on businesspeople. They go on-site to manage and assist construction. They're also responsible for marketing and managing the business.

The headquarter's role is to help Add-Venture franchises market the business—a skill woefully lacking in many contractors. For instance, Add-Venture supports its franchise owners by developing and distributing direct mail promotions to builders and real estate agencies in franchised territories. The company develops cable television advertising and teaches Add-Venture franchisees how to profitably price and spec out jobs.

"The biggest obstacle to a contractor's success is that many don't know how to price out a job and still make a profit," says Tom Sullivan, president. "They are so busy underpricing their competition that they price themselves out of business. Most contractors are good craftsman but bad businessmen."

For a $5,000 franchise fee, Add-Ventures teaches contractors how to market, manage, plan for future expansions or recessions, and bid profitably and competitively. The up-front fee also buys an exclusive territory with a residential population of 25,000 people and a five-year contract, which is automatically renewable at a franchisee's request. No other capital is needed.

Add-Ventures recommends that its franchisees operate from home.

The company charges a 3 percent royalty against a franchisee's gross sales, as well as a 3 percent advertising fee. Training time varies depending on the special needs of the franchisees.

Before contractors can become franchisees, the company comes to their site and inspects previous work that they have completed.

Add-Ventures requires certain building standards, and a major part of the franchise contract deals with assuring quality workmanship. Franchisees are also inspected annually, and company representatives visit completed job sites and talk with customers to ensure company standards.

FORECAST AND ANALYSIS

Add-Ventures is a solid concept considering how much contractors need the marketing and managing expertise that a franchise can provide. Company president Tom Sullivan is candid about the opportunity in that it's not a panacea for all that ails the contractor.

"Our programs take time and effort, but they work. Ironically, most contractors don't know what works in terms of marketing, pricing, and management." In that respect, Add-Venture can fill a niche in an industry that could benefit greatly from the power of franchising.

55. SOLID/FLUE CHIMNEY SAVERS

FRANCHISE FEE: *$15,800*
TOTAL INITIAL INVESTMENT: *$45,000*
FINANCING AVAILABLE: *None*
ROYALTY FEE: *None*
ADVERTISING FEE: *1½ percent*
ADDRESS: *370 100th Street S.W., Byron Center, MI 49315*
TELEPHONE: *1-616-877-4900*
CONTACT PERSON: *Doug LaFleur*
INDUSTRY OVERVIEW
- *Chimney relining is an extreme niche business that few people know about but which is in surprising demand.*

BENEFITS OF THIS COMPANY
- *Solid/Flue is the only franchise in the chimney relining industry and one of the most respected companies of its kind. The company uses a patented poured concrete material to replace a damaged chimney liner with one that properly vents fumes and heat from fireplaces and other heat-producing household appliances.*
- *Franchisees can either run the business from their homes or include it in an existing contracting or construction business. Most work comes from insurance companies and word-of-mouth referrals.*

COMPANY HISTORY
- **IN BUSINESS SINCE:** *1979*
- **FRANCHISING SINCE:** *1990*
- **NUMBER OF FRANCHISE UNITS:** *38*

Has specialization gone too far? How can a business that just repairs chimney liners (they aren't chimney sweeps) make a go of it in today's complex economy?

"We focused on what we knew best and perfected it," begins Doug LaFleur, president. "Millions of American homes and businesses, especially those in the frost belt of the country, rely on chimneys to vent fumes and heat from fireplaces, wood stoves, gas and oil furnaces, and other appliances. Inside these chimneys are liners often constructed of terra-cotta tile. Over years of use, the tiles crack and break. Heat can transfer to the home or business structure. Toxic fumes can escape."

The result is often dangerous fires or carbon monoxide infiltration.

Solid/Flue franchisees correct the problem. Using a patented product and proprietary process, the company replaces damaged chimney liners without tearing apart the brickwork. The process begins by inserting long balloons down the chimney and inflating them with air. The balloons, called formers, are spaced away from the sides of the chimney. This space is then filled with an ultra-light, highly insulative product. When it dries, it creates an impenetrable barrier between fumes and heat and homes and businesses.

Established in 1979, the company now sponsors thirty-eight franchises in the United States and plans to support seventy-five franchises by 1995.

Franchisees perform much of the installation work themselves, although many grow out of the hands-on labor and focus on managing the business. Some Solid/Flue franchisees employ three full-time crews and register sales of more than $1 million a year.

The investment in a Solid/Flue franchise ranges from $45,000 to $60,000 and includes equipment, supplies, opening advertising, and working capital. The company doesn't charge a royalty—its profits come from product sales—but it requires franchisees to pay a 1.5 percent advertising fee, which is used for local and national promotion.

Although franchisees need a vehicle to transport equipment, there are no office space requirements. Franchisees complete all work at the customer's site and carry only a small amount of inventory. These factors make it convenient for Solid/Flue franchisees to operate at home.

In a six-day training class, franchisees learn all aspects of the business, from the chimney lining and restoration service to bookkeeping, marketing, and operations management. Post-training telephone and personal support is available, and a field representative will accompany franchisees on their first jobs.

The company also makes routine, periodic trips to each franchisee several times during the course of a year.

FORECAST AND ANALYSIS

Chimney relining is certainly a niche business. But the franchisees we spoke with were adamant that demand for the product and service is strong. Solid/Flue delivers a unique service and product that is of high quality. The company assists franchisees in marketing this service to insurance adjustors and brokers. Solid/Flue's training is top-notch and its professionalism often wins insurance work that competitors can't touch.

56. THE SCREEN MACHINE

FRANCHISE FEE: *$15,000*
TOTAL INITIAL INVESTMENT: *$32,583 to $53,019*
FINANCING AVAILABLE: *No*
ROYALTY FEE: *5 percent*
ADVERTISING FEE: *3 percent (not implemented as yet)*
ADDRESS: *P.O. Box 1207, Sonoma, CA 95176*
TELEPHONE: *1-707-996-5551*
CONTACT PERSON: *Wayne Wirick*
INDUSTRY OVERVIEW
- *Most hardware and home-center stores no longer offer screening services. Consumers have few options when it comes time to replace door and window screens.*

BENEFIT OF THIS COMPANY
- *Screen Machine has managed to turn its competitors into referral sources. Hardware stores and home centers often refer screening work to Screen Machine franchisees as a way to serve customers and avoid having to do the work themselves.*

COMPANY HISTORY
- **IN BUSINESS SINCE:** *1986*
- **FRANCHISING SINCE:** *1988*
- **NUMBER OF FRANCHISE UNITS:** *5*

Wherever there's a house or apartment, there's at least one door and window in need of screen repair. The Screen Machine offers consumers a mobile screen service which measures, removes, repairs, and replaces screens at the customer's site.

Established in 1986, the company was started after company president Wayne Wirick realized how difficult it was to find screen repair services. Hardware stores and home centers were turning down the work because it didn't fit their product mixes. The Screen Machine offered its first franchise in 1988.

The company developed a mobile concept that brought the screen repair and replacement process to consumers' front doors. The idea worked so well that the company attracted five franchisees (it also supports a company-owned unit). The company estimates that by the mid-1990s there will be a minimum of twenty-five mobile repair franchises throughout California and the western portion of the United States.

Franchisees who enjoy working with their hands might find The Screen Machine to be an interesting opportunity. There's low overhead and work hours are flexible. Most of the work is performed outdoors.

The business has attracted full-time and part-time franchisees. Inventory and materials are stored in a specially designed Screen Machine van. All but one current franchisee operates from home.

Investment ranges from $32,583 to $53,019, depending on the size and number of territories bought. A minimum $15,000 fee purchases an exclusive territory based on a maximum of 30,000 households. Franchisees can choose to buy more than one territory for an additional fee of $7,500 per 30,000 homes.

Franchisees pay a 6 percent royalty fee on gross receipts, or $150 a month, whichever is greater. The company charges an advertising fee of 3 percent, but this clause of the agreement hasn't been enforced.

Costs for the equipment package vary depending on a franchisee's decision to purchase an optional telescoping, hydraulically operated trailer cover to provide shelter from bad weather.

The company trains franchisees for a minimum of thirty-five hours at headquarters in Sonoma. Franchisees learn how to perform the repair and replacement of screens using the company's equipment. The Screen Machine also provides instruction in sales, management, and administration.

As part of ongoing support services, The Screen Machine conducts annual visits to franchisee sites aimed at evaluating the franchisee's operation. The company also holds periodic marketing and sales seminars and financial planning and operational management classes.

FORECAST AND ANALYSIS

Niche home-repair businesses are becoming increasingly popular. Every home has at least one or two screens that could be repaired. The Screen Machine mobile concept provides consumers with an added measure of convenience.

This could be a sleeper franchise with little current competition. The Screen Machine's franchisees probably won't net six figures from their businesses, but for the right individuals this franchise could offer an interesting opportunity to work for themselves and with their hands by serving homeowners.

57. ABC SEAMLESS

■━━━■

FRANCHISE FEE: *$12,000*
TOTAL INITIAL INVESTMENT: *$25,000*
FINANCING AVAILABLE: *None*
ROYALTY FEE: *5 percent (sliding scale)*
ADVERTISING FEE: *½ percent*
ADDRESS: *3001 Fiechtner Drive S.W., Fargo, ND 58103*
TELEPHONE: *1-800-732-6577 or 1-701-293-5952*
CONTACT PERSON: *Don Barnum*
INDUSTRY OVERVIEW
- *Steel siding is an alternative to traditional aluminum and vinyl siding products.*
- *The products are long-lasting and more durable than standard aluminum and vinyl siding products.*

BENEFITS OF THIS COMPANY
- *ABC Seamless has a thirteen-year history in this industry and has become a recognized leader.*
- *The company is selective when choosing franchisees and looks for people with experience in either remodeling or construction.*
- *The company is financially solid, earning more than $100 million in revenue in 1990.*

COMPANY HISTORY
- **IN BUSINESS SINCE:** *1973*

- **FRANCHISING SINCE:** *1979*
- **NUMBER OF FRANCHISE UNITS:** *643*

With nineteen years of experience and 1990 revenue in excess of $100 million, ABC Seamless is considered the industry leader in manufacturing and installing seamless steel siding on residential and commercial buildings. The company currently supports 643 franchisees throughout North America.

ABC franchisees are responsible for marketing and installing the siding product. Critical to the franchisee's success is a sixteen-foot trailer which houses the company's exclusive seamless steel manufacturing machine. The seamless steel siding machine cuts patterns to fit even intricate building exteriors. Consequently, installation time is much quicker than traditional siding methods, which requires mix-and-match cutting procedures.

An investment of $12,000 buys an exclusive territory based on a minimum population of 60,000. The fee includes training and a computer to help with marketing.

ABC estimates that franchisees need another $13,000 for leases on the trailer and siding machine. The purchase of other equipment and tools, plus advertising and promotional materials, account for the rest of the initial investment.

ABC charges franchisees an ongoing royalty that declines from 5 percent to 2 percent as a franchisee's volume grows. There's a ½ percent advertising fee.

Because of the technical nature of the business, the company seeks franchisees with previous construction or remodeling experience.

Initially office space requirements are small: room for a telephone, answering machine, desk, computer, and small coil that attaches to the seamless machine. The trailer can be parked in a driveway.

Minimal office requirements allows more than half the franchisees to operate from home initially. Many of those lease outside office space as their business grows and they purchase more territories from the franchisor.

The franchise demands extensive training, including two to three weeks of on-the-job work and classroom instruction.

Franchisees receive ample marketing and post-training support. ABC conducts regular regional sales meetings, publishes a monthly newsletter, and holds an annual training convention.

FORECAST AND ANALYSIS

ABC Seamless volume has expanded considerably since its founding in 1979, and the company seems to be financially secure. Franchisees receive ample home-office support. The need for previous construction or remodeling experience eliminates many potential franchisees. Competition is stiff in the home and industrial siding markets with major retailers, such as Sears, and local contractors vying for the same market. Any advantage—and steel siding offers plenty—could translate into higher sales for franchisees.

58. PERMA-JACK CO.

FRANCHISE FEE: *$5,000 to $50,000 depending on size of territory*
TOTAL INITIAL INVESTMENT: *$75,000 maximum*
FINANCING AVAILABLE: *None*
ROYALTY FEE: *10 percent of monthly gross sales*
ADVERTISING FEE: *None*
ADDRESS: *9066 Watson Road, St. Louis, MO 63126*
TELEPHONE: *1-800-843-1888 or 1-314-843-1957*
CONTACT PERSON: *Joan Robinson*

INDUSTRY OVERVIEW
- *The foundation stabilization industry is very specialized, and methods of operation and their costs vary greatly.*
- *Foundation stabilization is not a "frill" or luxury service. When foundations are in trouble, the work must be completed, which makes the demand for work plentiful.*

BENEFIT OF THIS COMPANY
- *Perma-Jack's proprietary jacking system delivers quality service with less noise and disruption than traditional jacking methods.*

COMPANY HISTORY
- **IN BUSINESS SINCE:** *1974*
- **FRANCHISING SINCE:** *1976*
- **NUMBER OF FRANCHISE UNITS:** *22*

All houses settle. But when settling causes the foundation to crack, homeowners may find themselves in a dangerous situation. Perma-Jack, a family owned, St. Louis–based company, stabilizes foundations with its patented system that hydraulically drives steel pilings underneath troubled foundations.

Invented in 1974, the Perma-Jack system needs only two crewmen to perform an average foundation stabilization. This method is less costly than traditionally used methods that require eight to ten workers to mechanically drive pilings under the house. The patented Perma-Jack system also drastically reduces the amount of noise and demolition associated with this type of service.

To say Perma-Jack is specialized is an understatement. The industry is small, and few competitors have imitated the Perma- Jack system. The company does not actively recruit franchisees. New franchisees are typically employees or customers who have seen Perma-Jack in action.

Franchisees perform much of the work themselves. Crews include one or two other workmen who install the steel pilings under the foundation of the house. Franchisees can either hire part-time or full-time employees or they can hire labor on a temporary basis.

There is little promotional sales work involved with the franchise. Customers call franchisees when they realize their house's foundation may be in trouble. Franchisees sponsor direct mail or telemarketing campaigns focusing on the difference between the Perma-Jack method and competition.

The initial franchise fee ranges from $5,000 to $20,000 and purchases a territory with a residential population of 50,000. Territories are non-exclusive, and Perma-Jack reserves the right to put another franchisee in a territory if it is not being developed according to the company's standards. Perma-Jack also recommends that franchisees keep in reserve an additional $14,000 to $24,000 for the purchase of a van, hydraulic equipment, and basic office equipment.

Equipment for this franchise is portable and requires no extra storage space. Many franchisees initially run their Perma-Jack franchise as a home-based business since all work and sales calls are conducted at the customer's home. But most franchisees move to professional space as business grows, but this is not a Perma-Jack requirement.

A minimum training period of one to two days is mandatory for all franchisees, and it can either be completed in St. Louis or at the franchisee's location. The Perma-Jack technique is the center of the training, but instruction in marketing, promotion, and management is also provided. The company keeps in daily contact with new franchisees, and help for both new and established franchisees is only a phone call away.

FORECAST AND ANALYSIS

Perma-Jack is a company steeped in family tradition. However, the company is responsive to changes and improvements. The relationship between franchisor and franchisee is very important to both sides of the company and Perma-Jack selects franchisees who will blend well into its family culture.

59. ARCHADECK, INC.

■──■

FRANCHISE FEE: *$32,500*
TOTAL INITIAL INVESTMENT: *$47,500 to $82,500*
FINANCING AVAILABLE: *Yes; finances up to $12,500 of franchise fee*
ROYALTY FEE: *7 percent on residential sales and 5 percent on commercial sales*
ADVERTISING FEE: *1 percent*
ADDRESS: *2112 W. Laburnum Avenue, Suite 109, Richmond, VA 23227*
TELEPHONE: *1-800-722-4668 or 1-804-353-6999*
CONTACT PERSON: *Franchise Development*
INDUSTRY OVERVIEW
- *Wooden decks allow homeowners to cost-effectively expand their living space.*
- *Wooden decks add to the resale value of most homes.*
- *In a down economy, homeowners look to remodel rather than move. In an up economy, new construction sales lead builders to add extra features to homes which include both simple and elaborate decks.*

BENEFITS OF THIS COMPANY
- *Archadeck works with builders and homeowners. The company uses the highest-quality material, and works with vendors to bring the lowest-cost supplies to both its franchisees and its customers.*
- *Although Archadeck has been offering franchises since 1985, it didn't actively seek franchisees until 1989. Since September 1990, the company more than doubled the number of franchisees.*

COMPANY HISTORY
- **IN BUSINESS SINCE:** *1980*

● **FRANCHISING SINCE:** *1985*
● **NUMBER OF FRANCHISE UNITS:** *60*

It used to be when a family outgrew a home, they picked up and moved elsewhere. But an uncertain economy has left many property owners looking for an alternative way to find more space. Archadeck Inc., a Virginia-based company, accommodates the dream for expansion with its custom-made wooden decks.

Established in 1980, Archadeck includes 60 franchises throughout the United States, and the company expects that number to reach 250 by the year 1995. Franchisees work with homeowners and builders to design and construct decks, gazebos, and trellises that range in price from $1,500 to $50,000.

Franchisees do not need previous building or carpentry experience. The role of the franchisee is that of manager and sales professional. Archadeck teaches franchisees to design and sell the decks and wooden structures to real estate developers and homeowners. Franchisees then hire carpenters and contractors to build the decks.

For an initial $32,500 fee, franchisees purchase the right to use the Archadeck name and operating system for a minimum of ten years. Archadeck avoids exclusive territories and urges franchisees to cluster close together in order to maximize marketing through shared promotional programs.

The company estimates that franchisees need to invest an additional $15,000 to $50,000 to cover the expense of marketing, office set-up, insurance, bonding, and working capital.

The franchise generates no walk-in traffic, and all sales calls are conducted at the customer's home. Presently, 80 percent of franchisees operate from their homes.

Archadeck offers direct financing to qualified franchisees as well as financing through VET-FRAN. Under this program, veterans receive special discounts or financing for their investment in Archadeck. Archadeck encourages equity partnerships, but all partners must be approved by the company.

Training for franchisees is extensive and includes a six-part program which works to build a concrete business plan around the individual franchisee. The program begins with a home study course. Franchisees then spend three weeks in Virginia learning about the products, sales methods, and management techniques. After the initial training, franchisees receive ongoing support through personal visits, unlimited telephone assistance, and regular in-field seminars.

Archadeck offers franchisees drafting services as part of their contract as well. After they design the decks, franchisees send the drawings to the home office. The home office returns them to franchisees in blue-print form. The company also converts drawings to meet all municipal and construction specifications and lists all materials that will be used for the deck construction.

FORECAST AND ANALYSIS

This company has experimented with its franchise network to make it as support-oriented as possible. It stabilized itself financially first by taking on an equity partner in the mid-1980s. The partner, MELLCO, a manufacturer of high-quality treated wood, fit perfectly with the company's product and service line. Although Archadeck cannot force its franchisees to buy MELLCO products, it provides discounts to franchisees who use MELLCO products.

60. HOUSEMASTERS OF AMERICA

FRANCHISE FEE: *$17,000 to $35,000 depending on size of area*
TOTAL INITIAL INVESTMENT: *$27,000 to $50,000*
FINANCING AVAILABLE: *No*
ROYALTY FEE: *7½ percent*
ADVERTISING FEE: *2½ percent*
ADDRESS: *421 W. Union Avenue, Bound Brook, NJ 08805*
TELEPHONE: *1-800-526-3939 or 1-908-469-6565*
CONTACT PERSON: *Linda Sigman*
INDUSTRY OVERVIEW
- *Home inspections are becoming more common in today's shaky real estate market. Homeowners and potential home buyers require now more than ever the assurance of a quality property.*
- *Some states have passed regulations that require home inspection. This is obviously a boon to home inspection companies.*

BENEFIT OF THIS COMPANY
- *HouseMasters has the competitive edge in this industry because it is the oldest inspection service in the country. The company focuses on customers who are relocating to different states.*

COMPANY HISTORY
- **IN BUSINESS SINCE:** *1971*
- **FRANCHISING SINCE:** *1979*
- **NUMBER OF FRANCHISE UNITS:** *120*

HouseMasters of America relieves the fears of home buyers through its comprehensive visual inspections of houses' structural and mechanical condition.

The oldest and largest franchise company in the home-inspection industry, the twenty-one-year-old HouseMasters organization includes 120 franchises throughout the United States. Networkwide revenues total more than $7.3 million.

Franchisees are responsible for conducting visual house inspections which focus on the structure as well as all electrical, plumbing, and heating systems. The average inspection takes approximately ninety minutes to complete. The inspection costs customers an average of $250. Franchisees market and advertise their services locally through real estate and mortgage companies, and the home office provides an assortment of national promotions. HouseMasters also supports a full-service relocation department which helps franchisees land jobs from homeowners moving into their territory.

Franchisees pay an initial investment of $17,000 to $35,000 for an exclusive territory based on the number of owner-occupied homes in the area. HouseMasters estimates that franchisees will spend an additional $10,000 to $15,000 for tools, equipment, and the lease or purchase of a pick-up truck or van. The company also charges franchisees a 7½ percent royalty fee and a 2½ percent advertising fee.

The HouseMasters operation does not require a franchisee to rent professional office space in its first months of operation. The home office advises its franchisees to minimize overhead costs and run the business from home. Approximately 40 percent of franchisees move to commercial space as their business volume increases and they hire more staff to perform the inspections.

HouseMasters conducts an extensive two-week training class for all franchisees. Along with technical instruction, franchisees learn marketing and promotional techniques—all of which have been tested in other franchise territories. An ample amount of field support exists for both new and established franchisees. A full-service public relations department works to gain local and national exposure for the company and its franchisees. The company also publishes a newsletter and hosts regular training conferences. HouseMasters also supports a Franchise Owners' Advisory Council, an organization that communicates franchisee concerns to the home office.

FORECAST AND ANALYSIS

HouseMasters is a well-established organization that has worked diligently to promote its name throughout the real estate and financial industries. The industry will achieve future growth as more legislation requiring real estate inspections is enacted. HouseMasters offers its franchisees a great deal of experience and support—crucial for success in any business.

61. AMERISPEC, INC.

FRANCHISE FEE: *$18,900 if financed; $15,120 for a cash transaction*
TOTAL INITIAL INVESTMENT: *$20,000 to $30,000*
ROYALTY: *7 percent of gross monthly sales*
ADVERTISING: *3 percent of gross monthly sales*
ADDRESS: *1855 W. Kattella Avenue, Suite 330, Orange, CA 92667*
TELEPHONE: *1-800-426-2270 or 1-714-744-8360*
CONTACT PERSON: *Franchise Sales*
INDUSTRY OVERVIEW
- *Home inspection is a growing industry.*
- *As more and more states require full seller disclosure for properties, more companies will pop up trying to capture the home-inspection market.*

BENEFIT OF THIS COMPANY
- *AmeriSpec is a well-established company that tries to accommodate franchisees' needs. This is illustrated in their willingness to finance new franchisees and their underlying support network.*

COMPANY HISTORY
- **IN BUSINESS SINCE:** *1987*

● **FRANCHISING SINCE:** *1988*
● **NUMBER OF FRANCHISE UNITS:** *94*

Another company protecting the idea that the home is a person's most important investment is AmeriSpec, Inc. The Orange, California–based company includes ninety-four franchises throughout the United States, and it is the West Coast pioneer in the world of home inspections.

AmeriSpec franchisees perform a two-hour physical review of all types of residences, and then inform buyers and sellers of any danger signs which exist in the heating, plumbing, and electrical systems. AmeriSpec, like its competitors, will perform special environmental tests at a customer's request. The inspection costs approximately $200 to $300, which seems to be the industry norm.

AmeriSpec began franchising only three years ago, but it has expanded rapidly. The company, which now grosses $5.2 million, projects that 350 franchises will exist by 1995.

Headquartered in California, a state which legally requires full seller disclosure, AmeriSpec has taken advantage of the attention paid to the idea of home inspections. The company markets the service to real estate agents, banks, attorneys, and insurance companies through direct sales, telemarketing, and seminars.

A $20,000 to $30,000 total initial investment provides franchisees with an exclusive territory for a ten-year period as well as an abundance of promotional and educational material for customers. AmeriSpec finances 50 percent of the franchise fee for a period of two years, but it rewards franchisees who pay in cash with a 20 percent discount. The company also charges a royalty fee of 7 percent and an advertising fee of 3 percent. The company also urges potential franchisees to have at least three to four months' personal and living expenses in reserve as a cushion while building a market.

AmeriSpec claims to look for the non-technical entrepreneur and tries to recruit managerial or marketing executives. The success of the business depends on the professional image it projects to home buyers, realtors, and banks. Even with its national advertising campaign, the company reinforces the idea that local business is the backbone of a franchisee's survival.

No special equipment or inventory is required for the initial operation of the franchise, and more than 90 percent of new franchisees initially run their inspection business from home. The majority of franchisees are husband-and-wife teams, but most franchises eventually employ two or three people. AmeriSpec asks franchisees to view the home-office set-up as a temporary situation, and encourages them to lease commercial office space as the business expands.

The company provides a two-week training period for all franchisees where technical, sales, and management skills are taught with emphasis on professionalism and credibility.

FORECAST AND ANALYSIS

Home inspections will be a hot commodity in the 1990s. AmeriSpec provides a valuable service at a reasonable price, and it is accepted by realtors, consumers, and builders.

62. BUILDING INSPECTOR OF AMERICA, INC.

■————————————————————————————————————■

FRANCHISE FEE: *$15,000*
TOTAL INITIAL INVESTMENT: *$20,000 to $30,000*
ROYALTY FEE: *6 percent of gross monthly sales*
ADVERTISING FEE: *3 percent of gross monthly sales*
ADDRESS: *684 Main Street, Wakefield, MA 01880*
TELEPHONE: *1-800-321-4677 or 1-617-246-4215*
CONTACT PERSON: *Larry Finklestone*
INDUSTRY OVERVIEW
- *The new focus on home inspections can make the industry boom. Even in slow months, real estate sells and buyers want assurance that their house is in good shape.*
- *Many competitors are popping up. The increase in competition in an area can decrease profitability to a significant degree.*

BENEFIT OF THIS COMPANY
- *Building Inspector of America is a well-established company that knows how to market itself. The franchisor provides strong support for its franchisees.*

COMPANY HISTORY
- **IN BUSINESS SINCE:** *1976*

● **FRANCHISING SINCE:** *1985*
● **NUMBER OF FRANCHISE UNITS:** *74*

"Caveat Emptor—Buyer Beware." Words that have sparked fear in most home buyers since real estate became a marketable commodity. Building Inspector of America, Inc., is dedicated to educating home buyers to the existing or potential problems of a property before they settle on their dream house.

A two-hour visual inspection provides home buyers, sellers, and real estate agents with a concrete and objective evaluation of the condition of a property. Franchisees charge between $200 and $300 for the inspection, which focuses on a house's electrical, plumbing, and heating systems. Franchisees also evaluate the overall structural condition of the house for leaks, roof defects, and pest infestation. Building Inspector franchisees will perform special services such as water and radon testing at a customer's request.

Franchisees market their inspection services through real estate companies, banks, and attorney offices. The aggressive marketing tactics have awarded Building Inspector national recognition, and the company, which includes seventy-four franchises, grossed more than $3 million in 1991.

An initial $15,000 fee purchases the rights to an exclusive territory with a minimum of 250,000 homes for ten years. Franchisees will need an additional $5,000 to $10,000 to cover the purchase or lease of a pick-up truck plus carpenter tools needed to perform the inspections. Building Inspector provides as part of the franchise package all promotional material and stationery, plus price sheets and forms for 150 inspections. The company also charges franchisees a 6 percent royalty fee and a 3 percent advertising fee.

A Building Inspector franchise requires no inventory or special equipment, and franchisees complete all sales calls and inspections at the customer's location. More than 90 percent of franchisees do not lease professional office space and run the business from home.

The franchise may seem technical in nature, but Building Inspector of America claims that the inspection procedures can be easily learned. Initially, most franchisees conduct the inspections themselves, but many adopt a managerial role as their business develops.

Building Inspector emphasizes this to potential franchisees and attempts to attract business-oriented individuals with sales and management backgrounds.

Franchisees must be willing to knock on doors to make the service known. Many sponsor telemarketing and direct mail campaigns as well.

Building Inspector of America conducts a two-week training course which concentrates on the marketing end of the business as well as technical aspects. Franchisees learn to conduct sales presentations, and they also participate in actual home inspections. The company maintains an on-call field support system. It uses videos, slide presentations, and operating manuals to assist franchisees in the successful running of their territories. Building Inspector has also gained attention for the free manual it distributes to consumers explaining home inspections and what they should accomplish.

FORECAST AND ANALYSIS

There is now a great deal of national attention on home inspections. The National Association of Realtors is pushing for legislation which would demand full seller disclosure on property sales. California and Maine already have laws on the books which require full disclosure and Texas requires home inspections before the transfer of properties. Last year alone, more than 3.5 million houses were sold and 15 to 20 million houses were listed.

A franchisee must be a capable marketer. Presentations, cold calls, and follow-up are all part of the business.

63. EVER-DRY WATERPROOFING

■───■

FRANCHISE FEE: *$40,000*
TOTAL INITIAL INVESTMENT: *$110,000*
FINANCING AVAILABLE: *Yes*
ROYALTY FEE: *6 percent*
ADVERTISING FEE: *1 percent*
ADDRESS: *365 E. Highland Road, Macedonia, OH 44056*
TELEPHONE: *1-800-365-7295 or 1-800-775-3837 or 1-216-467-1055*
CONTACT PERSON: *Jack M. Jones*

INDUSTRY OVERVIEW
- *Water damage is a potential problem in both new and old homes. Eliminating the risk of water damage adds value to houses.*
- *There are several large waterproofing companies in business. All have their own high-tech procedures. Aggressive marketing is a must for anyone who wants to enter the field.*

BENEFIT OF THIS COMPANY
- *Ever-Dry spent time building its business and perfecting its waterproofing techniques. Franchising was a result of the company's popularity and reputation.*

COMPANY HISTORY
- **IN BUSINESS SINCE:** *1977*
- **FRANCHISING SINCE:** *1984*
- **NUMBER OF FRANCHISE UNITS:** *18*

The greatest hedge a homeowner has against expensive water damage is preventive maintenance. Each year, more homeowners realize this fact and invest in the Ever-Dry Waterproofing system. Based in Macedonia, Ohio, Ever-Dry uses its patented multistep waterproofing technique to effectively channel water that can seep into a building's basements and foundations. The company promotes its system internationally through eighteen franchises and three company outlets that gross more than $11 million annually.

For an Ever-Dry franchisee, a $40,000 franchise fee guarantees an exclusive county territory. Franchisees are responsible for local advertising and promotion of their services as well as the actual completion of the Ever-Dry waterproofing system. Franchisees need an additional $70,000 for the purchase of specialized equipment and inventory needed to conduct their businesses properly. Ever-Dry does not require its franchisees to rent commercial space initially. Most operate their franchises from home during their first year of operation and then relocate to commercial space.

Franchisees attend a six-week training session at the Macedonia headquarters, and then undergo an additional four weeks of personalized, on-site training which includes technical as well as marketing and management instruction. Ongoing, on-site support is also available with field consultations and monthly seminars designed to update franchisees on any marketing or technical advancements.

For entrepreneurs who want to remain in a home-based situation, an Ever-Dry franchise is probably not appropriate. Most franchisees outgrow their home offices within the first year of operation.

FORECAST AND ANALYSIS

If you are interested in a business that is likely to grow large enough to require commercial office space, Ever- Dry deserves your consideration. The strong support from the franchisor makes this franchise an option for franchisees who like to work with their hands and manage crews of workers.

64. B-DRY SYSTEM, INC.

FRANCHISE FEE: *$15,000 to $60,000 depending on territory*
TOTAL INITIAL INVESTMENT: *$44,000 to $94,000*
ROYALTY FEE: *6 percent*
ADVERTISING FEE: *None*
ADDRESS: *1341 Copley Road, Akron, OH 44320*
TELEPHONE: *1-800-321-0985 or 1-216-867-2576*
CONTACT PERSON: *Joseph Garfunkel*

INDUSTRY OVERVIEW

- *There are many homes in need of waterproofing services. Builders have a tendency to build in low-lying areas that are very conducive to flooding. The industry can be successfully marketed to consumer and insurance companies as well.*
- *Competition is out there. Extensive marketing programs are needed to keep a company on top.*

BENEFIT OF THIS COMPANY

- *B-Dry has been in existence for more than thirty years. The company takes pride in its ability to develop new products and services to customers. This drive toward excellence makes it a leader in the ever-increasing competitive market.*

COMPANY HISTORY

- **IN BUSINESS SINCE:** *1958*
- **FRANCHISING SINCE:** *1978*
- **NUMBER OF FRANCHISE UNITS:** *73*

April showers may bring May flowers but they also bring wet basements. If you live in a house that experiences water seepage problems every time it rains, you know this is not a minor inconvenience. Along with the hassle of mopping up wet floors, there is the fear that the excess water is damaging the house. B-Dry Thermo-Flo Drain System eliminates that fear with its waterproofing system that prevents basement leakage caused by either a high water table or the infiltration of ground water.

Founded in 1958 by Joseph Bevilacqua, Jr., B-Dry Systems has a long history as a pioneer in the waterproofing industry. Today, with seventy-three franchises throughout the United States and Canada and networkwide revenues totaling $23 million, it is recognized as one of the leading firms in the waterproofing industry.

B-Dry requires some large equipment, such as a dump truck, drills, and hydraulic jack hammers, but it is still considered a home-based franchise operation. The business generates no walk-in traffic and all sales calls are performed at the customer's home. Eventually, as the business grows, many franchisees do opt to move from their homes into commercial offices.

Franchisees pay between $15,000 and $60,000 for an exclusive territory based on county populations. An additional $35,000 is needed for the purchase or lease of equipment, inventory, and marketing materials. A franchisee needs only $50,000 to begin operation since financing is available through the home office.

The company provides a technical service, but B-Dry does not require franchisees to have experience in waterproofing or construction. The company offers a two-week training course at its home office in Akron, Ohio. Franchisees are taught how to install the Thermo-Flo drain system in homes and how to market their product successfully. The company also participates in on-site training for all franchisees and retains an in-field support staff to address concerns and problems.

FORECAST AND ANALYSIS

This company offers a needed service across the country. Both old and new housing developments display water seepage problems. The B-Dry name is known nationally, giving it a competitive edge over other smaller companies.

65. AMERICAN LEAK DETECTION

■━━━■

FRANCHISE FEE: *$20,000*
TOTAL INITIAL INVESTMENT: *$40,000 to $60,000*
ROYALTY FEE: *8 to 10 percent*
FINANCING AVAILABLE: *Yes*
ADVERTISING FEE: *None*
ADDRESS: *P.O. Box 1701, 1750 E. Arenas Road, #7, Palm Springs, CA 92263*
TELEPHONE: *1-800-755-6697 or 1-619-320-9991*
CONTACT PERSON: *Richard B. Rennick*
INDUSTRY OVERVIEW

- *Plumbers, carpenters, utility companies, and contractors may all dabble in this service. Each has its own method.*
- *Since leaks are an ever-present concern, demand is not likely to wane.*

BENEFITS OF THIS COMPANY

- *Due to the widespread appeal of its innovative, no-damage method of leak detection, this well-established company is expanding rapidly.*

COMPANY HISTORY

- **IN BUSINESS SINCE:** *1975*
- **FRANCHISING SINCE:** *1985*
- **NUMBER OF FRANCHISE UNITS:** *125*

■━━━■

A gas or water leak can be as elusive as the proverbial needle in the haystack. American Leak Detection, a Palm Springs, California–based franchise chain, uses state-of-the-art technology to isolate and repair water, gas, and sewer leaks in homes, commercial buildings, spas, swimming pools, and fountains.

Started more than twenty years ago, American Leak now includes 125 franchises throughout the United States and networkwide revenues in excess of $8.3 million. American Leak estimates that 200 franchises will be in operation by 1995.

The company's growth can be attributed to its unique method, which involves no demolition of walls and floors to find leaks. American Leak franchisees use electronic detection equipment to pinpoint leaks. The device allows franchisees to find leaks without tearing up concrete and punching through walls.

An initial investment of $20,000 secures an exclusive territory for ten years. American Leak estimates that equipment and inventory will cost franchisees an additional $20,000. The company provides some financing to qualified candidates. More than 90 percent of franchisees elect to establish home-based offices.

American Leak conducts a six-week training course which teaches leak detection, repair techniques, marketing, management, and public relations. Field representatives are available for on-site assistance after the initial training period, and an annual convention provides further education and information for all franchisees.

FORECAST AND ANALYSIS

American Leak is experiencing a major burst of growth as a result of its commitment to quality and customer service. Additionally, the company's cost-effective methods give it an edge over costlier competitors.

66. MR. ROOTER

FRANCHISE FEE: *$125 per 1,000 households with a $12,500 minimum*
TOTAL INITIAL INVESTMENT: *$24,000*
FINANCING AVAILABLE: *Yes*
ROYALTY FEE: *6 percent*
ADVERTISING FEE: *2 percent*
ADDRESS: *P.O. Box 1309, Waco, TX 76703*
TELEPHONE: *1-800-950-8003 or 1-817-755-0055*
CONTACT PERSON: *Robert Tunmire*

INDUSTRY OVERVIEW

- *Plumbing services will always be in demand. Smaller repairs, such as clogged drains and pipe cleaning (the bread and butter of a Mr. Rooter franchisee), are also the most common calls received by plumbers.*

BENEFITS OF THIS COMPANY

- *Mr. Rooter is the second largest franchisor in the drain-cleaning and plumbing repair industry.*
- *The company has been franchising since 1970, and it has developed a working support system for all its franchisees.*

COMPANY HISTORY
- **IN BUSINESS SINCE:** *1968*
- **FRANCHISING SINCE:** *1972*
- **NUMBER OF FRANCHISE UNITS:** *90*

Drain cleaning is nothing new to franchising. Roto-Rooter started in the 1940s and grew quickly by selling franchise opportunities to returning World War II GIs. Mr. Rooter was founded in 1968 and now supports more than ninety franchises throughout the United States and bills itself as the second largest plumbing franchise, behind the venerable Roto-Rooter. Mr. Rooter projects having 300 franchise units by 1995.

Mr. Rooter franchisees offer a range of drain, sewer, and pipe-cleaning services. Franchisees perform most of the work themselves and should have some plumbing or mechanical experience.

Franchisees invest about $24,000 to open and outfit their businesses. The figure includes a $12,500 franchise fee to acquire the rights to an exclusive territory with a minimum of 100,000 people and the right to use the Mr. Rooter name for ten years. At the franchisor's discretion, Mr. Rooter offers financing for up to one-half of the initial fee to qualified franchisees.

For their investment, franchisees get all plumbing equipment, a computerized business system, printed stationery, promotional materials, plus stripes and decals for their van.

Mr. Rooter also charges a 6 percent weekly royalty from all franchisees and a 2 percent advertising fee.

Franchisees are encouraged to work from home, but as volume increases they might want to find commercial space.

As part of their contract, franchisees are required to attend one week of training at headquarters. The company conducts annual visits to each franchisee and offers additional training courses to franchisees.

FORECAST AND ANALYSIS

Mr. Rooter has a catchy, well-recognized name which promotes consumer loyalty. The company provides ample support for all franchisees, which has been a key ingredient in its success. There's no "cure" for the occasional clogged drain or plumbing mishap. For this reason, Mr. Rooter's services will be in demand for years to come. Mr. Rooter is part of the Dwyer Group, a franchise conglomerate based in Waco, Texas.

67. DYNAMARK SECURITY CENTERS

■───■

FRANCHISE FEE: *$5,000 to $20,000*
TOTAL INITIAL INVESTMENT: *$10,000 to $30,000*
FINANCING AVAILABLE: *Yes*
ROYALTY FEE: *None (with special exceptions)*
ADVERTISING FEE: *1 percent*
ADDRESS: *P.O. Box 2068, Leitersburg Pike, Hagerstown, MD 21742-2068*
TELEPHONE: *1-800- or 1-301-797-2124*
CONTACT PERSON: *Marcus Peters*
INDUSTRY OVERVIEW
  • *Consumers are more concerned than ever with crime. Many are willing to pay for personal security.*
  • *The security industry grosses more than $10 billion annually. In this type of industry, there is room for many companies that provide quality security services.*

BENEFIT OF THIS COMPANY
  • *Dynamark has been established in the residential security industry for more than fifteen years. The company secures homeowners against burglary, fire, and other hazards.*

COMPANY HISTORY
  • **IN BUSINESS SINCE:** *1977*
  • **FRANCHISING SINCE:** *1984*
  • **NUMBER OF FRANCHISE UNITS:** *106*

■───■

The home should be a safe sanctuary for families. But in today's violent world, that's not always the case. Dynamark Security Centers restores that sanctity.

Established in 1977, Dynamark currently supports 106 franchises and projects that 350 franchisees will be operating by 1995. Dynamark works with homeowners to secure their houses against burglary, fire, and other dangers. The company's use of state-of-the-art alarms and monitoring devices have entrenched Dynamark as a leader in the $10 billion security industry.

The role of the Dynamark franchisee is initially two-fold. Franchisees sell the alarm systems to homeowners. They are then responsible for maintaining and installing the systems. Most franchisees begin operating the business from home by themselves or with one other person. Dynamark allows home-based operations initially, but as business volume grows and sales and maintenance staff increase, franchisees usually move to professional office space.

A $5,000 to $20,000 franchise fee purchases the rights to a territory based on a population ranging from 5,000 to 250,000 people. The territories are exclusive, and Dynamark encourages franchisees to expand their territory sizes as business develops. In addition to the initial fee, Dynamark estimates that franchisees will need $5,000 to $10,000 for the purchase of office equipment and promotional materials. The company will finance initial inventory for qualified franchisees.

Franchisees need no previous experience in security or law enforcement. The company works with franchisees during a one-week training course to develop and fine-tune sales and management skills. Franchisees must be able to interact comfortably with customers and instill trust and confidence.

Dynamark does not manufacture its own systems, and it offers products from many of the leading security manufacturers. In-field and on-the-job support are available for all franchisees, and telephone hotlines exist to address any immediate problems.

Dynamark offers franchisees ample post-training support with bimonthly seminars focusing on sales and technology. The company also sponsors yearly conventions, and it publishes monthly and quarterly newsletters as well.

FORECAST AND ANALYSIS

Dynamark is a thriving company. Homeowners are more concerned than ever about crime. The company's low franchise fees have also spurred growth.

But in the final analysis, sales ability is what determines success in this industry. It takes a sales professional to get homeowners to invest in a security system, when the same money could go to buying a new car or a home entertainment system. Those franchisees who can persuade and inform, and educate and motivate, typically lead the network in sales.

68. PROFUSION SYSTEMS, INC.

FRANCHISE FEE: *$20,500 minimum*
TOTAL INITIAL INVESTMENT: *$20,500*
FINANCING AVAILABLE: *Yes*
ROYALTY FEE: *6 percent*
ADVERTISING FEE: *1 percent (potential)*
ADDRESS: *2851 S. Parker Road, 6th Floor, Aurora, CO 80014*
TELEPHONE: *1-800-777-FUSE (3873)*
CONTACT PERSON: *Marketing Team*

INDUSTRY OVERVIEW

- *There's a preponderance of weekend vinyl repairmen and kits that are available for the consumer to do repairs.*
- *There's little competition for large commercial and wholesale accounts—everything from sports arenas to trucking fleets.*

BENEFITS OF THIS COMPANY

- *Profusion offers a surprisingly professional management and marketing program that has attracted a number of former white-collar executives to this seemingly blue-collar industry.*
- *The company was formed with entrepreneurial talent and motivation—forces that remain behind Profusion.*

COMPANY HISTORY

- **IN BUSINESS SINCE:** *1980*
- **FRANCHISING SINCE:** *1984*
- **NUMBER OF FRANCHISE UNITS:** *632*

Plastic abounds—it's in everything from space shuttles to Barbie dolls, but it isn't indestructible.

Profusion Systems provides a permanent solution to the breakdown of plastic at 20 percent of the replacement cost. Through a specialized process combining color computer technology and lasers to molecularly fuse plastics together, the company has risen to lead its industry and has become a $40 million company in only eleven years.

Formerly Western Vinyl Repair, Profusion spent $500,000 to upgrade its image and market position in 1988. The result? The company now holds contracts with the National Aeronautics and Space Administration (NASA), major airlines, and the U.S. Department of Defense.

Profusion currently sponsors 182 U.S. franchises, plus 450 franchises in twenty-five countries in Europe, Australia, the Middle East, and Asia.

Despite its fast growth, Profusion remains an affordable franchise. A franchise fee of $20,500 buys an exclusive territory based on a minimum population of 100,000. The investment covers most start-up expenses, including training and marketing assistance. Franchisees can choose a larger territory, which costs another $5,000 per 100,000 people. Profusion will finance up to 50 percent of the franchise fee. In addition to the initial fee, the company charges franchisees a 6 percent royalty and a 1 percent advertising fee.

The Profusion franchise system is easily learned during two weeks of training: one at the home office and one at the franchise location. The company sets up sales and accounts for franchisees before they open for business, and franchisees can see firsthand how jobs are performed locally.

Initially, franchisees are not required to lease office space, since most work is done at the customer's site. After one year of operation, Profusion encourages franchisees, who have territories of 250,000 people or more, to open retail stores and sell the vinyl repair kits and chemicals to consumers directly.

Profusion seeks franchisees with outgoing personalities and sales ability. The company emphasizes that the opportunity is a full-time commitment.

FORECAST AND ANALYSIS

Profusion was started in 1980 by Bob Gabbard, a then twenty-two-year-old college graduate, who used his 1979 Firebird for collateral on his initial small business loan. Eleven years later, the company has evolved into a full-blown manufacturer and franchise network.

Profusion doesn't rely on franchise fees to pay its expenses and stands on solid ground with realistic expansion goals. It isn't afraid to invest in itself and prides itself on the loyalty of its franchises.

23

INTERIOR DESIGN AND REDECORATING

---

69. FLOOR COVERINGS INTERNATIONAL

FRANCHISE FEE: *$10,000 for standard territory; $25,000 for executive territory*

TOTAL INITIAL INVESTMENT: *$13,500 to $29,500*

FINANCING AVAILABLE: *None*

ROYALTY FEE: *5 percent*

ADVERTISING FEE: *2 percent*

ADDRESS: *5182 Old Dixie Highway, Forest Park, GA 30050*

TELEPHONE: *1-800-955-4324 or 1-404-361-5047*

CONTACT PERSON: *Franchise Department*

INDUSTRY OVERVIEW

- *Home improvement is a top priority for every homeowner, and floor coverings, including carpet and tiles, are among the most popular form of improvement.*
- *Homeowners tend to redecorate often, and the floors are usually one of the first areas to get a different look. The room focuses on the carpeting or tile, and a new or updated look can increase the value of a house and make it more marketable.*

BENEFITS OF THIS COMPANY

- *Floor Coverings International is a totally mobile business. Customized vans carry an assortment of flooring and carpeting to the customer's doorstep, which attracts even the laziest of shoppers.*
- *The company takes the needs of the hectic consumer to heart with the shop-at-home service. This mobile franchise makes it easy for the franchisee to operate the business from home.*

COMPANY HISTORY
- **IN BUSINESS SINCE:** *1988*
- **FRANCHISING SINCE:** *1989*
- **NUMBER OF FRANCHISE UNITS:** *235*

Some of the most successful franchisors today focus on the consumer's number one need: convenience. Floor Coverings International (FCI) is no exception. It took its concept on the road, literally, in an effort to make its services convenient to homeowners.

Established in 1988, FCI's shop-at-home service appeals to today's time-strained consumer. That appeal accounts for the company's quick growth. FCI sponsors 235 franchises in forty-six states and Canada. The addition of forty-two franchises in the last quarter of 1991 alone led FCI to project that 2,000 franchises will exist by the mid-1990s.

Franchisees bring to customers' doorsteps, via a specialized van, more than 2,400 samples of carpeting, tiles, and vinyl flooring materials.

"Customers make better purchasing decisions when they are comfortable, and nowhere are they more comfortable than in their own homes," says Joseph Lunsford, FCI president.

"In their homes, customers can see firsthand what they want to do with their floors. They can actually put samples down on the floors to see what they look like. There is no better sales tool."

To help franchisees market products and services, FCI relies on a high-tech computer graphics package. Franchisees use a special camera to record the layout of a customer's house. The image is transferred to computer and displayed on a color monitor, which shows how the room would appear with various flooring and carpet options.

The franchise fees range from $10,000 to $25,000 depending on the size of the territory. The minimum territory consists of 8,000 households and the highest franchise fee covers up to 50,000 residences.

The franchise fee buys the rights to an exclusive territory for ten years, but franchisees should expect to have another $3,500 to $5,000 to cover the down payment on the "carpet van," which can be leased from either General Motors Corp. or Ford Motor Co. The only other expenses franchisees should expect are installation of a phone line and the purchase of promotional and advertising material. A $5,000 computer system may be added to the franchise package in the near future.

FCI charges a 5 percent royalty on all sales, plus a 2 percent advertising fee.

More than 95 percent of the franchisees reduce operating costs by working at home. The company encourages the practice. Few franchisees find it necessary to open a store or rent office space.

Franchisees are required to participate in a four-week training program, consisting of a one-week home study course including videotapes and manuals about the operation and marketing of the franchise. Franchisees then attend a second week of "Carpet College" at headquarters in Georgia. After initial training, franchisees are assigned a "coach" or an established franchisee who advises them on procedures and marketing strategy. FCI also holds quarterly training sessions for established franchisees at different U.S. sites. All franchisees attend two seminars each year—one held in Atlanta and the other at a different site.

The company also publishes *Wall to Wall,* a monthly newsletter and journal and other letters and memos as warranted.

FORECAST AND ANALYSIS

FCI provides franchisees with abundant support and assistance. It makes it easy for franchisees to get started and supplies them with an array of top-quality products. Although the company doesn't purchase inventory for the franchisee, it negotiates with major manufacturers to obtain the best price for its franchisees at 15 percent below "typical carpet stores."

70. DECORATING DEN

■——■

FRANCHISE FEE: *$6,900 to $15,900*
TOTAL INITIAL INVESTMENT: *$6,900 to $15,900*
FINANCING AVAILABLE: *Yes*
ROYALTY FEE: *11 percent decreasing to 7 percent as volume increases*
ADVERTISING FEE: *2 percent*

ADDRESS: *7910 Woodmont Avenue, Bethesda, MD 20814*
TELEPHONE: *1-207-783-2068*
CONTACT PERSON: *Patty Coons*
INDUSTRY OVERVIEW

- *Interior decorating is a multibillion-dollar business, with everyone from furniture stores to the neighbor next door claiming to be interior decorators.*
- *Americans typically have invested heavily in keeping their homes up-to-date and in good condition.*

BENEFITS OF THIS COMPANY

- *This is the granddaddy of mobile decorating businesses. By bringing samples to the doors of consumers, the company offers a level of convenience not often seen in the industry.*
- *Decorating Den franchisees receive four levels of training to make them experts. The company also employs a number of American Society of Interior Design–certified decorators to assist franchisees in their designing tasks.*
- *The company has had problems with franchisee turnover in the past. It claims to have solved the problem through tighter screening of potential franchisees and better support of operating franchisees.*

COMPANY HISTORY

- **IN BUSINESS SINCE:** *1970*
- **FRANCHISING SINCE:** *1984*
- **NUMBER OF FRANCHISE UNITS:** *1,150*

When Decorating Den introduced its mobile interior decorating concept in 1970, the company was credited with redefining an industry.

The story didn't end happily there. After experiencing tremendous growth in the 1970s and early 1980s, the company fell into trouble by growing too fast and alienating franchisees, many of whom never achieved their potential.

Things changed when Jim Bugg bought the company in 1984 and revamped its training and support systems. Today, Decorating Den is the undisputed champion of the mobile interior decorating industry. The company supports more than 1,150 franchisees (most of them women) throughout the world and recorded gross networkwide sales of $60 million.

Franchisees serve as consultants and confidants to consumers anxious to redecorate their homes and/or offices. Franchisees provide any number of services, from "specing" furniture, wallpaper, and painting requirements to acquiring and selling accessories.

Many franchisees are attracted by the affordable initial investment. Franchisees pay between $6,900 and $15,900 for a ten-year, exclusive territory, depending on the size of the territory. The fee covers all inventory, sample books, and the lease of the customized Decorating Den van.

Some franchisees begin as associate franchisees, meaning that another larger franchise operates in the area. Larger franchisees train and support smaller franchisees and get a 4 percent commission from the smaller franchisee's revenue.

There are no working capital requirements. However, the company recommends that franchisees examine their personal lifestyles and have enough money to carry them through the six-month start-up period.

Franchisees also pay an ongoing royalty of 11 percent, which gradually decreases to 7 percent as volume grows. Since the decorating van goes to customers' homes, franchisees aren't required to establish professional offices, and just about every Decorating Den franchisee operates from home.

The company requires franchisees to complete a four-level training curriculum. Initial training begins with a one-week home study course, which introduces franchisees to interior design. A mandatory three- to four-day training course at headquarters follows and must be completed before franchisees open for business.

Franchisees reinforce their decorating expertise through training courses conducted at headquarters several times a year. When franchisees reach level four of training, they're considered design specialists and receive advanced training in Europe and other cultural centers throughout the world at the expense of the Decorating Den organization.

Franchisees need not have decorating experience, but most possess an artistic or creative flair. Franchisees are predominantly women who are re-entering the workforce and need flexible schedules to raise families.

Decorating Den publishes newsletters as a means of passing information to its franchisees. The home office also employs a staff of certified interior designers who provide telephone support to franchise owners.

FORECAST AND ANALYSIS

Decorating Den's rediscovered commitment to training and support has made it easier for franchisees to build long-term, viable businesses. Women make the best franchisees because consumers feel more comfortable taking interior design advice from women.

The company's reported networkwide income of $60 million seems low, considering there are 1,150 franchisees worldwide. At this rate, the average franchise owner grosses less than $53,000 a year. After expenses, that doesn't leave much room for profit.

71. BLINDS ON WHEELS

■───■

FRANCHISE FEE: *$10,000*

TOTAL INITIAL INVESTMENT: *$17,000*

FINANCING AVAILABLE: *None*

ROYALTY FEE: *5 percent of gross sales*

ADVERTISING FEE: *None*

ADDRESS: *4012 Zahm Road, Belding, MI 48809*

TELEPHONE: *1-616-897-0200*

CONTACT PERSON: *Lon and Terri Ferguson*

INDUSTRY OVERVIEW

- *There are not many mobile window decorating services throughout the United States. Department stores have shop-at-home decorator services, but they do not specialize in window treatments and they have a reputation for being costly.*
- *Convenience is the key to this company. Consumers will spend money on durable, decorator window treatments if they are within easy reach.*

BENEFIT OF THIS COMPANY

- *Blinds on Wheels appeals to the busy consumer with its shop-at-home service. Overhead costs are minimal and franchisees maintain a high profit margin on each sale.*

COMPANY HISTORY

- **IN BUSINESS SINCE:** *1988*
- **FRANCHISING SINCE:** *1990*
- **NUMBER OF FRANCHISE UNITS:** *6*

■───■

In today's competitive market, convenience is often the cornerstone to success. Blinds on Wheels of Belding, Michigan, capitalized on the consumer's need for convenience and built a mobile, window-treatment franchise company around it. Established in 1988, Blinds on Wheels supports six franchisees throughout the United States. The company expects the shop-at-home service to attract consumer attention and estimates that fifty franchises will exist by 1995.

Franchisees use a specialized mini-van to bring to customers in their homes an assortment of designer window treatments including shades, blinds, and draperies. Customers order their merchandise from the franchisee, who delivers and installs the window treatments free of charge.

A Blinds on Wheels franchise is a one- or two-person operation. Franchisees market their service through direct mail and telemarketing campaigns and they install the window treatments as well. The van carries all material for the sale and installation of the window treatments, so the Blinds on Wheels office is literally the local road. No additional professional office space is needed and all franchisees run the base of their operations from home.

An initial investment of $10,000 purchases the rights to an exclusive territory based on population for ten years. The company estimates that a franchisee should expect to invest an additional $7,000 for the lease or purchase of a van, business supplies, and promotional materials. Blinds on Wheels also charges franchisees an ongoing 5 percent royalty fee.

All franchisees attend six to ten days of training at the company's headquarters in Michigan. During this period, franchisees learn sales and marketing strategies, as well as the procedures for the installation of window treatments. Blinds on Wheels also teaches franchisees how to purchase their merchandise from the various vendors and manufacturers. Company representatives work closely with each franchisee for six to eight weeks following the initial training class, and in-field assistance and daily phone contact is available to all franchisees.

FORECAST AND ANALYSIS:

Consumers today do not want to waste time shopping. They want services quickly, and they want them at their fingertips. Blinds on Wheels addresses both these needs, and the company has the potential to attract both residential and commercial customers.

72. MR. MINIBLIND

FRANCHISE FEE: *$28,000*
TOTAL INITIAL INVESTMENT: *Less than $40,000*
FINANCING AVAILABLE: *No*
ROYALTY FEE: *5 percent*
ADVERTISING FEE: *5 percent*
ADDRESS: *20341 Irvine Avenue, Suite 1, Santa Ana, CA 92707*
TELEPHONE: *1-800-877-7712 or 1-714-979-9221*
CONTACT PERSON: *Mark Huckins or Christina Huckins*
INDUSTRY OVERVIEW
- *Home shopping is increasingly popular as today's families find less time to fight department-store lines.*
- *Customers are fascinated by the lure of a mobile decorating service—especially when it provides a variety of quality products.*

BENEFIT OF THIS COMPANY
- *Mr. Miniblind was a pioneer in the mobile decorating industry and is well known among consumers. The company is dedicated to offering its franchisees ample support.*

COMPANY HISTORY
- **IN BUSINESS SINCE:** *1986*
- **FRANCHISING SINCE:** *1988*
- **NUMBER OF FRANCHISE UNITS:** *113*

Shop-at-home services provide consumers convenience. Mr. Miniblind of Irvine, California, demonstrates this point with its mobile window coverings concept. Established in 1986, Mr. Miniblind brings directly to the customer's home a broad array of micro blinds, wood blinds, vertical blinds, pleated shades, and shutters. Customers place their special orders, and Mr. Miniblind franchisees return and install the window coverings. Installation is free.

The company, which includes ninety-five franchises and master franchises throughout the world, reached $20 million in networkwide revenues in 1990.

For an initial fee of $28,000, Mr. Miniblind franchisees purchase the rights to an exclusive territory for five years. Franchisees incur other expenses such as van lease and lettering, as well as the purchase of office supplies and insurance.

Mr. Miniblind suggests that franchisees keep in reserve an additional $3,000 to $5,000 to cover these costs. The company also charges a 5 percent royalty fee and a 5 percent advertising fee. Mr. Miniblind encourages franchisees to operate their businesses from home. All sales calls are conducted in the customer's home, and all samples are stored in the van.

"We give consumers convenience—that is what is needed today," explains Mark Huckins, founder of Mr. Miniblind. "Convenience is also important to our franchisees. With Mr. Miniblind, they can make as many sales appointments as they want, and they can develop at their own pace."

Most Mr. Miniblind franchisees sell and install the products themselves. They market their shop-at-home service through direct mail and telemarketing campaigns. Mr. Miniblind also participates in national advertising programs.

Mr. Miniblind offers master franchisees to individuals who want to manage large territories and other franchisees. Investment cost for a master franchise depends on the size and location of the territory.

The company trains all franchisees in the brand-name products they sell. Franchisees also learn marketing and management strategies and procedures. The home office offers ongoing support and franchisees have at their disposal a full-service research and development department, and a wide array of promotional and management programs.

FORECAST AND ANALYSIS

In its thirteen-year history, Mr. Miniblind has become an internationally recognized corporation. The mobile store concept impresses consumers and provides them with attentive and personal service.

24

LANDSCAPING
AND GARDENING

---

73. FOLIAGE DESIGN SYSTEMS

FRANCHISE FEE: *$16,000 to $40,000 depending on size of territory*
TOTAL INITIAL INVESTMENT: *$30,000 to $50,000*
FINANCING AVAILABLE: *None*
ROYALTY FEE: *4 percent*
ADVERTISING FEE: *None*
ADDRESS: *1553 S.E. Fort King Avenue, Ocala, FL 32671*
TELEPHONE: *1-800-933-8751 or 1-904-732-8212*
CONTACT PERSON: *John S. Hagood*
INDUSTRY OVERVIEW

- *More businesses and shopping centers are returning to "real" plants in their interior design. Government and environmental studies prove that real greenery, which produces oxygen, can have a positive affect on employees and customers.*
- *It's more economical for businesses and shopping centers to hire plant rental, maintenance, and supply companies than to handle the task themselves.*
- *The interior plant design and maintenance industry now grosses more than $750 million per year. Exotic plants are becoming more popular, and along with that goes the demand for quality care.*

BENEFITS OF THIS COMPANY

- *Foliage Design Systems has been in existence for twenty years. The company sold one franchise, then watched its progress for one year. It evaluated its performance and corrected managerial and marketing mistakes before it offered a second franchise a year later.*

- *The company is located in Florida, which is the plant capital of the world. Most trees and exotic plants displayed in shopping centers are grown in the state. Foliage Design has established a network of plant vendors to distribute the highest-quality plant products to franchisees. Foliage Design also owns a subsidiary plant-supply company, which offers franchisees an assortment of ancillary products at lower cost.*

COMPANY HISTORY

- **IN BUSINESS SINCE:** *1972*
- **FRANCHISING SINCE:** *1980*
- **NUMBER OF FRANCHISE UNITS:** *44*

Exotic plants and flowers have become focal points in many shopping centers throughout the world. These tropical beauties may look as if they just magically sprouted; in truth, companies like Foliage Design bring this touch of the outdoors to the inside world.

Established in 1971, Foliage Design assumes the responsibility for plant life in commercial locations. Franchisees lease, sell, and maintain live and silk plants for malls, office buildings, restaurants, and other public places. The tasks include designing the interior "plantscapes" as well as feeding, watering, and transplanting foliage on a regular basis.

The company began as an interior landscaping service serving only central Florida. Less than ten years later it blossomed into the nation's first interior landscape franchisor, which now includes forty-four international franchise outlets and networkwide revenue in excess of $13 million.

"My father's hobby was plants. He loved them, and I would go with him to shows and nurseries," explains FDS founder John S. Hagood. "We worked on the concept for years before we set it in motion, and the franchise system seemed the most logical way to expand our service."

For the franchisee who can appreciate the beauty of interior plant design, FDS offers a unique business opportunity. An initial franchise fee of $16,000 to $40,000 buys the rights to an exclusive territory, which is individually negotiated between the franchisee and the company. FDS doesn't finance any part of the investment as yet, and the company estimates that each franchisee will need $30,000 to $50,000 to get the business started effectively.

The additional funds cover the cost of equipment, such as the lease or purchase of a van, a water machine, uniforms, and a computer.

Franchisees may also have to lease some mini-storage or warehouse space, especially if they elect to start their Foliage Design as a home-based operation. FDS doesn't discourage this practice, but cautions that more than 50 percent of franchisees eventually move to commercial or office space as their volume grows.

Along with the initial expense, franchisees also pay an ongoing 4 percent royalty to cover promotion and product development and research.

All franchisees complete a two- to three-week training course at headquarters. Franchisees learn plant identification and care, plus foliage design for interior spaces. The training also concentrates on marketing and management techniques to help franchisees promote their businesses and handle employee and client concerns as well.

FDS maintains a full staff of plant technicians and designers as well as horticultural specialists who confer or assist franchisees whenever needed. The company provides franchise support through a three-day annual convention as well as regional meetings. FDS also publishes a monthly newsletter for franchisees, which contains tips, leads, and general management information.

FDS prides itself on its franchise network. The company takes part in group-buying practices with more than 100 vendors, which helps cut franchisees' supply costs. It operates its own subsidiary company to offer franchisees an array of plant auxiliary products ranging from planters to mulch. FDS also owns more than 200,000 square feet of greenhouse space, which grows an abundance of plants that are available to franchisees at their request.

Foliage Design participates in several national trade shows and exhibits, and the company maintains contact with all accounts through a client newsletter and other customer-service programs.

FORECAST AND ANALYSIS

The interior plantscape industry grosses more than $750 million per year. Government studies that emphasize the health benefits of live foliage in the workplace have helped the industry to grow.

FDS is the first franchised plant-maintenance company. It boasts environmentally safe maintenance programs for plant care. The major competition is coming from large pesticide companies that see the profit in this industry and are buying plant-care chains.

The company only offered one franchise the first year it was able to sell territories and used it as a "test" for its methods of operation. The test helped FDS work out operating kinks before undertaking a full-scale franchise initiative. Although FDS is now in sixteen states, Canada, Europe, and the Bahamas, it's still cautious on its expansion.

74. SPRING-GREEN LAWN CARE CORP.

FRANCHISE FEE: *$12,900*
TOTAL INITIAL INVESTMENT: *$26,000 to $52,000*
FINANCING AVAILABLE: *Yes*
ROYALTY FEE: *9 percent on a sliding scale decreasing to 6 percent*
ADVERTISING FEE: *2 percent*
ADDRESS: *11927 Spaulding School Drive, Plainfield, IL 60544*
TELEPHONE: *1-800-435-4051 or 1-815-436-8777*
CONTACT PERSON: *Joe Nubie*
INDUSTRY OVERVIEW

- *Lawn maintenance is a specialty business that targets consumers who take pride in the appearance of their homes and properties. People may mow their lawns, but the tasks of fertilizing, pest elimination, and weed control are best left to professionals.*
- *Lawn-care firms are actively adding high-profile environmentally correct programs to attract customers.*
- *The industry is seasonal, so business owners need to prepare for these cycles.*

BENEFIT OF THIS COMPANY

- *Spring-Green is a national company with a good reputation for franchisee support. Franchisees are encouraged to take an active role in building their community and contributing to the local quality of life. This marketing strategy helps franchisees keep the Spring-Green name alive and thriving in local markets.*

COMPANY HISTORY

- **IN BUSINESS SINCE:** *1977*
- **FRANCHISING SINCE:** *1977*
- **NUMBER OF FRANCHISE UNITS:** *120*

Professional lawn-care service is on the rise in this country in both the commercial and residential markets. Spring-Green Lawn Service has grown along with this demand. The company—which began as a small local landscaping operation—now includes more than 120 franchises and twelve company outlets throughout the United States.

A reasonable franchise fee of $12,900 buys an exclusive territory for ten years. Initially, franchisees have the option of running the lawn-care service by themselves or hiring staff. Franchisees market a variety of lawn-care services from seeding to weed and pest control. Direct mail and telemarketing are the primary strategies for promoting the business.

Spring-Green estimates that franchisees will require an additional $12,000 to $40,000, depending on the type of franchise operation, to purchase or lease equipment. The company estimates that only 250 square feet of office space is needed initially to run the business—which can be easily managed from home. Spring-Green cautions that an increase in business volume could mean more equipment and more staff, which might require larger office facilities.

Spring-Green charges franchisees an initial 9 percent royalty fee, but this decreases to 6 percent as franchisee sales volumes grow. There is also a 2 percent advertising fee.

The company requires all franchisees to complete a two-phase training course. The first part consists of a one-week at-home study course. The second phase includes another week of classroom and hands-on training in lawn maintenance as well as marketing and management practices.

Franchisees receive ongoing support from the home office. Field representatives assist in the grand opening of new Spring-Green franchises. A toll-free hotline is available to answer franchisee questions, and a series of professional development seminars and regional meetings assist franchisees in building their businesses and reputations in the community. Spring-Green also publishes newsletters for its franchisees.

FORECAST AND ANALYSIS

Lawn care is a thriving industry. Two-income families have little time to tend to their yards, but they realize that a well-maintained lawn helps retain or even increase property values. Businesses are a growing segment of Spring-Green's customer base.

75. SERVICEMASTER LAWNCARE

FRANCHISE FEE: *$17,000*

TOTAL INITIAL INVESTMENT: *$16,200 (franchise fee down payment of $8,200 plus $8,000 working capital)*

FINANCING AVAILABLE: *Yes*

ROYALTY FEE: *8 percent*

ADVERTISING FEE: *None*

ADDRESS: *855 Ridge Lake Boulevard, Memphis, TN 38120*

TELEPHONE: *1-800-228-2814 or 1-901-684-7500*

CONTACT PERSON: *Bob Morris*

INDUSTRY OVERVIEW

- *The professional lawn-care business has grown in popularity during the last decade and has become an entrenched way of life in suburban America.*
- *More and more commercial offices are located in suburban environments which need professional lawn maintenance.*
- *Large franchises may have an advantage over local landscaping companies that can offer only a limited menu of services to customers.*
- *The larger lawn-care companies will have to become more environmentally responsible in order to thrive during the next decade.*

BENEFIT OF THIS COMPANY

- *ServiceMaster built its reputation solidly over forty-four years.*

COMPANY HISTORY

- **IN BUSINESS SINCE:** *1985 with lawn care; however, ServiceMaster has been in business since 1948*
- **FRANCHISING SINCE:** *1985*
- **NUMBER OF FRANCHISE UNITS:** *175*

Looks do count, especially in the world of real estate, where an attractive, well-kept lawn enhances property values. This philosophy spawned ServiceMaster LawnCare Systems of Memphis, Tennessee—an eight-year-old company dedicated to residential and commercial lawn maintenance. ServiceMaster has planted itself firmly as a national leader in the industry with 175 franchises—a number the company plans to double by 1995.

"ServiceMaster stands for quality," says Bob Morris, president of ServiceMaster. "We have pledged this ideal to customers since 1948, and that is the reason why we are so successful."

Franchisees offer customers a variety of lawn services including an exclusive soil testing process that maps out a specialized course of treatment for each lawn. Servicemaster is the only company in the lawn-care industry that performs this testing with the help of its own laboratory facilities in Memphis.

ServiceMaster's residential and commercial services encompass more than just lawn maintenance. The corporation, which last year surpassed the $352 million revenue mark, has forty-four years of successful franchising experience behind it in all types of service industries from commercial cleaning to carpet and upholstery cleaning.

An important advantage to the lawn-care arm of the company is its ability to accommodate the home-based entrepreneur. With no walk-in traffic and all services delivered or performed at the customer's location, little space is needed to conduct everyday business. Eighty-five percent of all ServiceMaster LawnCare franchisees work from home. Some of these franchisees elect to move to outside offices as their business grows.

A $17,000 fee establishes a franchisee as a lawn-care expert in the community. ServiceMaster offers no exclusive territories. As part of the franchise agreement, ServiceMaster will finance almost half the franchise fee for qualified individuals. Franchisees should still have in reserve an additional $8,000 in working capital for promotional brochures, marketing materials, uniforms, and an approved parts and equipment package.

ServiceMaster requires franchisees to complete four to six weeks of training which begins with a one-week, home study course. After the initial week, there is an additional period of classroom study which concentrates on the technical and business aspects of the lawn-care business. Franchisees learn effective promotional and marketing techniques, plus basic skills needed to run a profitable business. ServiceMaster offers ample ongoing support for franchisees, including post-training classes in safety, the environment, personnel recruitment, cash-flow management, and sales.

FORECAST AND ANALYSIS

ServiceMaster has a proven record of success. The company has proven that dedication to customer service and franchisee support produces profits. With its forty years of experience, ServiceMaster is among the most financially stable franchise opportunities available.

25

PET- AND
HOUSESITTING

━━

76. THE HOUSESITTERS

━━

FRANCHISE FEE: *$10,000 minimum*
TOTAL INITIAL INVESTMENT: *Varies depending on size of territory*
FINANCING AVAILABLE: *Yes*
ROYALTY FEE: *8 percent*
ADVERTISING FEE: *None*
ADDRESS: *530 Queen Street E., Toronto, Ontario, Canada M5A 1V2*
TELEPHONE: *1-800-387-1337 (Canada) or 1-800-388-1814 (U.S.)*
CONTACT PERSON: *Cameron Dalsto*
INDUSTRY OVERVIEW
- *Homeowners are becoming more cautious about the care of their pets and houses when they travel. They tend to trust companies with recognizable names rather than an acquaintance or "mom-and-pop" operations.*

BENEFITS OF THIS COMPANY
- *The company has more than ten years of experience. In the four years since it began franchising, the company has grown to include eighteen franchises throughout Canada and the United States.*
- *Housesitting is a service business which requires no professional office space. All franchisees run their operation from home. An increase in business volume doesn't mandate a move to professional office space.*

COMPANY HISTORY
- **IN BUSINESS SINCE:** *1981*

● **FRANCHISING SINCE:** *1987*
● **NUMBER OF FRANCHISE UNITS:** *18*

Anyone who has returned from a vacation to find their house burglarized knows the feeling of violation and fear that goes along with the crime.

Cameron Dalsto lived those emotions when he returned from vacation in 1981 to discover that vandals had broken into his home. When he tried to find a company to watch his home the next time he traveled, he came up empty. He did what entrepreneurs do—he started a business to fill a void in the market.

Since then, the company has added services for its clients, including live-in family care, occasional baby- and elderly-sitting, residential cleaning programs, and regular dog- walking services. The expanded concept generated $1.5 million in total revenue in 1991 and has spawned an eighteen-unit franchise network.

Housesitting franchise owners manage a network of people who housesit, babysit, clean, and provide other services. Most franchisees start out providing the services themselves. As the business grows, franchisees move on to managing the business with employees performing the in-house work.

New franchisees invest $10,000 to buy a territory of 100,000 people. The costs for equipment, start-up forms, invoices, and inventory, which are included in the franchise package price, also vary depending on whether a franchisee offers all or some of The Housesitters' services.

Training includes a one- to two-week introduction course at headquarters where franchisees learn marketing and management techniques. Franchisees also receive operation manuals and a computer software package to aid in administration of the business. The software allows a franchisee's computer to act as an answering machine, voice mail service, and information source to consumers.

All franchisees, no matter what size territory purchased, operate from home. Although franchisees hire an average of ten employees, most work schedules and arrangements are completed by telephone. There is little walk-in traffic, so an outside office is unnecessary. The Housesitters encourages its franchisees to remain at home.

FORECAST AND ANALYSIS

Consumers are looking for more ways to make all aspects of their lives convenient without sacrificing safety or quality. Calling a house-sitter is an option that more Americans might consider as travel becomes more a part of everyday life.

Still, there are a lot of unanswered questions regarding the demand for this service. Who can answer those questions? Current franchisees. Before investing in this franchise, do your homework. Call franchisees to ask about their volume. Are they making money? Is there a legitimate need for the service? If the answers are "yes," Housesitters may well be an inexpensive way to own a home-based franchise.

77. PETS ARE INN

■───■

FRANCHISE FEE: *$2,100 to $8,500*
TOTAL INITIAL INVESTMENT: *$5,000 to $21,000*
FINANCING AVAILABLE: *None*
ROYALTY FEE: *4½ percent*
ADVERTISING FEE: *1 percent*
ADDRESS: *27 N. Fourth Street, Suite 500, Minneapolis, MN 55401*
TELEPHONE: *1-800-248-PETS or 1-612-339-6255*
CONTACT PERSON: *Harry Sanders-Greenberg*

INDUSTRY OVERVIEW

- *Business and pleasure travel in the United States has increased, and the vast majority of those who travel are unable to take their pets along.*
- *Many pet owners are concerned about the care an animal gets in a kennel.*
- *The U.S. service sector is booming. People are searching for ways to make their lives less hectic and more convenient.*

BENEFIT OF THIS COMPANY

- *Pets Are Inn has a ten-year track record in the pet-care industry. The company places pets in other people's homes while their owners are away.*

COMPANY HISTORY

- **IN BUSINESS SINCE:** *1982*

- **FRANCHISING SINCE:** *1986*
- **NUMBER OF FRANCHISE UNITS:** *24*

To the 98 million cat and dog owners in the United States, vacation accommodations for pets are just as important as those for people. That's why in the past ten years the pet hotel and care industry has launched a fair share of franchises.

Such companies as Pets Are Inn put the industry on the map. Started only a decade ago, Pets Are Inn places a vacationing family's pet in the home of another family instead of a traditional kennel. Using its own computer software programs, Pets Are Inn matches vacationing pets with one of the "caretaking families" in its company network. The company estimates that the number of franchises will grow from twenty-four now to more than 200 by 1995.

Pets Are Inn offers an ideal home-based franchise opportunity. There's no inventory to carry and no in-office sales calls. In fact, all franchisees operate from home. No previous pet care experience is necessary, but a love of animals is a must for anyone examining this type of venture.

The initial franchise fee ranges from $2,100 to $8,500 and buys exclusive ten-year rights for a territory with a population of 50,000 to 500,000 people. Including the franchise fee, franchisees should expect to invest $5,000 to $20,000 to cover leasing or purchasing a van or mini-van, business stationery, computer equipment, training expenses, and promotional literature.

Franchisees receive four days of training at the company's headquarters. In addition, franchisees benefit from on-the-job training at a working franchise. The company also sponsors seminars on management, marketing, and computer operation. Operations manuals and an 800-number hotline provide support for established franchisees. Pets Are Inn communicates with franchisees via a regular newsletter.

FORECAST AND ANALYSIS

Pet care is a hot issue today. Kennels are under siege as unsanitary places for family pets. And fewer and fewer pet owners want to leave their keys with neighbors or in-home pet-sitting services. Even though Pets Are Inn overcomes some concerns associated with boarding pets, potential franchisees have to wonder whether the demand for pet-sitting services will stay strong in the face of more pressing family expenses.

78. HOMEWATCH

FRANCHISE FEE: *$19,500*

TOTAL INITIAL INVESTMENT: *$30,000*

FINANCING AVAILABLE: *No*

ROYALTY FEE: *6 percent*

ADVERTISING FEE: *1 percent*

ADDRESS: *2865 S. Colorado Boulevard, Denver, CO 80222*

TELEPHONE: *1-800-777-9770*

CONTACT PERSON: *Paul A. Sauer*

INDUSTRY OVERVIEW

- *There's increased interest from consumers in home protection and in-home services, such as baby- and pet-sitting. Consumers are willing to pay more for services that come directly to the home and free the busy schedules of two-career families.*

BENEFIT OF THIS COMPANY

- *Homewatch has been in business for almost twenty years, entering the market early, surviving and prospering through the years. Franchising began after more than twelve years of success as a company-owned operation.*

COMPANY HISTORY

- **IN BUSINESS SINCE:** *1973*
- **FRANCHISING SINCE:** *1985*
- **NUMBER OF FRANCHISE UNITS:** *20*

Consumers no longer have the time to take on chores that were once a part of typical American home life, so they hire companies like Homewatch to do the job. Offering consumers an assortment of services, from long- and short-term baby-sitting, adult companion, and pet care, Homewatch provides a menu of in-home services designed to accommodate the busy lifestyles of consumers.

Established in 1973, Homewatch sells trust, and it sells it to affluent Americans whose personal time is crimped by career and family commitments. The company offered its first franchise in 1985 and has grown from a one-man operation in 1973 to more than twenty franchise outlets across the United States. Homewatch sees growth continuing as more consumers discover its services. The company expects to include more than 300 franchises in the United States and Canada by 1995.

New franchisees perform most Homewatch services themselves, regardless of whether it's dog-sitting or taking in the mail and newspapers for vacationing homeowners. As the company grows, the Homewatch franchisee takes on a more managerial role and concentrates on orchestrating schedules and contracting for services.

Franchisees pay an initial fee of $19,500, entitling them, for ten years, to an exclusive territory determined by population. Homewatch recommends that franchisees keep in reserve another $10,000 for working capital and living expenses. The additional funds also pay for standard office equipment most franchisees need. Since Homewatch sells personal service, franchisees need little in the way of inventory or office space. With this in mind, most franchisees elect to run the business from home.

Homewatch franchisees attend a five-day training course focusing on marketing and personnel management. After the initial training period, franchisees can use an 800 line to contact the home office. The company also publishes a monthly newsletter for franchisees and conducts a yearly convention. A franchise consultant is available on an as-needed basis.

FORECAST AND ANALYSIS

Homewatch tested the waters for twelve years before offering a franchise. It took its time to overcome weaknesses and develop effective programs for franchisees. More franchises are popping up to offer similar services. Homewatch has the benefit of experience and stands committed to its franchisees.

79. PET NANNY

■──■

FRANCHISE FEE: *$7,100*
TOTAL INITIAL INVESTMENT: *$8,400–$11,400*

FINANCING AVAILABLE: *Yes*
ROYALTY FEE: *5 percent of weekly gross sales or $25 minimum*
ADVERTISING FEE: *2 percent per week but applicable only by regional vote*
ADDRESS: *1000 Long Boulevard, Suite 9, Lansing, MI 48911*
TELEPHONE: *1-517-694-4400*
CONTACT PERSON: *Rebecca Brevitz*
INDUSTRY OVERVIEW

- *The danger of infection to animals is diminished when pets are not forced to stay in kennels.*
- *Many copy-cat companies are cropping up in the market. The market may not absorb all the different services.*

BENEFITS OF THIS COMPANY:

- *Pet Nanny cares for pets in their homes. A Pet Nanny franchisee doubles as a guardian for the house when owners are away.*
- *This is one of the more established pet-sitting services, and many of the copy-cat companies have modeled themselves after Pet Nanny.*

COMPANY HISTORY

- **IN BUSINESS SINCE:** *1983*
- **FRANCHISING SINCE:** *1985*
- **NUMBER OF FRANCHISE UNITS:** *16*

For pet owners, vacations used to mean anxiety. Pet Nanny has eliminated the tension with a unique pet-sitting service that eliminates the need for kennels. For an average fee of $16 per hour, Pet Nanny franchisees not only visit a customer's home to feed and walk a pet, but they exercise, play with, and cuddle the pet as well. Pet Nanny sitters also take in mail and water plants for vacationing clients.

Pet Nanny is the most recognized name in the pet-sitting industry, and the company now includes sixteen franchises throughout the United States. The company estimates that more than forty franchises will exist throughout the United States and Canada within the next three years.

Part of the reason for the optimistic outlook is the company's comprehensive training program for Pet Nanny franchisees. All franchisees are bonded, trained, and insured, and they are taught the latest techniques in animal care including the administering of medications and injections.

Franchisees pay an initial franchise fee of $7,100 which purchases a five-year contract with an exclusive territory. The company estimates that franchisees will need an additional $2,000 for a general liability insurance policy, $1,000 for marketing and advertising material, and $1,200 for equipment and supplies. Since all sitting is done at the customer's home, franchisees do not need to lease professional office space. Company founder Rebecca A. Brevitz encourages home-based operation because it adds the personal touch for clients and franchisees alike. Initially, franchisees do the "sitting" themselves, but most develop into managers that hire others to take on that task.

Pet Nanny conducts a four-day training class for all franchisees which includes sessions with the company's veterinarian and an animal behaviorist. The home office provides continued in-field support for its franchisees and helps extensively with a new location's grand opening. The franchisor will also co-op booths at local dog, cat, and business shows during the initial year of operation.

FORECAST AND ANALYSIS

This is a reasonably priced franchise that fills a need in today's world of frequent traveling. The service eliminates boarding traumas for animals and protects them from the various infections and viruses contracted from kennels.

80. PET TENDERS

FRANCHISE FEE: *$9,500*
TOTAL INITIAL INVESTMENT: *$18,500*
FINANCING AVAILABLE: *Limited financing to qualified applicants*
ROYALTY FEE: *5 percent*
ADVERTISING FEE: *2 percent*
ADDRESS: *P.O. Box 23622, San Diego, CA 92193*
TELEPHONE: *1-619-283-3033*
CONTACT PERSON: *Cheryl Dagostaro*
INDUSTRY OVERVIEW

- *Pet Tenders and similar companies provide safe and healthy alternatives to traditional kennels.*
- *The industry is still in its infancy and many consumers don't know it exists.*

BENEFITS OF THIS COMPANY

- *Pet Tenders has a solid nine-year operating history even though it doesn't have a long franchising record.*

- *The company is an industry pioneer and therefore knows the ropes as well as, if not better than, competitors.*

COMPANY HISTORY
- **IN BUSINESS SINCE:** *1982*
- **FRANCHISING SINCE:** *1990*
- **NUMBER OF FRANCHISE UNITS:** *1*

Today's pet owners want more than a cage for the family pet when vacation draws near. They want a warm body to come in and care for their four-legged friends. Pet Tenders provides pet owners with on-site pet-sitting services. When a master's away, a Pet Tenders representative comes to the home and feeds, talks to, and visits the pet. Pet Tenders will also look after the house—picking up mail, watering plants, and turning off lights.

The company, which sold its first franchise in 1991, currently supports two franchises.

To become part of the Pet Tenders network, franchisees invest $9,500 in an initial franchise fee. Total investment costs can range from $11,500 to $18,500 depending on the amount of working capital, advertising and type of operation a franchisee wishes to operate. For the initial fee, a franchisee is assured of a protected Pet Tenders territory. The franchise contract runs five years and is renewable upon a franchisee's request.

Other initial costs include a 5 percent royalty and 2 percent advertising fee which is paid to the franchisor on a monthly basis. For the entrepreneur who may want to get in on the ground floor of a newly developing industry, Pet Tenders offers promise. The only experience required is a love for animals and a willingness to get on the phone and sell the service.

In order to use the Pet Tenders name, franchisees must complete the company's training course which consists of three to five days of classroom lecture, "hands-on" experience, plus instruction in telephone and sales techniques. The company hopes to conduct sales seminars more frequently in the future as its franchise network grows nationally.

FORECAST AND ANALYSIS

Pet Tenders is a new company in a relatively new industry. Animal rights are in the spotlight, and people are becoming more sensitive to their pets' needs. Kennels have also received bad press in recent years due to their unsanitary conditions and reputations as disease spreaders. The concept has promise. But investing in new franchising is always risky. Do your homework first before making a decision.

26

PHOTOGRAPHY

■━━━━━━━━━━━━━━━━━━━━━━━━━━━━━━━━■

81. THE SPORTS SECTION, INC.

■━━━━━━━━━━━━━━━━━━━━━━━━━━━━━━━━■

FRANCHISE FEE: *$14,500 to $29,500 depending on size of territory*
TOTAL INITIAL INVESTMENT: *$14,500 to $29,500*
FINANCING AVAILABLE: *Only on largest territory package*
ROYALTY FEE: *None*
ADVERTISING FEE: *None*
ADDRESS: *3120 Medlock Bridge Road, Building A, Norcross, GA 30071*
TELEPHONE: *1-800-321-9127 or 1-404-416-6604*
CONTACT PERSON: *Nancy Wood*

INDUSTRY OVERVIEW

- *The photographic industry contains many segments that don't compete against each other.*
- *Overall, the industry isn't overly competitive.*

BENEFITS OF THIS COMPANY

- *The Sports Section can be marketed to more than 300 groups ranging from children's athletic leagues to adult associations. Although sports leagues are the primary market, most franchisees go beyond this target audience to enhance their business.*
- *The Sports Section starts and remains a home-based business.*

COMPANY HISTORY

- **IN BUSINESS SINCE:** *1983*

- ● **FRANCHISING SINCE:** *1984*
- ● **NUMBER OF FRANCHISE UNITS:** *60*

Capturing the moment is what The Sports Section is all about. Established in 1983, The Sports Section takes ordinary photographs of organized athletic events and turns them into baseball cards, key chains, magazine covers, and other novelty items.

Geared initially for the children's sports market, the business also photographs non-sports groups, such as fraternities, businesses, and school groups. The company claims its franchisees now market to more than 300 types of organizations.

Franchisees serve as sales people and photographers. They divide their time between contacting and contracting with civic, sports, and social organizations and then setting up and conducting the photo shoots.

With sixty franchises throughout the United States and Canada and one in South Africa, the company is looking forward to extended international exposure and expects to have at least 400 franchises in operation by 1995.

"The franchise appeals to people who like children and don't want to wear suits and ties," says Nancy Wood, director of franchise sales. "This is a casual business with lots of weekend hours. That's appealing to some people, unappealing to others." Because of the business's flexible hours, the opportunity has attracted many female franchisees. No photographic background is necessary. The equipment is easy to learn and operate and compact enough to take just about anywhere.

The Sports Section strongly recommends that franchisees operate this business from home; all franchisees currently do that. The company offers three franchise packages: the first costs $14,500 and comes with an exclusive territory of up to 500,000 people; the second costs $19,500 and buys a population of up to 750,000 people; the third requires an investment of $29,500 and comes with an exclusive area of one million people.

The Sports Section emphasizes that no other up-front money is needed. The package price purchases all equipment including cameras, indoor lighting gear, tripods, and lenses.

The company charges no royalty or advertising fee, but it makes its profits on its wholesale developing services. Franchisees send film back to the home office, which operates a 27,000-square-foot photo-processing lab.

Before opening, franchisees receive two training sessions from field representatives. The first session teaches franchisees how to market their business to park and recreation departments, school groups, and other civic and voluntary organizations. The second session teaches franchisees how to handle the equipment and gear.

The Sports Section provides ample post-training support and maintains an 800 number for franchisees in case of problems or questions. The company also publishes a monthly newsletter and conducts bi-annual seminars at its headquarters.

FORECAST AND ANALYSIS

Much of the company's appeal is due to the baseball cards it produces and sells to parents of Little Leaguers and other youth sports programs. The company has diversified into other products and services that should strengthen its product offerings for franchisees.

Still, schools, department stores, and mom-and-pop photographers try to sell photography to families. To be successful, The Sports Section franchisee has to be a good marketer and a great people-person.

82. IDENT-A-KID

■———————————————————————————■

FRANCHISE FEE: *$12,500*
TOTAL INITIAL INVESTMENT: *$12,500*
FINANCING AVAILABLE: *None*
ROYALTY FEE: *None*
ADVERTISING FEE: *None*
ADDRESS: *2810 Scherer Drive, St. Petersburg, FL 33716*
TELEPHONE: *1-813-577-4646*
CONTACT PERSON: *Robert King*
INDUSTRY OVERVIEW
- *This is a specialized but simple business. The competition is scattered*

*and the company performs the photography and laminating service
on a full-time, part-time, or irregular basis.*

BENEFITS OF THIS COMPANY

- *Ident-A-Kid markets its identification service primarily to schools.
  Franchisees earn money by selling laminated photographs to parents
  who use them as permanent IDs for children.*
- *Ident-A-Kid is a complete turnkey operation and the company provides ample training and post-training support.*

COMPANY HISTORY

- **IN BUSINESS SINCE:** *1986*
- **FRANCHISING SINCE:** *1987*
- **NUMBER OF FRANCHISE UNITS:** *170*

Each year, 1.8 million U.S. children are reported missing. Some of
them run away, some are kidnapped, and some end up safely in the
hands of a divorced parent who doesn't have custody rights. The
scope of the problem has been debated, with some commentators
calling it a national epidemic and others terming it overdramatized.

Regardless of the view one takes, one fact is undeniable: a missing
child stirs panic in the hearts of any parent. Ident-A-Kid reduces this
fear by marketing laminated photo IDs that carry the likeness of the
child on one side and vital statistics on the other. If the child should
become separated from the family, parents can present police, security guards, the press, and anyone else with the ID that speeds the
search efforts.

"I started this business after a friend of mine told me about her
experience in losing her child in a shopping mall," says Ident-A-Kid
founder and president Robert King. "She had no picture to give to
the police, and that slowed down their search."

Since then Ident-A-Kid has added 170 locations throughout the
country, and the company plans on adding 230 franchises by 1995.

For an initial investment of $12,500, franchisees buy the right to
market the photo laminating and ID service to schools, day-care
centers, churches, and community centers. Ident-A-Kid franchisees
photograph children between the ages of two and fifteen. Prices for
the IDs range from $5 for one laminated card to $10 for three.

In return for their investment, franchisees receive the portable
photographic, fingerprinting, and laminating equipment, plus lights,
backdrops, and a computer system complete with software.

Ident-A-Kid provides two days of training at the franchisee's site. During the training, franchisees learn how to use the photographic equipment and how to market the Ident-A-Kid service to parents and schools.

There are minimal costs for the franchisee beyond the initial investment. Ident-A-Kid charges no royalty, but franchisees are required to purchase the equipment engraved with the Ident-A-Kid trademark and logo from headquarters. All photo sessions are done at the customer's site, which eliminates the expense of an office or studio.

FORECAST AND ANALYSIS

Ident-A-Kid maintains that it doesn't exploit a parent's fear of kidnapping in marketing the service; however, a parent's fear of losing a child is the motivating factor behind buying Ident-A-Kid products.

Other ID companies have cropped up in the United States, but only Ident-A-Kid is organized on the national level. The service provides a benefit to both police and parents and can aid in returning a missing child to his or her home. The reasonable retail price makes this product difficult not for a parent to buy.

27

PUBLISHING

━━━━━━━━━━━━━━━━━━━━━━━━━━━━━━━━━━━━

83. COMMUNITY PUBLICATIONS OF AMERICA—TV NEWS

━━━━━━━━━━━━━━━━━━━━━━━━━━━━━━━━━━━━

FRANCHISE FEE: *$28,500*

TOTAL INITIAL INVESTMENT: *$31,500 to $33,500*

FINANCING AVAILABLE: *Yes*

ROYALTY FEE: *4.5 percent per issue*

ADVERTISING FEE: *None*

ADDRESS: *80 8th Avenue, New York, NY 10011*

TELEPHONE: *1-212-243-6800*

CONTACT PERSON: *Allan Horwitz*

INDUSTRY OVERVIEW

- *The potential for profitability is strong in the publishing industry. Profit margins on ads are high, and the work needed to bring in ads carries low overhead costs.*
- *Local, targeted advertising appeals to small business owners—especially in tough economic times.*

BENEFIT OF THIS COMPANY

- *Franchisor Allan Horwitz's extensive history in the publishing industry includes experience with* The Wall Street Journal. *The company offers discounts for franchisees who buy* TV News *sister franchises:* Pennysaver *and* Buying & Dining Guide.

COMPANY HISTORY

- **IN BUSINESS SINCE:** *1973*

- **FRANCHISING SINCE:** *1979*
- **NUMBER OF FRANCHISE UNITS:** 9

Many Americans not only watch television, they live for television. It is on that premise that *TV News* is building its business. A weekly TV listing with a local twist, *TV News* is a free publication which combines an accurate listing of television events with regular articles, feature stories, puzzles, human-interest articles, and advertisements.

Based in New York City, *TV News* started in 1973 and now supports nine franchises. Community Publications expects to add several franchises by 1995.

"There may not be hundreds of *TV News* franchises in operation today," says Community Publications president Allan Horwitz. "But the market is growing, and the concept is gaining acceptance at the rate we projected years ago. We need franchisees who believe in the concept of television and, more importantly, advertising."

Franchisees earn their profits by selling advertising space in the weekly television-listing publication. Advertisers select the size of the ad they wish to place, and franchisees design the layout and write the copy, either alone or with the help of the home office. Franchisees deliver the printed guides to retail stores in their community which offer them free to customers. Community Publications provides additional support by offering low-cost printing services to its franchisees. The company also encourages franchisees to forgo the expense of commercial office space and instead operate the business from their homes.

A $28,500 franchise fee entitles a franchisee to an exclusive territory for seven years, and covers most initial operating expenses. Franchisees should expect to invest an additional $3,000 to $6,000 for the purchase of office equipment and the hook-up of a business telephone line.

TV News does not offer in-house financing to franchisees, but it has been successful in gaining outside loans for as much as 80 percent of the total investment. *TV News*, which charges franchisees a 4.5 percent royalty fee per issue, also supplies franchisees with a money-back guarantee on their investment. If a franchise does not become profitable, and the franchisee has marketed the service properly, Community Publications will refund the franchise fee.

Training for all franchisees is extensive and covers everything from making the initial sales call to laying out the publication. Community Publications supplies franchisees with promotional material, videotaped and printed sales-instruction manuals, money-back incentives, franchise expansion discounts, franchise sweepstakes promotions, and a hotline for emergency assistance.

FORECAST AND ANALYSIS:

Community Publications' money-back guarantee is unique in franchising. Franchisees need to be assertive and sales-oriented if they want to succeed in this type of business. Community Publications offers sales and technical support to new franchisees.

84. COMMUNITY PUBLICATIONS OF AMERICA—PENNYSAVER

■───■

FRANCHISE FEE: *$28,500*
TOTAL INITIAL INVESTMENT: *$31,500 to $33,500*
FINANCING AVAILABLE: *Yes*
ROYALTY FEE: *4.5 percent per issue*
ADVERTISING FEE: *None*
ADDRESS: *80 8th Avenue, New York, NY 10011*
TELEPHONE: *1-212-243-6800*
CONTACT PERSON: *Allan Horwitz*
INDUSTRY OVERVIEW
- *The potential for profitability is strong in the publishing industry. Profit margins on ads are high, and the work needed to bring in ads carries low overhead costs.*
- *Local, targeted advertising appeals to small business owners—especially in tough economic times.*

BENEFIT OF THIS COMPANY
- *Franchisor Allan Horwitz's extensive history in the publishing industry includes experience with* The Wall Street Journal. *The company offers discounts for franchisees who buy* Pennysaver *sister franchises:* TV News *and* Buying & Dining Guide.

COMPANY HISTORY
- **IN BUSINESS SINCE:** *1973*

- **FRANCHISING SINCE:** *Early 1980s*
- **NUMBER OF FRANCHISE UNITS:** *500*

"A penny saved is a penny earned" is the credo of *Pennysaver*, the free publication that matches seller and buyer with the best bargains. Established in 1973, *Pennysaver* is a weekly circular distributed free to consumers through local retail stores and restaurants. There are currently 480 *Pennysaver* franchisees throughout the country.

Franchisees pay an initial $28,000 franchise fee for the exclusive rights to produce and distribute the publication in their local communities for seven years. Franchisees generate profit by selling advertising space to local merchants, restaurant owners, and professionals. Most ads appear in display or classified form, but Pennysaver also sells space to professionals who wish to contribute by-lined articles. Community Publications also charges franchisees a royalty fee of 4.5 percent of ad revenue.

The successful operation of a *Pennysaver* franchise depends on the franchisees's willingness and ability to sell. Most sales calls are done via telephone or at the customer's location, eliminating the need for professional office space. Community Publications recommends the use of home-based offices to all franchisees.

Training for a *Pennysaver* franchisee encompasses sales, management, and production. Special training videotapes and manuals offer additional sales advice, and Community Publications uses role-playing techniques to help a franchisee become more comfortable in the selling environment. Telephone support is available for all franchisees who need immediate help with a client, and Community Publications provides printing assistance.

FORECAST AND ANALYSIS

As part of the Community Publications family of franchises, a *Pennysaver* franchisee can branch out and buy *TV News* and *Buying & Dining Guide* franchises at discounted prices. Community Publications provides a money-back guarantee policy for all franchisees who have tried to develop their territories properly, but did not attain profitability.

85. COMMUNITY PUBLICATIONS OF AMERICA—BUYING & DINING GUIDE

FRANCHISE FEE: *$28,500*
TOTAL INITIAL INVESTMENT: *$31,500 to $33,500*
FINANCING AVAILABLE: *Yes*
ROYALTY FEE: *4.5 percent per issue*
ADVERTISING FEE: *None*
ADDRESS: *80 8th Avenue, New York, NY 10011*
TELEPHONE: *1-212-243-6800*
CONTACT PERSON: *Allan Horwitz*

INDUSTRY OVERVIEW

- *The potential for profitability is strong in the publishing industry since profit margins on ads are high compared to the work needed to bring the ad to press.*
- *Local, targeted advertising appeals to small business owners—especially in tough economic times.*

BENEFITS OF THIS COMPANY

- *Franchisor Allan Horwitz's extensive history in the publishing industry includes experience with* The Wall Street Journal. *The company offers expansion discounts for franchisees, making it worth their while to investigate the purchase of another territory for either* TV News *or* Pennysaver.

COMPANY HISTORY

- **IN BUSINESS SINCE:** *1979*
- **FRANCHISING SINCE:** *1987*
- **NUMBER OF FRANCHISE UNITS:** *10*

To accompany its other publications, Community Publications created the *Buying & Dining Guide*, a free bi-monthly magazine geared to consumers who take pleasure in fine dining and entertainment. Franchisees sell advertising space to the restaurants, theaters, and retailers. Advertisers choose the type and size of advertisement they wish to place, and franchisees design the layout, create the artwork, and write the copy. The guide is distributed free through restaurants and upscale retail stores. Since its inception, the *Buying & Dining Guide* has grown by two franchises per year, and company president Allan Horwitz expects twenty-five franchises to be in existence by 1995.

"We reach the cost-conscious consumer through *Pennysaver* and *TV News*, and this guide is our opportunity to reach the consumer who is not as concerned with saving money," explains Allan Horwitz, Community Publications founder. "We do extensive research to make sure that we distribute the guide in areas that will attract the most customers for our advertisers. We're betting that this publication will be responsible for the majority of Community Publications' growth."

As with the other Community Publications, the $28,500 franchise fee purchases the rights to an exclusive territory for seven years, and the investment, which covers more than 80 percent of the start-up costs, comes with a money-back guarantee. The company will direct franchisees to outside lenders if financing is needed. Community Publications also charges franchisees of this guide a 4.5 percent royalty fee. Franchisees should have in reserve an additional $3,000 to $6,000 for the purchase of a computer, fax machine, and copier. As with its sister publications, the *Buying & Dining Guide* can be operated efficiently from home since all printing is done by Community Publications.

Community Publications trains its franchisees in all aspects of the sales process, from the initial call to closing the deal. The company also teaches franchisees the techniques of ad layout and design. Post-training support is also available to franchisees through ongoing sales programs, printing discounts, expansion options and bonus commissions. The company's hotline is also available for franchisees in need of immediate assistance.

FORECAST AND ANALYSIS

Because Community Publications takes care of printing the *Buying & Dining Guide*, franchisees can focus on selling ads and increasing their profitability. With the company's money-back guarantee, a franchisee assumes minimal risk. The money-back guarantee is only good if franchisees can prove they followed the operating procedures. Any new franchise owner should keep careful records if they plan to use the money-back guarantee to minimize their risk.

86. BINGO BUGLE (K & O PUBLISHING)

FRANCHISE FEE: *$1,500 to $4,000 depending on number of bingo games in franchise area*

TOTAL INITIAL INVESTMENT: *In addition to franchise fee, $75 to $1,000 for training and $2,000 in working capital*

FINANCING AVAILABLE: *None*

ROYALTY FEE: *10 percent*

ADVERTISING FEE: *None*

ADDRESS: *P.O. Box 51189, Seattle, WA 98115-1189*

TELEPHONE: *1-800-447-1958 or 1-206-527-4958*

CONTACT PERSON: *Warren Kraft*

INDUSTRY OVERVIEW

- *Local publishing allows local businesses to reach targeted audiences cost-effectively.*
- *Despite challenging economic conditions, merchants continue to advertise to promote their products and services and find new customers.*

BENEFIT OF THIS COMPANY

- Bingo Bugle *is recognized as the leading publication in the bingo industry. Its steady growth in advertisers and readers confirms the publication's popularity.*

COMPANY HISTORY

- **IN BUSINESS SINCE:** *1981*
- **FRANCHISING SINCE:** *1982*
- **NUMBER OF FRANCHISE UNITS:** *65*

Bingo may seem like a friendly little parlor game, but in reality bingo is the second largest commercial gambling game in North America. Fifty-eight million men and women wager more than $5 billion annually on bingo. The game draws more players than almost any other athletic and social pastime in the United States. Player commitment to the game sparked the introduction of *Bingo Bugle,* the industry's leading publication, in 1981. The company has grown to include more than sixty-five franchises nationwide.

Despite the recent recession, *Bingo Bugle* has increased its circulation and readership, and the company estimates that seventy-five franchises will exist by 1995.

An initial investment of $1,500 to $4,000 purchases a five-year exclusive territory, which is based on the number of organized bingo games in an area. Franchisees need an additional $2,000 to cover start-up costs, including the purchase of office equipment. *Bingo Bugle* also charges franchisees a 10 percent royalty fee on each issue.

The role of the franchisees is to report monthly on local bingo news about upcoming bingo tournaments and champion and celebrity players. Franchisees generate income by selling advertising space to local businesses and bingo clubs. The home office provides camera-ready photographs and artwork to franchisees for each issue. Issues are printed by local printers approved by the home office.

Franchisees need basic office equipment and a camera to run this business efficiently. Ninety percent of *Bingo Bugle* franchisees run their business from home.

Bingo Bugle trains franchisees for two and one-half days. Instruction focuses on sales, marketing, and management techniques. The company also offers ongoing support through regional meetings, annual conventions, and an in-depth publishing manual that aids the franchisee in writing copy, finding stories, and winning advertising contracts.

FORECAST AND ANALYSIS

Bingo Bugle has an established nationwide readership of avid bingo fans. K & O Publishing, the parent company of *Bingo Bugle*, has a long-standing track record for success and franchisee support, and *Bingo Bugle* has shown steady growth since its first issue in 1981. Bingo is considered the number one game of chance in charity and church organizations, and its growth in Atlantic City and Las Vegas has helped enhance its popularity. The game is inexpensive to play and provides a social activity that players take seriously.

87. FINDERBINDER/SOURCEBOOK

FRANCHISE FEE: *$1,000*
TOTAL INITIAL INVESTMENT: *$9,000 to $15,000*
FINANCING AVAILABLE: *None*

ROYALTY FEE: *15 percent to 5 percent depending on number of directories sold*

ADVERTISING FEE: *None*

ADDRESS: *4679 Vista Street, San Diego, CA 92116*

TELEPHONE: *1-800-255-2575 or 1-619-284-1145*

CONTACT PERSON: *Gary Beals*

INDUSTRY OVERVIEW

- *Media and association directories are needed by advertising agencies, public relations firms, fund-raising organizations, charities, and other civic associations.*

BENEFIT OF THIS COMPANY

- *The franchise is a perfect add-on business to an existing home-based publishing or sales franchise.*

COMPANY HISTORY

- **IN BUSINESS SINCE:** *1974*
- **FRANCHISING SINCE:** *1975*
- **NUMBER OF FRANCHISE UNITS:** *23*

The marketing professional relies heavily on print and broadcast media to sell a client's product or service. *Finderbinder/Sourcebook* of San Diego, California, publishes updated and accurate directories which list all media, associations, and organizations. These directories put important names, addresses, and phone numbers at a marketer's fingertips.

Franchises for the media directory, *Finderbinder,* and the association directory, *Sourcebook,* are sold separately, but many of the same requirements exist for both.

Franchisees are usually marketers and public relations specialists who already operate full-time businesses, whether it be from an outside office or at home.

Franchisees sell the directories directly to marketing professionals or through professional organizations and associations within their communities.

For the first edition, franchisees will need at least one researcher to gather names, addresses, and telephone numbers. After the first edition, the book is merely updated, and the need for full-time researchers diminishes.

Each directory ranges in price from $75 to $200. There is a moderate mark-up for each directory, but most franchisees do not reach the break-even point until they sell 200 books.

For either directory, the initial franchise fee is $1,000. Franchisees may need to invest an additional $8,000 to $12,000 to cover the cost of equipment and the hiring of a one- or two-member research staff. Franchise royalty fees for both directories start at 15 percent for the first 200 books sold. The fee decreases to 10 percent on the next 200 volumes and finally 5 percent on any sales after that point.

Finderbinder's content focuses on the media. *Sourcebook* is a directory of for-profit and non-profit organizations and associations. The *Sourcebook* franchisee is initially responsible for only an annual edition of the directory. After two years, franchisees must release the *Sourcebook* on a quarterly basis. *Finderbinder* franchisees are required to publish an annual directory as well as six newsletters per year.

Training for this franchise opportunity is short and requires only one day of at-home study. *Finderbinder/Sourcebook* provides operations manuals as well as camera-ready artwork and printing specifications for each directory. Franchisees hire outside contractors for the actual printing.

FORECAST AND ANALYSIS

This company has had a slow start in the franchise game. It targets public relations and marketing professionals who already operate successful home-based businesses.

The niche is an interesting one. Local directories are invaluable tools for sales people and marketers.

88. HOMES & LAND PUBLISHING CORP. (HOMES & LAND, HOMES & LAND RENTAL GUIDE, HOMES & LAND DIGEST)

FRANCHISE FEE: *$1,500 to $15,000 depending on publication*
TOTAL INITIAL INVESTMENT: *$20,000 to $75,000 depending on publication*
FINANCING AVAILABLE: *No*
ROYALTY FEE: *6 to 16 percent depending on publication and territory*
ADVERTISING FEE: *None*
ADDRESS: *1600 Capital Circle S.W., P.O. Box 5018, Tallahassee, FL 32310*
TELEPHONE: *1-904-574-2111*
CONTACT PERSON: *Roland Woosey*

INDUSTRY OVERVIEW

- *Local real estate publishing combines the potential for high profit with the simplicity of a small business. Sales ability is critical to succeeding in ad-based publishing.*

BENEFITS OF THIS COMPANY

- *A nineteen-year record of success is impressive for a company that depends on the whims of the fickle real estate market.*
- *The tighter the economy, the more realtors must advertise to sell their products.*
- *Homes & Land serves as the local link between sellers and buyers or owners and tenants. The company has a strong reputation for success as well as management skills.*

COMPANY HISTORY

- **IN BUSINESS SINCE:** *1973*
- **FRANCHISING SINCE:** *1984*
- **NUMBER OF FRANCHISE UNITS:** *246* Homes & Land; *29* Homes & Land Rental Guides

---

Selling a home is never easy. Realtors look for any advantage they can get. *Homes & Land* magazines provide that all-important advantage for many local real estate agencies.

Marketed to realtors and builders, the magazines list scores of homes for sale by local real estate agencies. The publications are distributed free of charge to consumers through banks, restaurants, and other local businesses.

Established since 1973, *Homes & Land* directories have assumed an important role in the real estate world. During its seven-year franchising history, the network has grown to more than 246 *Homes & Land* and 29 *Rental Guide* franchises throughout the United States.

Much of the success is due to each publication's ability to get results in targeted areas. Potential home buyers rely on *Homes & Land* and similar publications to learn what's for sale in a community. The publication also provides realtors access to a national referral service called Homeline which helps them serve distant and relocating buyers.

For an entrepreneur who enjoys seeing a project through from beginning to end, the Homes & Land Publishing Corp. may offer a valuable opportunity. Franchisees not only solicit ad space, but they participate in ad layout and design of the magazines.

An average franchise fee of $15,000 secures an exclusive territory for ten years which is renewable at a franchisee's request at no additional investment. The more elaborate the publication, the more money it costs to produce, and the total initial investment varies between $25,000 and $70,000.

Despite the many steps it takes to produce a magazine, *Homes & Land* is a relatively easy business to operate. The majority of the sales calls are done by phone or fax and layout of the publications requires only a tabletop. The actual printing of the magazines is performed by subcontractors. Because of this simplicity, 90 percent of Homes & Land franchisees operate their businesses from their homes. The company encourages this set-up because it cuts unnecessary overhead.

Homes & Land requires that franchisees attend a one-week orientation which teaches them the fundamentals of publishing the magazines. There is also two to three days of in-field training which helps to develop a franchisee's sales and closing skills. Homes & Land sponsors yearly sales meetings and keeps in touch with its franchisees with periodic newsletters and updated marketing aids and policies.

FORECAST AND ANALYSIS

Community real estate publications provide a vital link between buyers and sellers of property. It's an entrenched part of real estate sales in many communities. In fact, territories are hard to come by in many areas of the country. Homes & Land network has more than seven years of franchise experience and nineteen years of producing a tried-and-tested product. Its success is likely to continue well into 'he future.

89. THE EXECUTIVE FRANCHISING, INC.

FRANCHISE FEE: *$8,000 to $22,000 depending on size of territory*
TOTAL INITIAL INVESTMENT: *$15,000 to $28,000*
FINANCING AVAILABLE: *Yes*
ROYALTY FEE: *5 percent*
ADVERTISING FEE: *None*
ADDRESS: *4518 Valleydale Road, Birmingham, AL 35242*

TELEPHONE: *1-800-264-EXEC or 1-205-991-2970*
CONTACT PERSON: *Kevin A. Foote*

INDUSTRY OVERVIEW
- *Publishing can be a high-margin industry.*
- *Business-to-business advertising can be particularly lucrative.*

BENEFIT OF THIS COMPANY
- The Executive *doesn't target consumers; instead it focuses on business-to-business advertising, one of the most profitable segments of the advertising industry.*

COMPANY HISTORY
- **IN BUSINESS SINCE:** *1987*
- **FRANCHISING SINCE:** *1989*
- **NUMBER OF FRANCHISE UNITS:** *4*

No one should pass up a bargain, not even a business owner. That's the credo of *The Executive,* a business-to-business magazine that's 100 percent advertisements.

The complimentary magazine, which is published four times a year, is distributed free through other businesses in a franchisee's marketing area. The publication is filled with ads, coupons, and discount promotions geared toward the business consumer. Advertising is the sole source of a franchisee's income.

The Executive began franchising less than two years ago; today, there are four franchises and one company outlet. Although early growth has been slow, the company expects to have more than forty franchises by 1995.

Little office space is required and most franchisees find it convenient to run their franchises from home.

A moderate investment ranging from $8,000 to $22,000 secures an exclusive territory for a period of five years. Franchisees should expect to have access to an additional $6,000 to $7,000 to pay for equipment, inventory, promotional materials, and training.

A 5 percent royalty, which the franchisor collects on a monthly basis, is due only after the first issue is published.

The Executive Franchising trains franchisees for five days at company headquarters. Classes in marketing, management, and sales techniques focus on improving a franchisee's sales ability. Although no previous experience is needed, some sales background is helpful. The company provides ongoing support in layout, copy, and ad design.

FORECAST AND ANALYSIS

Publishing has been one of the industries hardest hit by the recession of the early 1990s. Business-to-business advertising is extremely competitive, with Yellow Pages, television, newspapers, and radio vying for the same ad dollars. Still, effective sales people may still find the right opportunity in business-to-business advertising, especially if they own the business and keep expenses under control.

90. THE BRIDE'S DAY MAGAZINE

FRANCHISE FEE: *$14,900*

TOTAL INITIAL INVESTMENT: *$14,900*

FINANCING AVAILABLE: *No*

ROYALTY FEE: *6 percent*

ADVERTISING FEE *None*

ADDRESS: *M.A.G. Publishing Company, Inc., 750 Hamburg Turnpike, Suite 208, Pompton Lakes, NJ 07442*

TELEPHONE: *1-201-835-6551*

CONTACT PERSON: *David Gay*

INDUSTRY OVERVIEW

- *Specialty publishing provides an effective way to reach targeted audiences. Directories offer consumers relevant information and real value without the hassle of having to conduct tedious research themselves.*

BENEFIT OF THIS COMPANY

- Bride's Day *gives engaged couples a wide array of information in a convenient and easy-to-use format. The traditional wedding is back, but the people getting married are more contemporary. Fewer people have the time to spend scouring their neighborhoods for purveyors of wedding services. Wedding consulting is now big business, and* Bride's Day *is in an excellent position to profit by providing a valuable service to those planning weddings.*

COMPANY HISTORY

- **IN BUSINESS SINCE:** *1987*
- **FRANCHISING SINCE:** *1990*
- **NUMBER OF FRANCHISE UNITS:** *11*

Weddings require a great deal of planning. One New Jersey–based publishing company helps couples avoid the hassles associated with weddings with its guidebook, *The Bride's Day* magazine.

Established in 1987, *The Bride's Day* magazine is a who's who in the world of wedding services. Distributed free to consumers through retail stores, the magazine was developed by M.A.G. Publishing Company, which opened its first franchise in 1990. Now eleven franchises exist throughout the country, and M.A.G. expects fifty franchises to be in existence by 1995.

"Traditional weddings have come back in style, and couples have more money to spend on the event itself," says M.A.G. founder David Gay. "What couples don't have is the time to hunt around for wedding services. Our guidebook does that for them."

The role of franchisees is to generate advertising dollars in their territories. Through telemarketing campaigns and person-to-person sales calls, franchisees sell advertising space in the publication to jewelers, caterers, photographers, bridal salons, formal-wear shops, and entertainment companies. Franchisees are free to design the ads themselves or enlist the help of M.A.G. for all artwork, proofreading, and printing services.

The initial $14,900 investment entitles franchisees to an exclusive territory based on population. Most franchisees need an additional $1,000 to $2,000 for a copier, fax machine, and typewriter. The company also charges franchisees a 6 percent royalty fee. M.A.G. requires franchisees to maintain a business telephone line that is separate from their personal lines. The company encourages franchisees to operate their businesses from home to cut down on overhead expenses—especially in the first six months of operation. *The Bride's Day* magazine seeks both men and women as franchisees, but at present 72 percent of franchisees are women.

Bride's Day franchisees need no experience in the publishing industry. The home office trains the franchisee for one week at its headquarters in Pompton Lakes, New Jersey. Training is provided in sales, customer account maintenance, bookkeeping, and advertisement design.

FORECAST AND ANALYSIS

The $14,900 franchise fee entitles franchisees to a host of support services. Franchise owners must be effective sales people. Generating revenue from ad dollars is the key to success in this franchise opportunity.

28

TRANSPORTATION

---

91. AIRBROOK LIMOUSINE

FRANCHISE FEE: *$10,500 to $15,500 depending on type of vehicle*

TOTAL INITIAL INVESTMENT: *Maximum of $15,500 plus lease payments on vehicle*

FINANCING AVAILABLE: *Yes*

ROYALTY FEE: *40 percent of gross franchise sales for sedan or wagon franchisees, 35 percent of gross for stretch limousine or van franchisees*

ADVERTISING FEE: *None*

ADDRESS: *P.O. Box 123, Rochelle Park, NJ 06772*

TELEPHONE: *1-201-368-3974*

CONTACT PERSON: *Conrad Rehill*

INDUSTRY OVERVIEW

- *Limousines used to be a luxury service that only the well-heeled could afford. But today, airport limousines are a standard in business and personal travel. Limos save customers valuable time, the costs of fuel, wear and tear on their own vehicles, and exorbitant airport parking rates. Travel-industry experts say that travelers who use limos are generally loyal customers who become repeat customers when they receive good service.*

BENEFIT OF THIS COMPANY

- *Airbrook has a long record of courteous and punctual service. The company is making plans to take the company public. This will increase Airbrook's visibility with travelers throughout the nation.*

COMPANY HISTORY
- **IN BUSINESS SINCE:** *1971*
- **FRANCHISING SINCE:** *1978*
- **NUMBER OF FRANCHISE UNITS:** *89*

The road to any metropolitan airport is fraught with pitfalls and obstacles. For twenty years, Airbrook Limousine, a New Jersey–based company, has taken the stress out of the airport commute for thousands of travelers.

Airbrook Limousine's network includes eighty-nine franchise vehicles and ten company limousines. In the past, the company has limited its franchise expansion to New Jersey only, but a recent push to take the company public could open up new franchise doors across the United States. Optimistic about its plan for national expansion, the company estimates that there will be more than 200 franchises by 1995.

"We are the best-known limousine service in the New York metropolitan area and now we're going public," says Conrad Rehill, franchise director for Airbrook. "That will open up a great deal of opportunities for our franchisees. Our franchisees include entrepreneurs who want to run a part-time business as drivers and those who want to build their own limousine fleet."

Each Airbrook limousine is considered one franchise, and the franchisees are not restricted to serving a certain mileage area. Franchisees serve as chauffeurs, driving customers to their destinations. Franchisees are not required to sell or contract for their services. The home office takes care of those responsibilities.

The initial investment for an Airbrook franchise ranges from $7,500 to $12,500, which entitles a franchisee to use all trademarks and logos of the company. The $7,500 investment purchases a franchise consisting of a sedan or station wagon limo. The $12,500 fee buys the rights to use a stretch limousine complete with bar and television. Airbrook estimates that an additional $3,000 is required for the purchase of a two-way radio for the limousine, uniforms, and a security deposit on the vehicle. The lease arrangements on the limousine are a separate expense and not part of the company's financial estimates. The home office receives 35 percent of each fare as royalty.

Franchisees do not need a professional office. Limousines can be parked in most driveways or garages.

Airbrook conducts a five-day training course for all new franchisees. No previous experience is required, but all Airbrook chauffeurs must meet state driver license standards.

FORECAST AND ANALYSIS

The company could receive a great deal of exposure if it succeeds in going public. Airbrook has taken the time to perfect its franchising skills locally and is likely to succeed in repeating its success nationally. Unlike many home-based franchises, this franchise does not require franchisees to have any sales ability.

92. WHEELCHAIR GETAWAYS

■━━━■

FRANCHISE FEE: *$12,500*
TOTAL INITIAL INVESTMENT: *$70,000 to $80,000*
ROYALTY FEE: *Flat fee of $500 per vehicle per year*
ADVERTISING FEE: *None*
ADDRESS: *P.O. Box 819, Newtown, PA 18940*
TELEPHONE: *1-215-579-9121*
CONTACT PERSON: *Ed Van Artsdalen*
INDUSTRY OVERVIEW
- *There is a growing need for short-term transportation for disabled and elderly Americans. The enactment of the American Disabilities Act will make it easier for disabled people to function in environments outside their homes. Transportation must be available for disabled persons to take advantage of these new opportunities.*

BENEFIT OF THIS COMPANY
- *Most of this company's franchisees are disabled themselves. The ability to relate with customers can provide a long-term customer-vendor relationship.*

COMPANY HISTORY
- **IN BUSINESS SINCE:** *1989*
- **FRANCHISING SINCE:** *1989*
- **NUMBER OF FRANCHISE TERRITORIES:** *32*

■━━━■

There are more than 43 million disabled Americans, many of whom use wheelchairs. Few of them can afford the $20,000 to $30,000 to buy a van made accessible for wheelchair users.

Wheelchair Getaways has changed all that. The Newtown, Pennsylvania–based franchise company rents, on a short-term basis, specially designed vans for wheelchair users. Equipped with wheelchair lifts, dropped floors, and wheelchair tie-down systems, the plush Dodge Ram vans hold one wheelchair user and five other adults.

A business that requires no inventory, Wheelchair Getaways is a prime example of a home-based opportunity. Customers contact the franchisee to reserve the van, and it is delivered to the customer's doorstep on the specified day. Daily rental rates range from $70 to $85 depending on the franchisee's location.

The initial fee for a Wheelchair Getaways franchise is $12,500, which purchases the rights to an exclusive territory based on population. Franchisees can expect to invest a total of $70,000 to $80,000, the bulk of which pays for down payments and leases on the specialized vans. Wheelchair Getaways also charges an ongoing annual royalty fee of $500 per van.

The company sold its first franchise only two years ago, and there are now thirty-two Wheelchair Getaways owners across the country. Much of this growth has come from increased public and government awareness of the plight of the disabled. The Americans With Disabilities Act, which was signed by President Bush in 1990, bars discrimination against people with physical and mental disabilities. Termed the Civil Rights Bill for disabled Americans, it requires easy access for the disabled to public buildings, telephone service, and mass transportation systems.

Since Wheelchair Getaways enjoys a "Good Samaritan" reputation, the business is not hard to promote. Franchisees must be willing to market their service to community organizations, hospitals, nursing homes, and extended-care facilities.

An interesting note to this company's expansion is that the majority of franchisees are disabled persons themselves. Most have set up shop in resort and retirement communities where there is a clear need for this specialized short-term transportation.

FORECAST AND ANALYSIS

Transportation for the disabled will always be in demand in this country. Wheelchair Getaways can provide high potential income, particularly in resort and tourist destinations. The company is negotiating with major airlines, hotel chains, and other facilities to provide the specially designed vans on an as-needed basis.

93. CAR CHECKERS OF AMERICA

■——■

FRANCHISE FEE: *$20,000*

TOTAL INITIAL INVESTMENT: *$70,000 to $80,000*

ROYALTY FEE: *5 percent of monthly gross sales*

ADVERTISING FEE: *2 percent of monthly gross sales*

ADDRESS: *1011 Route 22 W., Bridgewater, NJ 08807*

TELEPHONE: *1-800-242-CHEX or 1-908-704-1221*

CONTACT PERSON: *Lee Geller*

INDUSTRY OVERVIEW

- *This type of service provides used-car buyers with an unbiased evaluation of a car before its purchase. The comprehensive inspection eliminates the fear of the unknown when buying a car.*
- *It takes an aggressive marketing strategy to make people aware of the service. There are no walk-in or drive-by customers. Clients must be cultivated.*

BENEFIT OF THIS COMPANY

- *This is a new marketing concept. All calls and sales presentations are done at the customer's location. There is no need for a franchisee to rent office space, and most franchisees run their businesses from home.*

COMPANY HISTORY

- **IN BUSINESS SINCE:** *1986*
- **FRANCHISING SINCE:** *1989*
- **NUMBER OF FRANCHISE UNITS:** *124*

■——■

There are more than 18 million used cars on the road in the United States today, and that number is expected to climb dramatically over the next three years. The popularity of used cars is growing, and unsuspecting car buyers need someone to look out for their interests. This is the philosophy behind Car Checkers of America, the Bridgewater, New Jersey–based franchise company that uses state-of-the-art, computerized equipment to identify problems with a used car before a customer takes it off the lot. Dubbed the "Lemon Busters," Car Checkers offers potential car buyers a quick, complete, objective, and inexpensive evaluation of more than 3,600 components of a vehicle's electrical, emission, and on-board computer systems.

The Car Checkers' service is mobile—it goes to the customer or, more accurately, to the car. All the equipment used in the diagnostic check is aboard a white, Chevrolet Lumina van, which fits into any standard-sized garage. This mobility makes Car Checkers the ultimate example of a home-based franchise.

A baby in the world of franchising, Car Checkers sold its first territory only two years ago—three years after its own jump-start into the automotive world. Now, the company grosses almost $2.5 million per year, and it includes more than 124 franchise territories throughout the continental United States and Hawaii.

A Car Checkers franchise is neither for the lazy nor the "get-rich-quick" fortune seekers. The success of the operation depends on a franchisee's willingness to market and promote the inspection services throughout an exclusive territory predetermined by population. The bulk of the promotion centers on credit unions and financial lending institutions that use the service to obtain a "clean bill of health" on a car before financing it. Some franchisees have marketed the service to used-car dealerships that offer the inspection to customers as part of price negotiation.

With such an intense focus on promotion, Car Checkers attracts mostly former sales and marketing executives as franchisees. More than 90 percent of its franchisees are men, but several husband-and-wife teams exist. The company has made every effort to highlight its twenty-five-year-old female founder and president as a way of recruiting women franchisees into its network.

An estimated $70,000 to $80,000 covers all initial costs of the franchise including the leasing of specialized equipment needed in the operation of the business. Car Checkers does not finance any part of the investment, but it does assist new franchisees in obtaining the leased equipment, which includes the Chevy Lumina van, a diagnostic analyzer, a paint-coating thickness analyzer, and a suspension analyzer. The company also insists that franchisees have at least six months in financial reserves to pay for personal and living expenses.

Car Checkers charges franchisees a 5 percent royalty fee and a 2 percent advertising fee as well.

The company conducts a two-week training course for all franchisees. Car Checkers teaches franchisees how to perform the inspections and market the service to credit unions and bank officers. Field representatives are always available to answer franchisee questions, and the company maintains a twenty-four-hour hot line for franchisees' emergencies.

FORECAST AND ANALYSIS

The used-car market has never been so popular. The car inspections are analogous to the home inspections of the 1970s, which led to legislation in many states requiring inspections before purchase. Could this happen to the used-car industry as well? If it does, Car Checkers will be on the cutting edge of a major windfall.

If the franchise is marketed exclusively to consumers, there is little hope of growth since the repeat business factor is very limited. Most consumers buy only two to three used cars in a lifetime. Car Checkers has countered this situation by marketing to banks and credit unions. One closed deal with a bank or financial institution can result in hundreds of car checks for franchisees.

29

VIDEO, DJ SERVICES, NOVELTY ANNOUNCEMENTS, AND ENTERTAINMENT

---

94. VIDEO DATA SERVICES

FRANCHISE FEE: *$15,950*

TOTAL INITIAL INVESTMENT: *$17,950*

FINANCING AVAILABLE: *None*

ROYALTY FEE: *$250 every six months*

ADVERTISING FEE: *None*

ADDRESS: *30 Grove Street. Pittsford, NY 14534*

TELEPHONE: *1-800-836-9461 or 1-716-385-4773*

CONTACT PERSON: *Stuart Dizak*

INDUSTRY OVERVIEW

- *Videotaping has many uses, ranging from entertainment to business to law. Uses for this technology are expanding, so companies who offer this service are expanding too.*

BENEFITS OF THIS COMPANY

- *Video Data Services was one of the first entries into the video industry. The company offers training to franchisees that allows them to do entertainment, corporate, and legal video services.*
- *Video Data also allows franchisees to begin part-time until they feel comfortable giving up their full-time jobs. Few franchisees find it necessary to rent office space; most start and remain home-based.*

COMPANY HISTORY

- **IN BUSINESS SINCE:** *1981*

- **FRANCHISING SINCE:** *1982*
- **NUMBER OF FRANCHISE UNITS:** *286*

Video services encompass more than a weekend of weddings and bar mitzvahs. Today's "videographer" produces sales motivational tapes for companies as well as mock trials for legal firms planning courtroom strategy.

Video Data came into the marketplace in 1981 before the hand-held video camera was a part of many American homes. It grew quickly due to demand for wedding and bar mitzvah videotaping. When consumers began buying video cameras, parts of the business started to dry up. Still, other parts, especially commercial work, took off. Video Data repositioned itself and is firmly entrenched in the profitable corporate, sales, and legal sectors of the videotaping field.

"Franchisees still videotape weddings, but that's an increasingly smaller portion of our business," says Stuart Dizak, president. "Our franchisees are working with corporations and professionals who need videotaping services for sales presentations, facility brochures, and documentation of legal proceedings, both real and rehearsed."

Video Data currently sponsors 286 franchises throughout the United States and has franchisees in Canada.

The range of services offered by its franchisees is wide. For instance, some franchisees are part-timers who still live off wedding business. Others own full-service production facilities complete with computer graphics and all the bells and whistles needed to produce broadcast-quality videotapes.

Headquarters maintains a database of each franchisee's specialty and refers work to franchisees based on their expertise and the types of work they feel comfortable completing.

Franchisees need no previous technical experience. Video Data seeks franchisees who are comfortable interacting with people and aren't intimidated by electronic equipment. Franchisees come from all walks of life. They all must be willing to conduct direct mail and telemarketing sales programs. Some franchisees choose to start part-time and keep their current jobs until the business is generating enough cash flow to pay a professional salary.

An initial fee of $15,950 buys the equipment franchisees need to open the business, including cameras, lights, and an exclusive territory of 250,000 people. The agreement runs for ten years, and franchisees can automatically renew it upon its expiration date.

Video Services recommends that franchisees have an additional $2,000 in working capital for office supplies, telephone hook-up, and advertising expenses. The company charges a flat royalty of $250 payable every six months.

All franchisees start their video business at home, and most choose to stay there.

Training consists of a three-day seminar at the company facility in Rochester, New York, or in Phoenix, followed by a six-week home study course. As part of that course, franchisees complete a documentary film promoting their home communities as relocation sites for businesses. The production must include footage and interviews with merchants, Chamber of Commerce members, and residents.

After a year of operation, Video Data offers franchisees advanced training on the Amiga computer system, which is used to edit legal productions. Franchisees who produce mock trials must receive advanced certified legal training before adding this to their list of services.

FORECAST AND ANALYSIS

Videotaping services is a competitive industry. One of the great advantages of Video Data is that it provides individual franchisees with a network of other videotaping professionals who share ideas, referrals, and strategies with one another.

Video Data franchisees contacted for this profile were extremely positive about the business. The company lets them grow as businesspeople and encourages them to learn about technology, marketing and management. The home office was cited as staying on the cutting edge of an evolving industry and providing franchisees with a plethora of seminars, conventions, newsletters, and meetings to keep people involved and up-to- date.

95. COMPLETE MUSIC

FRANCHISE FEE: *$9,500*
TOTAL INITIAL INVESTMENT: *$22,500*

FINANCING AVAILABLE: *Yes*
ADVERTISING FEE: *Zero to 2 percent*
ADDRESS: *8317 Cass, Omaha, NE 68114*
TELEPHONE: *1-800-843-3866 or 1-402-391-4847*
CONTACT PERSON: *Jerry Maas*
ROYALTY FEE: *8 percent*
INDUSTRY OVERVIEW

- *The professional disc-jockey industry gains more credibility each year. Customers like the variety of music that disc jockeys provide.*
- *Disc jockeys compete with live entertainment as well as other disc-jockey services. Franchisees must be good sales people and personable entertainers.*

BENEFIT OF THIS COMPANY

- *A well-established entertainment company, Complete Music has been in business during all kinds of music and entertainment trends, weathered them, and prospered. Not many other companies in this field can make the same claim.*

COMPANY HISTORY

- **IN BUSINESS SINCE:** *1973*
- **FRANCHISING SINCE:** *1979*
- **NUMBER OF FRANCHISE UNITS:** *94*

Music is a central part of a formal party, prom, or wedding. Complete Music of Omaha, Nebraska, provides a wide assortment of music along with its professional disc-jockey service. Established in 1973, the company is a national franchise network consisting of ninety-four franchises and one company-owned outlet.

The franchisee's role is that of an entertainer. Each DJ uses an audio library of more than 2,000 songs, representing major eras in music as well as music representative of various ethnic cultures. The goal of the DJ is to lead audiences in dancing, singing, and playing party games. Although most franchisees start out as DJs themselves, many soon become managers and hire others to cover the weddings or parties for them as their businesses grow.

"We have one rule and that is DJs can't be shy out there—they have to be willing to let go and have fun," says Complete Music president Jerry Maas. "It's hard to tell who will be good and who won't be good at this. Sometimes it is the most reserved people— the ones with hidden personalities that explode when they are put in front of a microphone."

The initial franchise fee of $9,500 purchases the lifetime rights to an exclusive territory. Franchisees need an additional $11,000 to pay for sound and lighting equipment, which fits comfortably into the trunk of a compact car. Most franchisees do not need to invest in a commercial office. Complete Music does not require any minimum office space and advises its franchisees to run the business from home.

The company trains its franchisees for ten days at its headquarters in Omaha and four days at the franchisee's location. Franchisees learn to set up and use the equipment, plus they receive coaching instruction in performing. Complete Music also teaches franchisees effective marketing and management techniques including how to hire and train DJs. Franchisees must also attend yearly training seminars as part of the contract.

FORECAST AND ANALYSIS

Franchisees do not need a musical background to succeed in this franchise opportunity—good management skills are what count most. A Complete Music franchise costs a fraction of what it takes to set up this type of business independently. The industry's growth is expected to continue, and aggressive, sales-oriented franchise owners can look forward to building profitable businesses.

96. STORK NEWS OF AMERICA, INC.

FRANCHISE FEE: *$7,000 to $12,000*
TOTAL INITIAL INVESTMENT: *$10,000 to $15,000*
FINANCING AVAILABLE: *Not yet (company plans to implement programs in future)*
ROYALTY FEE: *$500 to $1,500 per year*
ADVERTISING FEE: *None*
ADDRESS: *5075 Morganton Road, Suite 12-A, Fayettesville, NC 28314*
TELEPHONE: *1-800-633-6395 or 1-919-868-3065*
CONTACT PERSON: *Franchise Department*
INDUSTRY OVERVIEW
- *The American public loves babies and novelties. No matter how weak the economy, the birth of a baby is a time to celebrate—and spend money.*
    BENEFIT OF THIS COMPANY
- *Stork News tested its concept extensively before franchising. Having babies is back in vogue in the family-oriented 1990s.*

COMPANY HISTORY

- **IN BUSINESS SINCE:** *1984*
- **FRANCHISING SINCE:** *1985*
- **NUMBER OF FRANCHISE UNITS:** *115*

The parents of the late 1980s and early 1990s have spawned more new arrivals than any other generation.

Stork News of America is a front-runner in the baby-announcement novelty business. Started in 1984, the company's franchisees market eight-foot wooden storks that new parents plant in their front yards to announce a new baby to friends and neighbors.

The business is simple to operate and market. Word-of-mouth generates the majority of interest in the product. The business's focus on new births has attracted mostly female franchisees; presently, 95 percent of the franchisees are women.

Although the stork yard sign is the company's primary product, the franchise is integrating other novelty items into its product mix, included delivered candies and flowers. The franchisor also plans to establish Stork News Baby Boutiques to sell clothes for the newborns and assorted announcement products.

Stork News expects to support 235 franchises by 1995.

Franchisees invest $7,000 to $12,000 to open their franchises. Franchisees also expect to invest $2,000 to $3,000 in equipment, marketing, and advertising materials.

Since most franchisees do most of their business via telephone, the business can be effectively managed from home. Ninety-eight percent of the franchisees presently work at home. Training runs from one day to two weeks, depending on the size of a territory. Franchisees also receive an operations manual as part of their initial investment.

FORECAST AND ANALYSIS

As long as babies are being born, parents will want to announce the news. But there is competition. Florists and party stores sell cardboard storks and novelty announcements. Stork News' plans to open retail stores suggest that the company needs to broaden its concept to improve franchisee sales.

97. AMERICAN POOLPLAYERS ASSOCIATION

FRANCHISE FEE: *None*

TOTAL INITIAL INVESTMENT: *$8,250*

FINANCING AVAILABLE: *No*

ROYALTY FEE: *20 percent*

ADVERTISING FEE: *None*

ADDRESS: *1000 Lake St. Louis Boulevard, Suite 325, Lake St. Louis, MO 63367*

TELEPHONE: *1-314-625-8611*

CONTACT PERSON: *D. Renee Lyle*

INDUSTRY OVERVIEW

- *Organized pool tournaments is definitely not a competitive industry as yet.*
- *Pool is gaining momentum as a participation sport, and leagues are needed to organize this activity.*

BENEFIT OF THIS COMPANY

- *The league's founders are pool professionals and experts. They bring innovation, organization, and knowledge to the league system.*

COMPANY HISTORY

- **IN BUSINESS SINCE:** *1981*
- **FRANCHISING SINCE:** *1982*
- **NUMBER OF FRANCHISE UNITS:** *147*

The sport of pool or billiards once conjured up images of smokey bars on the seedy side of town. All that's changed. Today, pool is the second largest participation sport in the United States with more than 35 million players, and its participants are predominantly upscale, college-educated professionals.

The resurgence of pool has spawned a need for organized amateur leagues and governing bodies to oversee them. From this need, the American Poolplayers Association (APA) and its league system, the American Pool/Busch League, were formed.

Established in 1980, The American Pool/Busch League is the largest amateur league in the country with more than 75,000 active players. Under the corporate sponsorship of Anheuser-Busch, the league network has grown to include 147 franchises, and the APA expects that number to increase to more than 200 by the mid-1990s.

Franchisees are responsible for organizing the leagues, collecting dues, and sponsoring tournaments, complete with cash prizes.

The company's founders, Terry Bland and Larry Hubbart, are both nationally ranked professional players who have developed and incorporated programs such as a unique handicap system that allows players of all abilities to compete against one another.

A total investment of $8,250 assures a franchisee an exclusive territory based on population and county boundaries.

There is no franchise fee, but the investment covers the costs of a computer system, software, and any additional equipment and supplies, plus APA league jackets and tee- shirts. The computer helps manage the league and track the business. APA charges franchisees a hefty 20 percent franchise fee.

Franchisees should be committed to building the league, and that requires motivation, a love of sales, and most importantly a love of the game of pool.

With the computer as the base of operations, a franchise can operate in a space as small as 150 square feet. Consequently, 94 percent of franchisees operate from their homes.

As part of the contractual agreement, each franchisee must attend an initial three-day training seminar at company headquarters in Missouri. Along with the hands-on computer training, franchisees receive an operations and computer manual. The APA also conducts several regional meetings per year as well as an annual convention.

FORECAST AND ANALYSIS

More than 300,000 people play in unorganized pool leagues throughout the country. Pool playing is on the rise. Pool players are young, old, male, and female. For a person who loves the sport, this opportunity could be exciting. But beware. Fads come and go quickly. Could pool's resurgence be short-lived? Pool will always be around. But it's yet to be seen whether pool's mass popularity will continue.